101

GREAT WAYS
TO IMPROVE
YOUR LIFE

— VOLUME 2 —

Selected and Introduced by
DAVID RIKLAN

A PRODUCT OF

SELFGROWTH.COM

101 Great Ways to Improve Your Life: Volume 2
By David Riklan

Published by
Self Improvement Online, Inc.
http://www.SelfGrowth.com
20 Arie Drive, Marlboro, NJ 07746

Copyright © 2006 by David Riklan
All rights reserved.
ISBN 0-9745672-7-2
Manufactured in the United States

Cover Design:
Peri Poloni
Knockout Design
http://www.knockoutbooks.com

This book is dedicated to my father and mother, Manuel and Gloria Riklan. Their love, support and encouragement have been, and continue to be, a great source of inspiration.

ACKNOWLEDGEMENTS

When I began working on Volume 2 of our *101 Great Ways* series, I realized that I had a difficult task ahead of me. My team and I had already created Volume 1, which included what I felt were 101 *really* great ways to improve your life. How could we possibly come up with another 101 great ways?

My team and I went to work—and in doing so, we found that there were dozens of self-improvement experts who each had some gem of wisdom to impart that could ultimately lead to an enriching, fulfilling life. As a result, I've come up with what I truly believe are another *101 Great Ways to Improve Your Life.*

First off, I'd like to acknowledge every author that contributed to this book. Thank you to John Gray, Jack Canfield, Richard Carlson, Bob Proctor, Alan Cohen and the 96 other authors that made this book a powerful tool to help improve our lives.

In addition to all of the contributors to the book, there were three people involved in this project that deserve a very special thanks. Stephanie Anastasio, Kristina Kanaley and Jerry Kimbrough made the creation of this book possible. This three-person team worked closely together to create this powerful self-improvement book—and, in many ways, was more responsible for the completion of this book than I was.

I would also like to thank many other members of our self-improvement team. Todd Lesser and Jamie Albert provided many hours of valuable feedback and insights which were instrumental in the creation of our *101 Great Ways* book series. Joe De Palma provided staunch support for this project and helped me stay focused on this endeavor. Adriene Hayes has assisted in countless aspects of our business. Gary Dong, Douglas Pak and Greg Aronne have all helped to expand our self-improvement message around the world.

There are also several other people that have been a continual source of inspiration for my books, my website and my business. The list is too large to print verbatim in this section, but some of these key people include: Peggy McColl, Mike Litman, Mike Brescia, Pete Bissonette, Gay Hendricks, Karim Hajee, Vic Johnson, Scott Martineau, Hale Dwoskin, Bill Harris and Brad Antin.

Many special thanks are due to my friends and family, who have provided much-needed support and encouragement throughout the process.

Finally, a special thanks to my wife, Michelle, who is a continual source of motivation for everything that I do.

TABLE OF CONTENTS

Contents

Contents

Contents

Contents

Contents

Contents

Contents

Contents

Contents

Contents

INTRODUCTION – BY DAVID RIKLAN

Have you ever lain awake at night, asking yourself how life turned out the way it did? Would things have been different if you took that other job... married that girl next door... invested that money in the can't-miss stock? Do you regret your decisions? Do you want to turn things around?

You can look back, analyze, and regret the things you've done... or you can pick yourself up and vow that the future will be full of happiness, prosperity, and good times.

There are many *decent* ways to improve your life; then again, there are many *Great Ways*! This book is the second edition in our series of *101 Great Ways to Improve Your Life*. No one can narrow self-improvement to a defined list of advice, methods, and techniques. And that's why we couldn't stop at just one book.

Life-improvement is in your hands. How strong is your vow to change? Are you focused? Are you determined? Good... because we are too.

ABOUT VOLUME 2

Many people believe that learning only takes place in the classroom, that the only real teacher is someone with a certain degree or occupational background. But the truth is, we can learn something from just about anybody: the high-school dropout who started his own million-dollar business; the waitress who fulfilled her dreams of Hollywood stardom; the office secretary who finally published that book of poetry.

I follow the credo that *everyone* has a pearl of knowledge to impart, and it doesn't matter if that person is someone you see every day or someone you've only heard about.

In Volume 1 of *101 Great Ways*, we had to exclude many qualified authors and important philosophies on personal growth. That's another reason why we turned this into a series. There are too many valuable experts who long to impart their wisdom onto you. Thus, we bring you Volume 2, with another edition soon to follow.

In *101 Great Ways to Improve Your Life: Volume 2*, we have once again compiled an amazing collection of 101 great chapters, all written by unique experts in self-improvement. Each author has a distinctive voice and a method of teaching that is all his or her own.

You may know many of the experts already. Others you may be reading for the first time. But there's one common thread that ties all of these teachers together—they're all phenomenal educators who *know* how to help people improve their lives.

WHAT YOU CAN LEARN FROM THIS BOOK

You *can* find a satisfying career.
You *can* conquer negativity.
You *can* improve your health naturally.
You *can* get out of debt.
You *can* age with style.

In short, you *can* do a lot of things, and this book will show you how. These 101 articles are written on a wide range of topics: humor, fate, self-esteem, love and relationships, and dozens of others. There's something in here for *everyone*.

If you're looking for a specific subject, simply check out the table of contents. All 101 articles are listed by topic, and the topics are arranged in alphabetical order. For instance, if you want to read an article about "anger," you'll find it near the beginning of the book.

Please know that you *don't* have to agree with an author's philosophy. Not every chapter of this book will apply to each individual person—one reader might think a particular section is inspiring, while another might not. But we've provided you with a number of different vantage points, so hopefully you'll find one that fits your way of life.

Please also know that you *don't* have to agree with only one author. You may find that you agree with the message of 10 authors, or 20 authors, or you may feel that they *all* have important things to say. That's natural too. Again, self-improvement is in your hands. Only you can decide how to do it—no one else.

A PRODUCT OF SELFGROWTH.COM

I'm very excited about Volume 2 because we can now expose you to even more terrific authors from the SelfGrowth.com community. So many good writers submit content to SelfGrowth.com—our self-improvement super-site—yet it's hard for the average visitor to find them amongst the hundreds we feature daily. So here you have it: 101 very unique articles, from very unique people, that can help you achieve a bright future.

Hopefully, after reading *101 Great Ways: Volume 2*, you'll come away with the confidence to put the past behind you, make good decisions, and try new things. There are so many books that have had this effect. Volume 1 sure did. Volume 2 does as well.

So, on behalf of everyone here at Self Improvement Online, Inc., I wish you the best of luck. Remember, you have the power to improve your life... and we have some *Great Ways* to do it!

1

Healing, Forgiving, and Overcoming Abuse

Nancy Richards

The soul cannot forgive until it is restored to
wholeness and health.
In the absence of love—how can one forgive?
With an abundance of love, starting with one's self,
forgiveness becomes a viable opportunity.

At some point in every abuse survivor's healing journey, he or she must face the question of forgiveness. Are there some abuses too atrocious to forgive? Is it possible, or even healthy, to forgive someone who has never asked to be forgiven, someone who has never acknowledged any wrongdoing, and someone who continues to practice the same abusive behaviors?

I questioned how I could forgive my mother for granting her approval when my stepfather burned my 10-year-old hands. Year after year, the betrayal felt incomprehensible as I watched my mother silently witnessing my abuse, defending my stepfather, and even participating in the abuse as my stepfather beat and tortured my brothers and me. How could I forgive a litany of unacknowledged emotional and physical abuses?

Many survivors recovering from abuse, including physical, emotional, and sexual abuse as well as neglect, rejection, and abandonment, often wrestle with the conflicting senses of a longing to forgive versus not feeling forgiving. Many times, survivors feel a responsibility or a social pressure to forgive even when they have not healed sufficiently for that step to have an emotionally healthy outcome. All too often, well-intentioned friends and relatives ask individuals to forgive and forget. Survivors of family abuse often succumb to this pressure and embark on a path of superficial forgiveness that does not honor the depth of the injury or enable authentic healing and forgiveness.

Any of us who have heard the words "you have to forgive" knows that this added burden can actually impede our recovery. When a survivor denies his feelings and sets aside his wounds, pain, anger, and grief in order to forgive, he often finds that he is not able to heal. Ultimately, in the absence of healing, forgiveness doesn't last.

Sometimes it is necessary to place a moratorium on forgiveness until healing has taken place. This affords us the opportunity to validate our stories with sympathetic listeners, express our anger in appropriate ways, mourn our losses, and protect others and ourselves from re-injury. Surprisingly, it is often the very process of not forgiving, of acknowledging the pain and taking the steps to heal, that can free the abused to forgive. How then do we acknowledge our pain?

One way to acknowledge our pain is to receive emotional compensation and acknowledgment from our abusers. "Our greatest opportunity for healing comes from the offender. When the person who harmed us is willing to offer restitution, we are truly blessed. This means the wrongdoer must be willing to acknowledge the harm they caused us, offer a genuine apology, demonstrate a willingness to restore what was taken and change their abusive behavior."[1] However, because of the chronic nature of abuse, most victims do not have their abuse acknowledged by the offender. When survivors do not receive acknowledgment from the person who harmed them, they need to have their abuse acknowledged by other individuals. It is extremely difficult to forgive something that, in the eyes of their families and communities, never happened.

Another way to acknowledge our pain and move toward the possibility of forgiveness is to feel as if justice has been served. This an important part of the healing journey, and validation and acknowledgment are part of the justice-making process. Justice can be as limited as receiving support and validation or as substantial as criminal prosecution.

Third, expressing anger is a necessary step toward authentic forgiveness. Forgiveness is not a single act but rather takes place in layers, as other individuals, whether they be our abusers, our friends, our families, or our communities, are willing to share our burden of pain. Once our stories are heard, the door opens to recognizing our anger. All too often, victims try to deny or suppress their anger, yet finding appropriate ways to express their painful experiences is necessary in order to heal. Survivors need to find safe methods and environments in which to discharge their repressed rage. Discharging anger frees the individual to honor her pain and mourn her substantial losses.

Finally, a victim of abuse must be free from abuse to acknowledge her pain and move toward forgiveness, and this often requires placing our trust in others to help us move away from abusive situations. "An important and often overlooked aspect to healing is that of protecting others and ourselves from further harm. In order to heal, we must be free from the anxiety of re-injury."[2] In other words, forgiveness is not possible if there is ongoing abuse, and in order to protect ourselves, we need the support of others.

Healing requires a great deal of time, self-examination, hard work, and pain. Yet once an adequate amount of healing has been accomplished, forgiveness becomes a viable opportunity. Forgiveness doesn't mean that we "excuse" offensive behavior; it doesn't mean forgetting or even trusting the person who harmed us. Nor does it require us to "let go" of our safety. Rather, forgiveness means to let go of resentment and find peace.

Endnotes

1. Nancy Richards, *Heal and Forgive: Forgiveness in the Face of Abuse* (Nevada City: Blue Dolphin, 2005), xii.
2. Ibid., 121.

About the Author

Nancy Richards is the author of Heal and Forgive: Forgiveness in the Face of Abuse. Richards is an adult survivor of childhood abuse. She is the single parent of two thriving adult daughters and is a successful businesswoman as vice president and general manager of a large wholesale food processing company in Seattle. Visit http://www.healandforgive.net.

2

ACCOMPLISHMENT

Accomplish 20 Times as Much

Donald W. Mitchell

Once there was a busy shepherd. She was always gathering strays. Her father taught her that if she focused on the strays, her sheep would always be safe.

Her sister joined the shepherd one day to help with the endless task. The sister asked, "Do all the sheep stray?"

"No," responded the shepherd. "Only 16 ever stray."

"Why don't you build a little fenced area in each part of the pasture for those 16 to use when you bring the flock to that area? Then you'll never have to chase strays again."

She followed her sister's advice. The shepherd then used her time watching the docile sheep to trade commodity futures by cell phone and increased the family fortune manyfold.

That was a 2,000 percent solution for increasing her income. A 2,000 percent solution is any way of accomplishing 20 times as much with the same time, effort, and resources . . . or accomplishing the same results with 1/20 the time, effort, and resources.

Many people are stalled from making 2,000 percent solutions because they are stuck with bad habits based on tradition, disbelief that there could be a better way, misconceptions about what the task is, wanting to avoid something unattractive, misunderstanding what's been said, unintentionally confusing others, becoming bogged down in red tape, and procrastinating. A good way to overcome such stalled thinking is to examine your progress in the most important areas of your life. Ask yourself these questions about your activities over the last year.

- What did you learn to do better?
- Which activities take up more of your time than you would like?
- Do you have enough time for the people you love?
- Are there things you'd like to be doing that you don't do?
- Do you know how to make much faster progress in each of these areas?

If you are dissatisfied with your answers, you may feel a little overwhelmed about how you can make so many changes. That's because each improvement usually requires learning lots of new things, spending time practicing those new activities, and still getting everything else done.

Relax. There's a simpler, more effective way. Learn to be a 2,000 percent solver. This easy-to-learn method can be applied to every area of your life. You learn one process that you can apply to do anything. Sound good?

Okay, here are the steps.

1. Understand the importance of measuring your performance. If you don't measure it, you don't know how you're doing . . . or if you're getting better or worse.
2. Decide what to measure. The shepherd was measuring whether she lost any sheep; she should have been measuring how she much time she spent tracking down each sheep. Then she would have realized that she could just pen up the constant strays and free up all that time for complementary activities while she watched the docile animals.
3. Identify the future best practice. Dog trainers use electronic fences to encourage dogs not to stray. Perhaps something similar could be used for sheep so that the shepherd wouldn't have to build so many pens.
4. Implement beyond the future best practice. If the shepherd sold off any sheep that were constant strays, she wouldn't need to put up any fences.
5. Identify the ideal best practice. This is the best anyone could ever do. If we only raise sheep predisposed to stay with the herd, shepherds could focus on other things.
6. Pursue the ideal best practice. The shepherd should keep breeding records and observe which sheep never stray. She should then only breed sheep that

are the most reliable in not straying, while selling off the occasional maverick.

7. Identify the right people and provide the right motivation. The shepherd could look around to see if any sheep raisers have been doing this kind of breeding already so that she could buy their stock.
8. Repeat the first seven steps. Having found one solution doesn't mean that there's not a better one. The second time around, the shepherd could look at how pasture choices affect straying.

But you're not a shepherd. How does this lesson apply to you? Well, you may have children that need to be looked after. The purpose is to keep them from straying away from you and into trouble . . . both when they are with you and when they aren't. The solutions will obviously be different than for tending sheep, but the same thought process can be employed. You'll probably end up focusing on eliminating dangers in advance, monitoring access to dangers, and encouraging involvement in safe situations. You'll be careful of who your children's friends are and encourage your children to invite their friends to your house so you can see what's going on.

You may also have employees to supervise to be sure they don't stray from what they should be doing. Or you may be responsible for keeping customers loyal so they don't stray to the competition. Or you may simply have big time wasters that distract you from what's important, and you need to learn how not to stray into those areas.

Obviously, it takes time to learn this new skill. How can you make that time? We encourage everyone to begin by keeping a diary for two weeks of how every moment is spent 24 hours a day, seven days a week. At the end of two weeks, add up the time for each activity. Then see where you could make changes.

Many people will discover they are watching television more than necessary. Take out time-wasting shows, and you'll have more time to learn. Others will discover that during commuting and travel time they aren't doing anything else. You can listen to a self-improving message during those moments. Those with jobs may find they are working long hours because of inefficiencies at work. Delegate some of those tasks or get rid of the inefficiencies, and you'll be home sooner. Some people discover they are sleeping 10 hours a night and could get by on a little less if they exercised more. The average person who does this exercise finds 25 hours a week to do something new.

If you apply some of that redirected time to learning about and creating 2,000 percent solutions, you'll soon have even more time and resources. You can then choose to either spend that increased time in self-improvement, or self-enjoyment. In many cases, time can be substituted for money, and vice versa. Soon, many of your greatest dreams will be within your reach.

What are you waiting for?

ABOUT THE AUTHOR

Donald W. Mitchell is a coauthor of *The 2,000 Percent Solution* and *The 2,000 Percent Solution Workbook*.

He can be reached by e-mail at ultimatecompetitiveadvantage@yahoo.com. You can read all but two chapters of *The 2,000 Percent Solution* for free at http://www.2000percentsolution.com. Each chapter begins with a one-paragraph summary and ends in questions to help you apply what you learned in the chapter. If you would like to have even more guidance, you can also purchase and read *The 2,000 Percent Solution Workbook*.

3

The Passionate Warrior

Cathi Watson

Some time ago, I think it was in the 1980s, someone asked me to give myself a title that would support my mission statement—my mission in life is to help everyone look and feel younger and better longer than they ever thought possible . . . men, women, people of all ages and ethnicities. Almost immediately, like a rocket zooming, I got my title: "The Passionate Warrior."

Don't ask me where it came from because I don't know. Well, maybe I was a *passionate warrior* in a former life (who knows?), so I decided to look up "passionate" in the dictionary:'

1. "Having or showing strong feelings" — that's me.
2. "Hot-tempered" — what? I see myself as calm, even-tempered. Well, not according to my friends and associates, who label me a type A+ personality . . . *how rude*!
3. "Ardent; intense" — okay, I could live with that.
4. "Sensual, devoted to the pleasures of the senses" — with passion, I encourage anyone who is inclined to make pleasurable changes in their lives that support *my mission statement.*

On the basis of my track record, I have strong feelings on what the concept of aging is and should be. I definitely become disenchanted with those who have "settled in to give in." Raymond C. Barker, a theologian, put it this way: "The danger of middle age is that most people accept where they are and stop visioning where they want to go." *How dismal*!

I definitely champion changing old, worn out trends that are not in sync with current discoveries and proven principles related to enjoying every minute on this planet—in good health and good everything—longer than you ever thought possible.

I invite you to join me with an open mind, to embrace the new and eradicate old, archaic thinking and trends that will keep you locked up and a prisoner, forever living in the past.

The Form Is Changing

Twenty-Somethings: Seeking and Searching

Life is theirs to dare! They are bulletproof in mind, body, and spirit.

Thirties: Twinkling and Thriving

By the age of 30, you've reached cellular maturity. Think of how you look and feel. Now, I want you to imagine that you're a rosebud about ready to blossom, opening up to drink and embrace the elixir of youth. Don't you want to keep that blossom alive and healthy for as long as possible? You water and nourish a rosebush, and this is what you're going to have to do with your body. *Water, nourish,* and *love* your body . . . if you wear your body out, where will you live?

Forties: Flashing and Fleeting

Some call this "mid-life," but that is relative. . . . Is this a wake-up call? Are you beginning to reevaluate your previous choices? Do you smoke, party too much, maintain a poor diet . . . and exercise? Forget it! Is this going to be your mid-life crisis? Resolve to make changes. *Don't despair! Help and hope is on the way!*

Fifties: Fabulous and Flirty

Are you 50 and fabulous, or 50 and feeble? Is it time to rethink your reluctance to exercise? According to all the experts, exercise is the closest thing we have to an antiaging pill. Getting into shape may be easier than you think.

Sixties: Sexy and Sizzling

A new era is emerging for the "ageless": aging with *glamour*, *style*, and *vigor*. Did you know:

- you *can* have a sizzling, sensational second half of life
- you *can* energize your life
- you *can* have a fulfilling life regardless of age
- you *can* *refire*, not *retire*, the passion in your life
- you *can* look and feel younger and better longer than you ever thought possible!

Aging has been theorized, intellectualized, and spiritualized, but never *glamorized*! That's about to change. Who said you can't be sexy and sensationally glamorous after 60 and beyond?

Seventies: Simply Sensational

A call to action: get in the mix in 2006—the *year of renewal and choices*. The new aging paradigm redefines aging, and the *dynamic* 70-year-old is the *new* 40- to 50-year-old.

Eighties: Enduring and Enchanting

Congratulations, you've made it—you're a survivor. You're living life to the fullest. The best is now . . . and *better is yet to come*!

ABOUT THE AUTHOR

Cathi Watson's mission is to teach dedicated, proven methods and techniques to all who want to look and feel younger through her antiaging "Ageless for Life" concept. She is the coauthor of two books, an international speaker, and the producer/host of two weekly radio shows currently on WJJG am1530 and WYLL.com am1160 in Chicago. Special presentations are also done with Comcast TV 19 and 35 and with Chicago cable TV 19. Visit Cathi's Web site at http://www.cathiwatson.com or e-mail her at cathistudio@sbcglobal.net.

4

ANGER

Unbend Your Anger with "Stop, Drop and Roll"

John R. Rifkin

Everyone seems to understand the destructive power of anger. That's because everyone equates anger with aggressive behavior, and aggressive behavior hurts people. Once we are injured by someone who is angry, it is an easy next step to thinking it is the anger that injures us. Anger, however, is only an emotion. It takes a person to change the emotion into an aggressive behavior.

Emotions take place in our bodies and minds, in an interactive manner. When trying to understand anger, you must first place it in the context of emotion, especially negative emotion. At the most basic level of emotion, there are really only two: pleasure and pain.

Pain is the primary negative emotion. Without pain or injury we really don't experience any problems. Secondary to pain or injury, there are three negative emotions that follow, in greater or lesser amounts. The amount of each of these will vary from person to person and for differing injuries. Sadness is a secondary emotion to injury that I define as an honoring of that injury. Fear is energy that the body generates to avoid being hurt again. Finally, anger is energy that the body generates to attend to or fix the injury.

When you begin to look at anger as energy instead of dangerous aggressive behavior, you begin to become compassionate for the emotion. You begin to look at your anger and the anger of others as a reflection of the human experience of injury. Instead of making the judgment that anger is bad, you begin to investigate it as what it really is: energy that is meant to heal the injury.

After having worked with this energy of anger in healing for 30 years and seen how powerfully it can work, both in the dysfunction in peoples' lives as well as in their healing processes, I've developed a simple system for unbending anger from dysfunction into functional behavior. I call this system "Stop, Drop, and Roll."

Stop, Drop, and Roll is what you're told you're supposed to do when you catch fire. Of course, if you don't notice that you're on fire, you won't stop, drop, and roll, so it is actually a four-step system.

The metaphor I like to use to demonstrate Stop, Drop, and Roll applied to the idea of bent anger is what I call "the mosquito." If you imagine a mosquito landing on your hand, you can see this as a metaphor for the injury: a bloodsucker, with a potentially life-threatening illness, is preparing to attack you. This information gets transferred by the nerves in your hand and eyes to your brain. You respond by generating energy, the fight or flight energy of fear and anger.

A functional response to that injury would be to utilize the energy of your fear and anger to wipe off the insect. Bent anger would be represented by taking that same energy and the same hand and, instead of wiping off the bug, slapping yourself in the face! Such an act would represent, metaphorically, depression, addictions, anxiety, explosive anger, and extramarital affairs, to name but a few.

In using Stop, Drop, and Roll the first step is for you to identify the problematic thoughts, feelings, and behaviors that make up the bent anger in your life. Once you have identified them, you need to begin to train yourself to notice them before you get overwhelmed by them. This may take a lot of practice.
Once you can notice them in a timely way, it is time to begin the Stop step. This involves taking time out from your place of injury. This step may take quite a bit of practice as well.

When you have been able to complete the Stop step, you will have the opportunity to Drop. Dropping means preparing to take action. You do this by becoming cognitive and by beginning, through investigation, to understand why you are about to slap yourself across the face instead of wiping off the insect. This will require understanding what has injured and upset you in the present as well as how these injuries may relate to your childhood.

Finally, the Roll step involves taking that angry energy that used to be bent into dysfunction and using it for some form of healthy activity. You may find a different healthy use for your functional anger in every situation, but there are only two broad categories for the functional use of anger: self-nurturing and empowerment. Self-nurturing is where you use the energy of anger to care directly for yourself, and empowerment is where you act on the world so that the world can empower you. Every other use of anger is dysfunction.

Let's look at how Sheila learned to use Stop, Drop, and Roll. Sheila identified her particular brand of catching on fire as her depressive thinking. Sheila was a single, 27-year-old elementary school teacher. In her mind her self-talk was self-abusive at times. The most negative thought that she identified was thinking "nothing's ever going to work out for me." Self-abusive thinking becomes clearly angry when you imagine how angry it would sound if you said the same thought to someone else.

Sheila first trained herself to be on the look out for this thought. She had to notice it when she heard it in her mind. It took a little practice before she noticed it regularly.

Once Sheila had learned to recognize this dysfunctional, angry thought, she began to practice the Stop step of intervening in this depressive cognitive behavior. She would try to stop thinking the thought. In order to do this, she had to understand that she was in an emotionally injured state and to be ready to start thinking about why.

For the Drop step Sheila needed to investigate what was hurting her in the here and now and how that injury resonated with injuries from childhood. She had recently gone out on a date with a young man and had enjoyed her time with him. She'd been hoping to hear from him, but it had been several days since he'd called. Her experience of waiting to be called resonated with her experience of her father's gradual disappearance from the lives of her and her mother after her parents' divorce when she was seven years old as well as other dating disappointments throughout her life.

As Sheila came to understand the sources of her injury, she was ready to do the Roll step. She began to think about how to use her angry energy to attend to herself and to the pain she was experiencing. She decided to call a friend and find some fun things to do as well as to attack some hills on her bike.

The Stop, Drop, and Roll system is relatively easy to explain, and yet hard to do. It takes practice, and mastering each step can be challenging. However, if you keep working at it, you will be successful. It can help to journal your progress and your process as you work at the steps. If you don't give up, you can't fail. Learn to use your anger to carve out the life you want for yourself!

ABOUT THE AUTHOR

Dr. John Rifkin is a licensed psychologist with a private practice in Boulder, Colorado. His book, *The Healing Power of Anger: The Unexpected Path to Love and Fulfillment*, was published in 2004 and has been nominated for the prestigious William James Book Award. It is an extremely accessible self-help book which can be helpful for therapists and accelerates treatment for clients. Dr. Rifkin is the former chair of the Committee on Professional Practice for the Colorado Psychological Association and a former member of their Board of Directors. His Web site is http://www.EmotionalSuccess.com.

5

APPROVAL

You Don't Need Their Approval: Who Are They Anyway?

Ehryck Gilmore

What is approval? It is the acceptance as satisfactory. The act of giving validity. We seek approval to satisfy our desire to be loved. If someone approves of some event or occurrence that happens in our lives, we feel appreciated. Whether this appreciation comes from our parents, spouse, or friends, we feel acceptance and make a mental note to ourselves saying "I did something, and they're pleased."

Why we look outside ourselves for this approval is one of the mysteries of life that plays out every day in our world. It is like being in grade school, where the teacher passes out stars for exemplary work. Stars were, even then, classified in order of acceptance—gold, silver, bronze, etc.

Most people, on an intellectual level, don't believe they need anyone else's approval. But have you ever asked someone at one time or another, "How do I look?" There you have it! For those who are self-assured, the phrase would have been "I look good, don't I?," accompanied by a big smile. When you are sure of yourself and sure of your path in life, you do not look for or seek another's approval.

Acknowledgment is different from approval. Allowing someone else to say you look great does not change who you are nor the mood or spirit you are in at the time. Seeking approval can paralyze your life because you become dependent on others to tell you whether you are doing the right thing at the right time. It is like sitting in the driver's seat of your car waiting for someone to give you the keys so you can rev it up and hit the road. Isn't it foolish to believe, to take the analogy further, that you can live your life waiting for someone else to give you the keys?

19

Ask yourself, "Do I know what I know now because someone gave me the knowledge or his approval?" Is there ever a time when approval from another is necessary? Yes, if you work for an employer who wants a task performed in a certain manner. But in life scenarios where outside approval is not required, why would you seek another's approval when he is on a path of life that may not be the same as your own?

> The soul never seeks approval, only man.

If you still want approval, then approve of yourself and how you want to live your life. Now, with an inner knowing, say to yourself, "There is no one above me other than the Universe that I seek approval from." If this is the case, how can anyone give you the approval you crave other than the Universe?

I often question the term "they" because I want to know who "they" are. Who are these Universally appointed, highly evolved, all-knowing, intelligent people that keep a person from moving forward? Digging a little deeper will likely reveal that the "they" most people talk about are their own fears. And amidst this search for praise from others, what most people are looking for is a way to put off the choice of making a decision, a decision that requires the energy of a self-assured, self-aware, and confident person. How might you look at approval? Well, when you regularly seek approval, it shows that you are not sure about yourself, so how can anyone be sure about you?

Sometimes we are so concerned about the way approval is supposed to look or be packaged that part of ourselves that craves approval totally misses it. We then continue on a path of self-sabotage, trying to recreate the emotion of approval in another way.

Like letting a writer pen the screenplay to your life while you sit and anticipate the outcome, some people turn their lives over to others to dictate what, how, and when they should feel. Then as you read the screenplay of your life, you want to cry. Why? Because the "they" have given you a script that you can't live up to or have created a character that you don't want to be. Wouldn't it just be easier to accept the fact that you don't need anyone's approval other than your own and your Creator's?

Most people have not taken the time to become whole within themselves. While searching for a confirmation of who they are and what they believe, they constantly look to sources outside of themselves for acceptance and thus slowly relinquish personal responsibility to others.

Think of yourself as a cup. When the water in the cup is not filled to the top, there is room for something else or someone else to fill it. Whether those empty spaces are filled with love, light, or negativity, it does not matter to the Universe, as long as they are being filled. What does matter is that you choose what your cup is filled with because if you are not filling it with much-needed love, understanding, and the teachings of infinite wisdom, anyone can come fill your cup with whom and what they are (negative or positive), whether you need it or not and whether you like it or not.

In your quest to become whole, doesn't filling your cup with self-love sound better than allowing someone to pour mud into it? Whoever fills the cup gains control of the mind and hence your life. Whose cup is it anyway? Filling your cup on your own, with your own truths, your own acquired knowledge, desires, goals, and dreams, can bring you a sense of peace. If you are fulfilling these obligations to yourself, you will no longer need to search for answers outside of those already springing forth from your inner self.

There are many ways to find out who you are: through work, art, literature, music, and the earth. However, we tend to look toward others when this journey should be one of a personal, spiritual nature. It is important to know that those to whom you look for guidance are probably looking, too! The spirit, the ever-flowing part of the Universe that connects all of us and every living thing and inanimate object, must be the source that fills us, not the Guru on the mountain.

Who Are You? The more you become aware of who you are, the greater your signal out to the Universe . . . and the greater the signal, the greater the connection. It's up to you to keep your connection to the Universe. No one else is responsible for your life.

Words are not essential; it is the essence of who you are that is moving the energy. It is focused thought and energy in motion that creates. If you want to keep real momentum, you must constantly reeducate and reprogram yourself on what is happening now. Otherwise, you will struggle, physically and mentally, from that lower level. That struggle and stress will take their toll on the body sooner or later, resulting in illness and disease.

How might you make a smooth transition? Do your homework. Do the research to disclose the latest trends, processes, and data. Let go of old habits and beliefs that do not apply to the now. Start implementing tangible changes in your environment that stimulate productivity; get advice from a life coach or another professional who has a specialty in your area of interest; and network-exchange and share information.

ABOUT THE AUTHOR

Ehryck F. Gilmore is a Certified Hypnotherapist, life coach, empowerment coach, intuitive counselor, and author. He is also a master practitioner of neuro-linguistic programming. He has studied at the Omega Center in Rhinebeck, New York, the NLP Institute of Chicago, DePaul University, Moody Bible Institute, and the School of Spiritual Psychology of Milwaukee. His Web site is http://www.ehryckgilmore.com.

6

ASPIRATIONS

Bring Your Dream to Life in Seven Focused Steps: The "Heroes" Story

Donna Goldstein

Have you ever had a big exciting dream but not taken the steps you needed to make it a reality? Maybe you said to yourself, "It'll take too long" or "I've never done this, I don't know how." Do you currently have a product you would like to produce, a poem you just need to write, or a children's book series just waiting for you to bring it to life? I suspect nearly everyone has a dream that could use some help down the birth canal.

This article will give you a clear and easy seven-step approach for making your dream a reality. You will find key questions to answer and areas to plot your own scenario. I'll use one of my big dreams as an example to help you to see how you can use this approach to activate your own dream!

As a professor of multicultural education back in 1992, I became distressed about how little my students (all prospective teachers) knew about Black history. Once we got beyond Dr. Martin Luther King and Rosa Parks, they knew nothing at all! One evening, I had a riveting dream wherein my students and I toured an African American portrait gallery, and magnificent, full-size portraits of heroes and heroines such as Sojourner Truth and Benjamin Banneker came alive. They stepped right off the wall and shared their struggles and triumphs with us, and we were mesmerized. I knew that one day I needed to somehow make that dream a reality.

What helped me to make it happen, and how can you use these seven steps to bring your dream to life?

1. **Clarify your intention.** What is your intention? Who can you speak to about its viability? Who can help you clarify your intention?

The first step is to clarify your intention. Is it a song or a story? A new product or product adaptation? Can you clearly articulate it in a few sentences? What value does it bring? For example, your dream might be to open a literary coffeehouse that houses poetry readings and book discussions, while catering lunches to downtown businesses.

To bring my own dream to life as a theatrical production, in late 2003, after a long, dormant period, I began to meet with dozens of educators, artists, funders, and community leaders. We explored the needs and constraints of schools, libraries, and other likely audiences and determined that a one-man, one-act touring show would best suit the needs of our communities. We then hired one of south Florida's leading African American actors, who enthusiastically collaborated on the project .

2. **Call in potential opportunity partners.** Who in your world could help you make your dream a reality? How will it also benefit them?

Bringing your dream from concept to fruition can often be hastened by seeking out opportunities and developing partnerships. We hired a skilled playwright and director with a similar vision. We wanted to spotlight lesser known African American heroes as role models. Then we searched diligently for individuals and organizations that saw a need for, or would support, our concept. Since that time, we have partnered with dozens of corporations, nonprofits, and educational and community organizations to bring this dream to life.

3. **Develop resourcefulness.** What other skills/resources does your dream require? What are the small business resources in your community? Check SBA, SCORE, etc. Who in your circle would help you if you asked them?

Perhaps you will need to borrow some tools or take out a small business loan to bring your dream to reality. Since we started on a "shoestring" budget, we acquired, made, and borrowed our initial props and costumes, sourcing family members, colleagues, friends, and even our own closets! As the show has evolved, we have purchased and commissioned the additional pieces we needed.

4. **Upgrade your product or service continuously.** How could your dream be even better? Reach more people? Touch more lives?

Even after you give birth to your initial concept, keep refining and improving it. Very few successes spring forth fully realized. Our actor and our playwright rehearsed and revised the show tirelessly, adding more humor, audience interaction, and music, adjusting sound cues, and deepening the characters. For a show at the Langston Hughes Library in New York, we added one of his poems, and most recently added multimedia effects and additional characters.

5. **Be responsive and flexible.** Can you adapt your dream in response to your target market? Who else can use or benefit from your big idea?

Remember, Starbucks began as a single coffeehouse in Seattle! Always stay attuned to the needs of your audience or consumers, even if it means retooling your dream. Though we had originally planned a show targeted at the 6th to 12th grades, we quickly saw that the show was of great interest and relevance to younger audiences, college students, and even seniors. So we adapted the play and now have several versions for both younger and more mature audiences.

6. **Give something back.** How can your dream benefit the greater good? Could giving your product or service away (samples or small sizes) be beneficial?

There are many ways to "enhance your karma" and increase your exposure. An opening of an art show could be provided as a benefit for charity. Many restaurants provide food and supplies to organizations like Second Harvest. We initially provided free shows to audiences ranging from homeless adults and children to inner city schools and our Young at Art Children's Museum. The phone started to ring soon afterward for the paid performances! We still donate several shows a year to worthy audiences.

7. **Build your referral base.** What's the "buzz" on your dream? How could you generate more interest and referrals?

Once you are up and running, you'll need referrals to keep you going. Many of our initial shows were provided to personal and business associates, people who knew of the caliber of our work, then shared their excitement with others. Later referrals have also come from individuals who read one of our five full-page newspaper reviews. (See http://www.daint.org/WorldArts/Heroes.)

My mother recently gave me a cap that says "Producer," and I guess now I am. Though I was an experienced educator and event creator, I had never produced a

25

play before this one. In just two and a half years we've performed our play, "The African American Portrait Gallery: Discovering Timeless Heroes," to over 30,000 people in five states, and it all started with my dream in 1992! Many clients have asked what other shows or programs we have available. We now have created several more programs through a new division of our firm, World Arts, and so that takes us back to step one.

What is your big dream, and will you follow this plan to make it a reality?

ABOUT THE AUTHOR

Dr. Donna Goldstein, the Managing Director of Development Associates International, is a pioneering career and life success coach, author, and educator who assists individuals, teams, and organizations. She has helped clients worldwide to achieve balance and focus and to excel in many ways: starting new businesses, completing books, videotapes, and CDs, and improving sales and service. For more information on the Heroes project, visit http://www.WorldArtsNow.com. To book a consultation to discuss your big (or little) dream, e-mail her at DrDonna@DAInt.org, or call her at (954) 893–0123. For a free copy of her dynamic approach to goal setting, visit http://www.DrDonnaGo.com.

7

AWARENESS

Breaking the Cycle

Jo-Anne Cutler

> You must be the change you want to see in the world.
> – Gandhi

When I was younger, I always knew that I wanted to be two things in life: a teacher and a mom. The first came true for me as I taught swimming throughout my high school and university summers. In 1991, after three long years of trying, I finally realized my dream of being a mom! Giving birth to my daughter, this beautiful bundle of love and joy, was an unforgettable moment in my life, as was the miraculous birth of my son just 19 months later. It wasn't until I became a parent that I realized that my most sought after desires were so connected.

As my children grew through the infancy, toddler, nursery, grade school, and middle school years, I began to see how important a role model I was for them, and I did the best I could with the knowledge that I had; however, the increased stress that accompanied this new role was sometimes difficult, and I believed at that time that it was my children who caused some of the stress and discontentment in my life!

One day, I sent my son to his room for misbehaving, and he was so mad at having to stay in his room that he began to slam his door . . . repeatedly! I could feel my blood boiling as I rushed to the bottom of the stairs and yelled at the top of my lungs for him to stop. I realized in that moment that I was acting in a way I vowed that I never would, but something came over me that was so strong and uncontrollable that I couldn't stop.

I remember another experience with my daughter when she was three. She had very proudly made her bed before going to nursery school, and as I went about my morning routine, I straightened out her bed. My godmother was visiting us, and as she witnessed what I had done, she said, "Don't you think she's going to notice that she didn't make her bed that way when she gets home? What she will take from that is that she didn't make it good enough for you. Who needs the bed neat and tidy, you or her?" She then commented, "There is no need to worry, Jo-Anne. By the time she is 30, she will know how to make up a bed!" I laughed at the silliness but also saw the huge message that I was sending my daughter. The notion of having to be perfect was my issue!

So many times I had a rough day at work, was exhausted from running on the treadmill of life, was frustrated with having to do it all myself as a single mom, or was heavy with worries about money or relationships issues. My kids might have wanted to share something exciting with me, needed some attention, or were maybe fighting with each other, and I would react by either yelling at them or withdrawing. Then I would feel guilty for my behavior, but it was too late— the damage had already been done. I love my children with all my heart, and my intention was never to hurt them.

Others have shared similar experiences with me, and I have compassion for them as I know that I, too, was behaving the only way I knew how. I have witnessed, both privately and publicly, the emotional and physical abuse that takes place on a regular basis in our world, and we need to do something to break this cycle.

We teach our children how to behave by our example, and the cycle we are continuing could be one that we learned as a child. We have long forgotten or maybe buried how we felt as children when we were yelled at, scolded, or felt disapproval, disappointment, or lack of love from our parents. I believe our children are experiencing the same thing now and that they can't find the voice, any more than we could, to say to us, "Please don't yell at me—that doesn't feel good" or " Mom, Dad, why are you always disappointed in me? Why won't you listen to me? Why can't you love me just the way I am?"

I know that my life became easier and less stressed when I took responsibility for my feelings and saw how I imposed those feelings onto my kids: the control, resentment, projection of anger, the shutdown, disapproval, and disappointment, all because they weren't doing what I wanted them to or behaving the way I thought they should. In wanting to be the best parent I could be, I started to take a good look within myself and through the eyes of my children. My mentor helped me to see how I could have done things differently and how my behavior and reactions impacted how they behaved . . . not only as children, but how my behavior created a template that they would follow when they became parents themselves. I saw how I was a container of all sorts of feelings that I had never felt safe enough to express, and when my children, or anyone else, for that matter, triggered me, all of those unfelt emotions exploded out of me, and I, of course, blamed them! I had continued a cycle of unhealthy behavior, and I wanted to do it differently.

I am no different than any other parent and thought I was doing a great job, and I was! I was doing the best I could with what I knew. My children and I now joke about the fact that they didn't come complete with a manual, and I fully admit to them that I'm not perfect! I am open to listening to my children now, and when they feel me getting agitated (remember, I'm not perfect) or when my "recovering control freak" side starts to rear its ugly head, my children feel safe to point it out, which reminds me that I am stepping back into my old patterns. This is my issue to take care of and to let go of. It feels good to be able to laugh now at my own behavior, and I am grateful and continually thank my children for sharing their observations.

There is a familiar phrase that says, "When the student is ready, the teacher will appear."

Our children can teach us so much if we let them express themselves and create a safe place for them to share their feelings and when we try not to take their expressions personally or view them as a sign of disrespect or back talk.

I can honestly say that I don't yell at my kids anymore. I am so blessed to have such wonderful children, as we all are—they are such gifts, and mine taught me how to look at and take ownership of how I showed up in life. Once I shifted, everything in my life did as well! It's an ongoing process for me to healthily take care of my emotions, and it is so clear to me now that my ultimate desires of being a mom and a teacher had to occur in that order: to learn how to be the best mom I could be so that I could teach my children. This has inspired our family to break the cycle.

ABOUT THE AUTHOR

Jo-Anne Cutler is committed to making a difference as a writer, speaker, and facilitator. Her vision is to empower and inspire you to be the parent, teacher, and role model the children of this world need you to be. One of the many ways that Jo-Anne supports this vision is through an audio program called "Breaking the Cycle." It contains insightful perspectives and stories as well as practical techniques that you can use to begin breaking the cycle of unhealthy behaviors and to connect with more peace and happiness in your life. For more information, please visit http://www.jcconnections.ca.

8

Balance Your Body, Mind and Spirit in Five Minutes a Day

Theresa Murphy & Dennis Mahoney

The alarm goes off in the morning. You want to roll over and go back to sleep, but you get up and go through your rushed morning routine to get ready for the day. Whether you jump into the car to make the commute to work or you stay at home with the children, there is always too much to do.

There's no such thing as a nine-to-five workday anymore, and there are still the daily chores, like getting to the bank or grocery store, doing the laundry, washing the dishes . . . and don't forget dinner. After all this you try to squeeze in time for a family and social life along with a little exercise, whether it's going to the gym, running, or using that piece of fitness equipment in the corner.

There just always seems to be too much to do and not enough time, money, or energy to do it. Stress—we all have it, and we all know what causes it. We know we have to reduce it to improve our health, but how? You can start to change your stress levels with one simple action done every day.

In five minutes a day you can reduce your stress, improve your self-esteem, build more confidence, and improve your quality of life. This may sound too good to be true, but it's not. It only takes putting yourself first, doing something just for you, once a day. It's easy; here's how.

Put three small, distinctive objects, like colored stones or marbles, into a container. One represents body, one mind, and one spirit. Each day, pull out one and spend at least five minutes on that category, doing something for you. It could be in the morning, at lunchtime, or at the end of the day. Everyone can find

31

five minutes to put himself or herself first. The act of physically picking one of the three objects will help you to make it a daily habit.

You may wonder what you can do for yourself in five minutes. The possibilities are endless, and here are some ideas to start you off.

For Your Body

Go for a walk, do five minutes of exercise or stretching, massage your feet, eat something healthy, climb stairs instead of using the elevator, rub lotion on your hands, do a few yoga or Pilates exercises, shoot some hoops, take a nap, or just lean back, close your eyes, and rest.

For Your Mind

Read part of a book, magazine, or newspaper, work on a puzzle for five minutes, play a hand of solitaire, do a crossword puzzle or play sudoku, learn a new skill like knitting, quilting, juggling, magic, or card tricks, learn a few words in a new language, or even just look up a new word in your own language.

For Your Spirit

Sit and breathe deeply or meditate for five minutes, go outside into nature, visit a museum and look at art, listen to music, read poetry, philosophy, or a spiritual text, buy yourself flowers, call a friend, laugh, hug someone, write a letter, or do something unexpected for someone—it will lift both your spirits.

Once you get into the habit of doing this each day, you'll begin to look forward to your five minutes. You may find that as your life improves, you can find 10 minutes, 15 minutes, or more.

When you take time for yourself, you'll find that the rest of your day isn't so difficult—you actually become more productive with the time you have. No matter how crazy or busy your day is, find five minutes, and do something for you.

ABOUT THE AUTHOR

Theresa Murphy and Dennis Mahoney are the creators of LIVE: Lessons In Violence Evasion, an educational system developed to help women and children evade and escape violence without having to fight. For more information, please visit http://www.lessionsinviolenceevasion.com.

9

BARRIERS TO SUCCESS

Breaking Through Self-Imposed Barriers to Success

Karen A. Jones

I waited patiently for the attractive woman seated before me to answer my question. Neatly groomed and well dressed, Andrea appeared every bit the successful, polished businesswoman confidently perched on an upper rung of the corporate ladder. Yet, when she did answer, her voice belied a confused frustration.

"I don't exactly know why I'm here. I mean, I never thought I'd be retaining a business coach at this point in my career. All I can say is, I just feel stuck." Andrea punctuated this announcement by crossing one arm over its mate and settling back into her chair.

"Congratulations," I said, my gaze unwavering and my voice gentle, with no hint of sarcasm or condescension as I continued. "Inertia takes a great deal of energy to work against the constant motion of this ever-vibrating world in which we live. You must be very consistent." Andrea uncrossed her arms and watched me as I explained.

"Contrary to what you may think, being stuck is really quite an active process. It means that you have been making the same choices over and over again, in order to remain precisely where you are. The key is to figure out what is keeping you from making different choices."

This scenario is quite common. At some point in life, everyone feels stuck, and many of us make the mistake of thinking it is due to external forces or conditions. With everything from quantum mechanics and cellular biology to Ayurvedic medicine and metaphysics validating the notion that we create our own reality, it is surprising that many of us still feel victimized by the very circumstances within which we find ourselves. *For things to change, we must change.*

Turning a loving but critical eye inwardly takes courage. Knowing what to look for takes a strategic plan. Attending to three aspects of our inner worlds will shake loose those self-imposed barriers to success preventing us from stepping into our full power. Targeting these three areas will set us free: counterintentional behaviors, self-defeating beliefs, and feelings of unworthiness.

Counterintentional Behaviors

When we find ourselves behaving in ways that are contrary to our intentions and values, we create cognitive dissonance and emotional discomfort. In fact, the smaller the chasm between our intentions and our actions, the better our self-esteem. When we live consciously, we cannot tolerate the disparity between the *intention* of working out five mornings per week and the *behavior* of lying in bed day after day, hitting the snooze button and blowing off the gym. We must design the kind of support we need in our lives to consistently answer the following question in the affirmative: Do my actions match my words?

Self-Defeating Beliefs

Otherwise known as negative self-talk, the critical inner parent, or the harsh superego, self-defeating beliefs usually begin in childhood and, if left unchallenged, can reverberate throughout the life-span. They can be based on interpretations and conclusions we drew through the limited perspective of a child's eyes. They can be words and actions directed toward us by parents, other adults, and other children. More often than not, they contain some sort of comparison to another and the word *enough*: tall enough, smart enough, man enough.

Self-defeating beliefs draw their power from the sheer number of times we have unquestioningly repeated them in our heads, unconsciously employing the Law of Attraction to solidify them even further. A belief is merely a thought that has habituated over time. Every time we limit ourselves with a self-defeating belief, we actually reinforce a specific interference in our own success.

The good news is that whatever we learn, we can unlearn. As we live more consciously, we can identify self-defeating thoughts, disprove them at a rational level, and develop the new habit of a more positive, self-affirming cognition. As we break the pattern, in time, we simply don't feel the same way about ourselves.

Feelings of Unworthiness

The difference between worthlessness and unworthiness is not merely semantic. In my 25 years of practice, I can honestly say that I have never known anyone to feel completely worthless. However, I have worked with quite a few people who are fairly successful but who stop their forward progression just short of achievement. It's amazing how skillful they are at teetering on the tightrope of never failing, but never really succeeding either.

I have also worked with others who, as they become more and more successful, amassing larger and larger fortunes and realizing more and more of their dreams, begin to feel unworthy of such great prosperity. They seem to illustrate the adage "be careful what you wish for."

If they head in a negative direction, they begin to self-sabotage in obvious ways, such as excessive spending or other excessive hedonistic pursuits, and in subtle ways, such as questioning or testing the love and loyalty of those closest to them. It is as though they have a thermostatic set point for the level of success they can tolerate, and they begin to turn down the heat rather than step up to greatness.

Those who head in a positive direction develop a healthy humility and a sense of deep gratitude regarding their accomplishments. Greater purpose, philanthropic endeavors, and considerations of meaningful legacy occupy the space previously held by concerns about worthiness. Ego and its fear-based defenses give way to a deeper understanding of one's place in the larger scheme of universal order.

In an abundant world the only real barriers to success are self-imposed. If we are the ones who put up the roadblocks, we can also remove them. It is simply a matter of deciding: deciding to live consciously, look inwardly, identify cognitive patterns we wish to change, and persevere through the transition of replacing old thoughts with new ones until the latter become habits. It is about designing the kind of support systems we need to help us through this lifelong process. And it is about closing the gap between our words and our actions, our intentions and our behaviors. We are the creators of our own reality, and everything that comes to us does so by virtue of that to which we have given our attention. The choice is ours: to live with deliberate clarity, or unconsciously by default.

ABOUT THE AUTHOR

Karen A. Jones, MFT, is a licensed psychotherapist and professional coach who has maintained a successful private practice for the past 25 years in Orange County, California. She brings a holistic approach to the *Business of Wellness*™ through her motivational and business coaching, working with corporate executives, entrepreneurs, and network marketers. She is a nationally recognized lecturer in the fields of team building, personal growth, leadership, and behavioral change. Karen is a published researcher and coauthor of Inspiration to Realization, volume 2. She may be reached at http://www.karenjones.com.

10

BELIEFS

What the Heck Is Wrong with Her?

Teri Rose

I had learned to cringe when I heard the word *September*. This response was constantly reinforced by friends and family who knew my history of repeated calamities, mostly in September. Some of them seemed to relish asking the rhetorical question, "What's it going to be this year?" They knew it was coming and waited with expectation for the continuing drama.

I'm not sure exactly when it started, only that one day, we connected the dots and saw that September meant I would be going to the hospital. The first time may have been when I was a teenager and worked at a summer camp. I had gone to the infirmary with back pain. The nurse gave me someone else's prescription medicine, and I had a drug reaction and couldn't breathe. They rushed me to the emergency room.

Then there was the time I was horseback riding with a friend. She started having trouble, and we decided to switch horses. As I landed in the saddle, the horse started backing into some tall weeds. I was about to find out there was a section of barbed wire fence camouflaged by the weeds. What happened next wasn't pleasant, and once again, I headed off to the emergency room.

I got over that incident, but not over my love of horses. I lived to be around them and spent a lot of time riding around the summer camp where I worked as a teenager. One day, I volunteered to ride out through the fields to check on something for an outside contractor. I bridled a horse and jumped on bareback. It was one of those beautiful days that people dream about for their outdoor activities. I wanted to be on a horse, feeling the wind in my hair and the sun on my face as I moved along, looking at the clouds overhead. Unfortunately, that is exactly what I was doing as I rode along a dirt road that had been cut through some corn fields. We kicked up some pheasants, and with a great commotion, my horse jumped for the sky. Suddenly, I was feeling air instead of horse and somehow caught a hoof as we landed. Once again, I was off to the emergency room.

Each experience caused more and more people to inquire, "What is it going to be this September?" I'm sure they were also thinking, "What the heck is wrong with her?"

Ever since my childhood, I had loved to think about life and attempt to solve its mysteries. That interest was sparked when I first heard my mom tell a story about her twin sister, who had died of heart failure at 11. Mom had gone to the grocery store with a friend when suddenly she stopped what she was doing and said, "I have to get home." She turned toward home and ran all the way. Shortly after walking through the door, her sister died.

I begged my mom to tell the story over and over again, hoping to satisfy my desire to know what caused her to run home. The answer was always the same. Something told her to get home. She just knew she had to.

Because of my insatiable hunger to learn more about how this could be possible, I read, studied, and listened. I discovered that everything is made up of energy and that all energy has a frequency. Think about a radio: you push a button on a box in your car and hear the weather report. How does that happen? Information is carried on electromagnetic waves. You don't see them, but frequencies are all around you. They are also received by and emitted from you. We now have the technology to prove that as fact.

I heard versions of the same message over and over again, and here's what it boils down to: what we think, believe, and expect becomes our reality. Our thoughts are things that cause a different physiological response that corresponds to the emotion we are feeling at the time. The frequency of joy and expectation of good creates a much different frequency than the feeling of fear or lack of self-confidence. The frequency created carries a message out into the world. That frequency attracts back to us what we send out as belief and expectation. It is called the Law of Attraction.

When it finally sunk in, I got mad at myself for allowing this expectation of disaster every September into my thoughts. When it hit me, I slammed my fist down and said, "No more!" I made a decision to change the way I thought about things. I made a proclamation that next September, I would find myself in perfect health, accident-free, and full of thoughts of hope and expectations of good.

I changed my thoughts; I refused to be around anyone who even wanted to kid me about accidents. I constantly said things like "cancel" when a thought hit me that allowed the "September Phenomena" to be a part of my conscious thoughts. I removed the title and insisted that my thoughts of September be filled with anticipation of the beautiful fall colors and all the fun activities associated with fall and winter.

An amazing thing happened. My "September Phenomena" stopped! I never had another horse accident or went to the hospital again. I had made a conscious decision to change my thoughts in order to change what was happening in my world, *and it worked*!

I was beside myself with excitement. I had made a decision and followed through by removing myself from people and situations that weren't supportive. I made the effort to become very conscious of my thoughts and expectations. That was easier than going through all the stitches, aches, and pains I had endured. I was really on to something.

Next came the rude awakening. I couldn't get it to work consistently. I used the same techniques on many things; some worked, and others didn't. I struggled for years to understand why all the affirmations, visualizations, determination, and expectations in the world didn't seem to make a difference in some situations. While I was able to attract some of my goals, some things, very important to me, just wouldn't materialize.

My research led to fascinating new discoveries about cellular memories and a new understanding of how the brain works. Then I began to understand the concept that perception is reality. I began to understand that a vast amount of information is being processed very rapidly at the subconscious level. These data, both new and what have been stored from past experiences, are referenced to give meaning to what is happening moment by moment. Activated cellular memories from the past reinforce beliefs and expectations of the future. You will continue to attract what you believe about yourself at that cellular level. That information is running the show. If you allow yourself to run on autopilot, you will constantly recreate the past or what you do not want. What you think about, believe, and expect becomes your reality. You must be aware of your thoughts, correct misinformation, and spend time creating the future you desire.

The important thing is to take the necessary steps to change the part of your story that causes you to be unhappy or unfulfilled. That will allow you to attract and then live the life of your dreams.

What do you think about most of the time and expect to happen today, tomorrow, and in the future?

ABOUT THE AUTHOR

Teri Rose is a success coach and also works with Dr. Alex Loyd Services with her "Success Unlimited" program. Her greatest asset is the fact that she has used what she teaches to transform all aspects of her own life. Her passion is teaching others to do the same. Visit her Web site at http://www.PeaceOfSuccess.com.

11

BODY LANGUAGE

The Top 10 Body Language Tips

Robert Phipps

It doesn't matter how much you know in your personal or professional life; your knowledge is quite useless, unless you know how to communicate it to others, and I don't just mean with the words you use. I'm also talking about the nonverbal communication, or body language, that goes on in every face-to-face situation.

Here are my personal tips on how to use your body language to assist you in communicating your message more successfully.

How to Make a Good Impression

Eye contact in any culture is one of the most important aspects when dealing with others, especially people we've just met. Maintaining good eye contact shows respect and interest in what they have to say. In the United States, the United Kingdom, and Australia we tend to keep eye contact around 60 to 70 percent of the time. We tend to look directly at the face more when we're listening than talking.

By allowing your gaze to drift away from the face some of the time, you won't make yourself or other people feel self-conscious. Instead, it will give them a feeling of comfort and genuine warmth in your company and will allow you to gather your thoughts. Any more eye contact than this, and you could come across as too intense; any less, and you give off signals that perhaps you're losing interest in them or the content of their conversation.

Posture is the next thing to master—get your posture right, and you'll automatically feel good. Next time you notice you're feeling a bit down, take a few moments to notice how you're sitting or standing. Chances are you'll be slouched over with your shoulders drooping down and inward. This collapses the chest and inhibits good breathing, which in turn can make you feel nervous, uncomfortable, and low. Good posture should be easy and relaxed on the spine, and there should be no tension in the muscles—just imagine a thread running through your spine and being gently lifted upward.

Head position is a great one to play with, both with yourself and others. When you want to feel confident and self-assured, keep your head level, both horizontally and vertically. You can also use this straight head position when you want to be authoritative with people and you want them to take you and what you're saying seriously. Conversely, when you want to be friendly and in the listening, receptive mode, tilt your head just a little to one side or other. You can shift the tilt from left to right at different points in the conversation as well as nod your head to encourage people to continue speaking.

Arm movements let people know how open and receptive we are to them. We use them to hug and to push away, so keep your arms relaxed at the side of your body or behind your back. This shows you are not scared to take on whatever comes your way and you meet challenges full-on. In general terms the more outgoing you are as a person, the more you tend to use your arms outwardly and away from the body. The quieter you are, the less you gesticulate, and the movements are smaller. Try to strike a natural balance and keep your arm motions midway. When wanting to come across in the best possible light, a very simple rule is not to cross your arms. Obviously, if someone says something that you disagree with, then by all means, show your disapproval by crossing them, but otherwise, don't.

Legs are the furthest point away from the brain, and consequently, they're one of the hardest parts of the body to consciously control. They tend to move around a lot more than normal when we are nervous, stressed, or being deceptive. In most situations, especially interviews or work meetings, it's best to keep them as still as possible. Be careful, too, in the way you cross your legs. Do you cross at the knees or ankles, or do you bring your leg up to rest on the knee of the other? This is more a question of comfort than anything else. Just be aware that the last position mentioned is known as the "figure four" and is generally perceived as the most defensive leg cross, especially if you do it just after someone says or does something you don't like, because the natural tendency is to grip the ankle and squeeze, which shows people your tension.

Orientation, or angle of the body, gives an indication of our attitudes and feelings toward others. We naturally angle ourselves toward people we find attractive, friendly, and interesting and angle ourselves away from those we don't. This includes the way we lean in and out from people, as we will often just tilt from the pelvis and lean sideways or forward to share a bit of conversation. Being directly face-on to someone can be adversarial, like a game of chess. In situations where there may be tension or stress it is better to approach softly from the side than straight on.

Hand gestures are so numerous that it's hard to give a brief guide. Palms slightly up and outward is seen as open and friendly. Palm-down gestures are generally seen as dominant, emphasizing, and possibly aggressive, especially when there is no movement or bending between the wrist and the forearm. This palm up, palm down is very important when it comes to handshaking, and where appropriate, you should always offer a handshake when meeting new people. The handshake should be upright and vertical, which will convey a feeling of equality.

Distance or proximity to others is crucial if you want to give off the right signals. Stand or sit too close, and you'll be marked as "pushy"; too far away, and you'll be "standoffish." Neither are what we want, so observe when in a group situation how close all the other people are to each other. If you move closer to someone and he backs away, you're probably just a little too close to his comfort zone. You've "overstepped the mark" and should pull back a little to your previous position.

Mouth movements can give away all sorts of clues as to how we're feeling. We purse our lips, bite them, and sometimes twist them to the side when we're thinking or maybe holding back a sarcastic or angry comment we don't wish to reveal. Nevertheless, it will probably be spotted by others, and although they may not know the comment, they will get a feeling you are not pleased. There are also different types of smiles, and each gives off a corresponding feeling to the recipient. Genuine smiles show the teeth and wrinkle the corners of the eyes.

Your ears are also important, even though, in general terms, most people can't move them much. However, if you've got two ears and only one mouth, try to use them in that order. If you listen twice as much as you talk, you'll come across as a good communicator who knows how to strike a balanced conversation without being self-centered or, at the other end of the scale, a wallflower.

Practice these 10 simple ways to improve your communication skills, and you'll reap the rewards in your personal and professional life. People will find you more attractive, more open, more presentable, and more professional. Go ahead—you have nothing to lose and everything to gain.

ABOUT THE AUTHOR

Robert Phipps is probably the United Kingdom's best known expert in the field of nonverbal communication, a.k.a., body language. Robert is in constant demand by the media world, with more than 300 TV and radio appearances on a variety of shows, and by commercial business, where he has worked with some of the world's largest companies. As a certified hypnotherapist, his 20 years of experience have helped him develop a truly unique approach to getting the very best out of people by understanding the constantly changing emotions running through the mind and body. To find out more, visit http://www.robertphipps.com or http://www.bodylanguagetraining.com.

12

BOREDOM

Unbearable Boredom:
A Call to a Magnificent Life

Annette Colby

"Life is okay, but I'm bored with it all. I get up, go through my morning habits, and generally keep going. During the day I smile, engage in friendly conversations, attend to the requirements of my work. After work, it's home to watch television, eat, and sleep. In between, there's the movies, gym, music, and shopping. My days are predictable and routine. What is joy? What is excitement? I think I'm missing the meaning of my life."

If you ever find yourself dealing with unbearable boredom, treat it not as an undesirable invader, but celebrate the arrival of an important messenger. Without boredom we'd comfortably vegetate in neutral, passing time by doing the same things in the same ways over and over again. Boredom's appearance is a glorious sign of impending growth. New interests, passions, talents, or strengths seek expression. It's a wake-up call indicating a readiness for more: more self-love, self-leadership, self-expression, pleasure, passion, and spontaneity.

Boredom is an invitation to allow an old self to fade away and a new potential self to emerge. Certain facets of self-control and repetitive behaviors are ready to be released in favor of expanded imagination, creativity, inspiration, and spontaneity. What was once an effective, useful routine has now become stagnant, stale, and passive. Boredom is the interim period; a place neither here nor there. On one side lies the safe, comfortable, and dependable, yet outgrown past. On the other side lies an intriguing, daring, more passionate future. Boredom identifies the natural resistance we all have toward letting go of the known and entering the unknown.

Once boredom reveals its presence, several options are available: we can sink deeper into passivity and dullness; the physical edginess can be temporarily concealed with greater levels of entertainment, distractions, and diversions; or the boredom can be sedated with food, drink, or choice addictions.

Another alternative exists: embrace the message of boredom. Beneath the uncomfortable discontentment lies a natural, inherent call to the lifelong process of individuation. It is time to broaden personal horizons beyond past former levels of conformity and social adaptation. Greater individuality, power, love, and creation beckon from within. A readiness is brewing to connect more deeply with the heart of our existence.

The chains of boredom are more easily shed by allowing time to welcome ideas that spark the imagination and expand the heart. What is truly important; what fascinates and engages our spirit? We have the ability to go inside, sort through some ideas, and decide what an exciting life would look like. We feel good, and our bodies feel good, when we assume responsibility for choosing to focus on stimulating desires, personal interests, and inner passions. Only we know what feels good within, what excites, ignites, and enlivens. We gently allow for the emergence of new potentials and new possibilities—and decide to feel good in the process.

Instead of letting life just happen, we can go inside and ask, "What do I want?" Typically, the first answers are filled with details about what is not wanted. Accept this as an excellent starting point. But our responsibility is to make sure we take the extra step and actually find an exciting vision to focus on. We become what we think about, and it is up to us to determine what thoughts and visions dominate our mind. We take control of our lives as we spend more time with thoughts that increase excitement and less with those that decrease excitement.

Will an exciting life happen instantaneously just because we shift thoughts from boredom to more passionate visions? Obviously, the answer is no. Some individuals will wonder how in the world they can possibly imagine exciting outcomes when they are currently just barely getting through the day. They don't have a clue what to imagine; they are frustrated and mad at themselves for being in this position. For anyone, creating a larger life requires effort, patience, and time. Yet not much changes without first engaging imagination and intention. Excitement is the element that moves us toward unfinished business and unfolding potential. It is what we want to be doing right now, while providing the energy necessary to do it.

Who we are and what excites us matters. The irritation of boredom simply reminds us, in a very noticeable way, that energy is swirling about without passionate direction or purpose. Rather than permitting our lives to be blown about like leaves on the dirt, victims of circumstance, we allow imagination to set the foundation for direction and purpose in life. Boredom is an indication of a certain readiness to become increasingly loyal to internal passions, desires, and values. We can decide we are worthy of forming enthusiastic relationships with what we care about.

Feeling good, feeling alive, and being a radiant human is important for us and for the world. We consciously develop our divine natures through the joyful manifestation of dreams and desires. A loving community begins first with a party of one. It begins by forming excited relationships with our bodies, thoughts, emotions, and ideas. Our inner dreams are the joy of life, the salvation of earth, and the future of the people of this planet. Bringing paradise to earth is more than just a lofty concept; it is an individual endeavor, a personal responsibility. As human beings, we suffer when this physical connection between spirit and earth is no longer expanding and evolving as it is meant to. Our most important task is to first give permission to love, excite, and empower ourselves. We take the time to ensure we are the ones balanced, enlightened, and joyful.

To share and expand love with all life on this incredible earth, we begin with ourselves. We serve others when we become living, breathing, walking examples of inspired, excited lives. We inspire others to greatness when we ourselves have come to realize that happiness, success, abundance, empowerment, and joy are possible. The magic spreads as we become the magic. Personal success is allowed, so our beautiful concepts are no longer lofty spiritual abstractions, but tangible, physical manifestations.

The next time you are perpetually bored, realize the beautiful magic wishing to unfold. An invitation has been issued to venture beneath the surface and investigate new and exciting potentials and possibilities. Inspiration spreads as the success of one individual ignites the desires and dreams of another. It makes a difference that we, you and I, carry excitement once more. Boredom asks us to become the living, breathing embodiment of joy. Our joy brings light into the world.

ABOUT THE AUTHOR

Helping people create joy, excited physical aliveness, and a grounded spiritual connection has been the lifework of Dr. Annette Colby, RD. Her fascination with the power of the mind, emotions, spirituality, and physicality has led her to become a leader in the field of personal growth and consciousness. As a nationally known consultant, educator, and author, her contagious passion for life is shared in her private practice, where she inspires people to believe in themselves and find themselves worthy of receiving their dreams. This article is based on her soon-to-be-published book, The Highest Potential. Visit http://www.LovingMiracles.com for a free, weekly, life-changing newsletter.

13

Creating Personal Boundaries: Commanding Respect in Love, Work, and Life!

Lisa Angelettie

Many people walk through life making career, relationship, and other life decisions in response or in reaction to others around them. This is an extremely toxic way of living because these people will never live based on their own life designs. If you never realize that you are following this pattern, it is possible that you will live the majority of your life at the mercy of others—never really doing what you want to do, and possibly never even knowing what it is you actually want out of life.

Ask yourself these questions:

1. Would people describe me as a mystery or complicated?
2. Do people walk all over me at work? In my family? In my relationships?
3. Do I make it clear to those around me what I expect from them through either my words or my actions?
4. Do people often misinterpret what I mean?
5. Am I all talk and no action?

If you answered yes to any of these questions, then you are missing some personal boundaries in one or more areas of your life.

For instance, Veronica (whose name was changed for privacy) is a very strong and self-assured person—she is on the fast track at the technology company where she works. People know what and what not to ask of her as well as what to expect of her. She has a great relationship with her supervisor, and Veronica's coworkers respect her. The rules are very clear at her job, and there is clarity and little confusion. It's a perfect setting for a work environment, and that is why Veronica thrives there.

But follow Veronica after work into her personal life, and she isn't as clear about her boundaries. Veronica was in a relationship with a man 10 years her senior and allowed him to set the boundaries for the both of them. Veronica had never told or shown him what her personal relationship boundaries were but was shocked when he picked up another woman for a ménage à trois while they were both out at a bar.

What's even more interesting, Veronica said nothing and assumed that her boyfriend would figure out that he was hurting and embarrassing her and then drop the whole thing. Of course, he didn't make that realization; the fact that she said nothing and allowed the woman to come home with them was a green light in his mind. He only realized what a huge mistake he had made when Veronica couldn't take it any longer and exploded both emotionally and physically. She started pushing the woman out of the house, then packed her things and left in a fury. This was when she reached out for some professional help and began to learn the concept of *recognizing and then communicating what her personal boundaries are* within a relationship.

After Veronica answered the five questions listed earlier and assessed her answers, she began to see that she had always had personal boundaries but never effectively communicated them to any of her boyfriends because she always assumed that they "should know" based on who she was as a person. What a falsity! Most people are not mind readers—especially men! We had to change Veronica's way of thinking; we taught her to use some of the positive communication skills she had gained from her work environment and apply them to her personal life.

While her current relationship couldn't be salvaged based on such huge sexuality differences, she began seriously seeing a new man, with whom she did set personal and relationship boundaries. With him, she:

- made it clear that she was looking for a monogamous relationship;
- expressed what the rules were for people interacting with her pets;
- communicated that her patience for lateness had its limits;
- verbalized clearly that physical or emotional abuse was nonnegotiable and unacceptable;

…and a couple of other, smaller things. The end result was that this new man in her life was clear about what she would and would not accept and, of course, would learn more as their relationship progressed. There were things she may not have said to him in the beginning but that he would learn as new situations arose.

Veronica *no longer feared* that setting personal boundaries in her relationship would scare men away. In fact, it was empowering for her to say to men, "Hey, this is who I am—either accept me, or don't." She took the power back and, consequently, is involved in a much more reciprocal and rewarding relationship.

While this may seem an extreme example to some, it can be applied to almost any situation and any relationship because the bottom line is that many people will test your limits, especially if they don't know what your limits are and how far they reach.

I advise people to assume that the people in their lives are clueless! We tend to give the people we love way more benefit of the doubt than they deserve. You need to spell things out. Make them clear. And do not avoid setting your personal boundaries and limitations because you are afraid of what comes next. You have one life and once chance to live it according to your personal truth. If you do that, you will live a life more rewarding than you can imagine—no matter what so-called opportunity, job, relationship, or friend you lose along the way.

Homework Assignment: Get your favorite drink from the fridge, sit at the kitchen table, and write out a list of 10 rules, limits, or boundaries you would like to live by in your life. Do it now, before you get distracted. *Set your boundaries* today!

ABOUT THE AUTHOR

Lisa Angelettie is the Director of GirlShrink, Inc. (http://www.GirlShrink.com), an author, therapist, and online advice authority. This article is based on her most recent book, *Relationship 911! (7 Steps to Saving Your Sinking Relationship)*. Lisa created the Relationship 911! Program, a simple, "step-by-step" course that has helped couples repair their relationships. If you need help setting personal boundaries, she also offers private coaching, writes a syndicated advice column, "Ask GirlShrink," writes articles, and publishes the popular "Better Choices" online newsletter. Get her *free* Relationship 911! introductory e-course at http://www.AboutMyRelationship.com.

© Copyright 2006, Lisa Angelettie.

14

BREATHING EXERCISES

Energy Breathing: Be Healthier, Feel Happier, Have More Energy, and Achieve Peak Performance in Everything You Do!

Chunyi Lin

The single most important action in all our lives is one we seldom, if ever, think about—breathing! If we don't breathe, none of the rest of life is even possible. Yet when was the last time you paid any attention to the way you breathe? You know breathing is essential to keeping you alive. What you may not know is that the way in which you choose to breathe is essential to how fully you live. Opera stars know the importance of breathing. So do great actors. So do champion swimmers. Sadly, most of the rest of us, including most athletes, simply take breathing for granted.

It is through breathing that we take in oxygen to fuel our minds and bodies. The more fuel we have, the better we function. The more effectively we breathe, the more effectively we live. The benefits of effective breathing include:

- increased oxygen intake
- increased oxygenation of the blood, tissues, muscles, and organs
- relaxation of the body
- calming of the mind
- balance of the emotions
- enhanced mental focus, clarity, and creativity
- relief of stress.

Put simply, proper breathing can make you faster, stronger, calmer, and smarter, which is pretty wonderful when you stop and think about it—something so simple can be so powerfully helpful and healthful.

Conversely, if you are not breathing effectively, you simply cannot be as fast, as strong, as calm, as smart, or as healthy as you could be.

What I want to share with you here is a simple yet powerfully effective method for enhancing the benefits of breathing. Call it "energy breathing." Energy breathing is an easy way to enhance your mind-body-spirit connection. That is the key.

Your mind and body are not separate things. Your mind affects every part of your physical body, just as your physical body affects your mind. If your body is tense, if your breathing is shallow or rapid, your mind cannot be focused and calm. If your mind is focused on all the stress in your life, your body will be stressed, also. You need to have your mind and body working in concert to get the most out of life. This is especially true of your breathing.

Your spirit is your connection with the infinite. In energy breathing you connect your mind and body with the limitless power of the universe. You *are* mind, body, and spirit. It only makes sense to make the best use of all three aspects of you.

I use the term energy breathing because everything in the universe is a form of energy. Albert Einstein established this principle in the Western world more than a hundred years ago. Ancient scholars in China and other cultures have created health and wellness systems based on this principle for thousands of years.

When I say everything is a form of energy, I mean this literally. A rock, a tree, the air, every cell in your body, these are all forms of energy. You are an energy being. Even your thoughts are a form of energy, and a very powerful one. Every thought you have sends electrical impulses somewhere in your body, and your body responds accordingly.

The ancient Chinese scholars saw energy as two main components: yin and yang. Think of yin and yang like female and male, like the positive and negative poles of a magnet, or like the positive and negative charges at either end of a battery.

They are opposites that attract each other. For optimal performance, yin and yang need to be in good balance.

That is some of the background behind energy breathing. How you do energy breathing is very simple.

Energy Breathing Step-by-Step:

- Sit or lie down in a comfortable position.
- Put a smile on your face (this helps relax your mind and body).
- Place the tip of your tongue gently against the roof of your mouth (this connects the two main energy channels in your body).
- Breathe through your nose in slow, gentle, deep breaths.
- As you breathe in, gently pull your lower stomach in a little.
- As you breathe out, let your stomach out.

(The upper part of the body belongs to yang energy; the lower part of the body belongs to yin energy. Breathing in is a part of yin energy; breathing out is yang. One of the reasons we get sick is that yin and yang energies are not communicating well. By pulling your lower stomach in as you inhale and letting it out as you exhale, you are enhancing the communication of the yin and yang energies.)

This is the body part of energy breathing. Now we connect it with the mind and spirit by utilizing simple visualization and mental focus. Say in your mind the "password":

> I am in the universe. The universe is in my body. The
> universe and I are one.

If you choose to use a different password, that is fine. The words are not as important as their meaning—you are not alone. You are connected with the infinite.

- As you breathe in,
    - imagine you are using your entire body to breathe
    - see and feel the air, the limitless energy of the universe, flowing into your body through every part of your body.

- As you breathe out,
    - o visualize any tiredness or stress, pain or sickness, any doubt or worries changing into smoke
    - o and visualize it shooting out of your body to the ends of the universe.

As you continue breathing in this way, feel your mind and body becoming completely relaxed. Know that every cell in your body is being restored to its perfect, balanced state, revitalized and rejuvenated.

To end your energy breathing session:

- take one final, slow, gentle, deep breath
- slowly open your eyes
- rub your hands together, palm to palm
- gently massage your face . . .
    - o running your fingertips gently up each side of the bridge of your nose to your forehead, then out and down to your chin in a circular motion
    - o repeat this motion several times.

That's all there is to it. Energy breathing is just that simple.

The key is to allow yourself to relax and enjoy the experience. Do not concern yourself with whether you are "getting it right." There is no right. There is only good, better, and best. The more you practice energy breathing, the better off you will be, and the more you will empower yourself to be your best.

Why not take a few minutes now to practice energy breathing. Even just five minutes of energy breathing is helpful. If you can do it several times a day or for a longer period of time, that is even better.

Breathing is what you must do to stay alive, but the way you choose to breathe can empower you to truly live.

ABOUT THE AUTHOR

With a master's degree in holistic healing, Chunyi Lin is a certified International Qigong Master and the founder and creator of Spring Forest Qigong. He has taught his techniques to nearly 100,000 people through classes or home-learning courses. He is also Director of the Spring Forest Qigong Healing Center in Minneapolis, where he provides healing assistance to more than 7,000 people from all over the world each year. He is a frequent keynote speaker at medical conferences and is the coauthor of a #1 Amazon.com best-selling book, *Born A Healer*. Visit him on the Web at http://www.SpringForestQigong.com.

15

Money Management for the New Millennium: Four Reasons Why Managing Money Today Is So Hard and What You Can Do about It

Judy Lawrence

Have you ever wondered why managing your money seems so hard? Not only is it challenging knowing which method will work, but more significantly, the real issue is determining which method will bring a long-term, sustainable, satisfying lifestyle change.

You would think, with the abundance of available information, that it would be a no-brainer to effectively manage your personal finances. So what gives? Why is it so hard to manage money? Could it be related to the current pace of your life?

Think about the following modern obstacles and consider how they may apply in your life.

Choice Overload

Would you like boiled ham, or Italian ham? American cheese, or Provolone? Wheat, or white bread? Should you pay off your debt, or put more money into savings? Buy a no load or load mutual fund?

Believe it or not, there actually was a time when choices were limited to things like ham and cheese, silver or black eyeglass frames, vanilla, chocolate, or Neapolitan ice cream, one long distance carrier, 30-year mortgages, and paying either with cash or check. Where in your life right now do you have the simplicity of two choices?

Even though these many options are designed to make you happier, this ongoing daily accumulation of the most mundane choices eventually causes such "overwhelm" that there is little energy left for the more important financial decisions. Have you ever been so overwhelmed that you just picked *anything* to get the decision over with? And if so, what did this decision cost you in terms of money, disappointment, frustration, or time?

Lifestyle Overload

Can you think of the last time you had an evening or weekend when you had nothing to do? If you are like many, your life is probably crammed with family, work, and community obligations. So just when do you squeeze in the time to pay bills, research major financial decisions, compare prices, record and evaluate your spending, prioritize your financial needs, or take time to discuss financial matters with your spouse and family? Many times, the expensive late fees and bounced check fees are not about lack of money or money skills but instead are due to a lack of time to pay the bills, deposit the paychecks, or get financially organized.

Media Overload

Would your 12 year old really care as much about shopping at Victoria's Secret if she wasn't reading teen magazines and wanting to dress like Britney Spears? Would you still have bought that Dell computer if you weren't told 100 times you "gotta have a Dell"?

It's hard to maintain a simple, manageable life with the daily bombardment from TV sitcoms, commercials, celebrities, movies, computer games, Web sites, and magazines influencing spending in every facet of our lives. To feel trendy, we notice how to dress, style our hair, feed our pets, furnish our homes, travel, play, and invest our money.

The cost of this media overload can be financial as well as emotional. Even if you are able to "keep up with the Joneses," are you able to keep up with the payments? Notice how much energy goes into putting on the brakes for your children or for yourself every time you are in the mall and see something you just have to have. After all, how can you pass up that tempting, convenient, fabulous product for yourself, child, home, vehicle, or pet? Yet if you weren't aware of this product, you probably would not even feel like you were "missing out" if you didn't have it. Also, your monthly budget would not be disrupted by this unplanned expense.

Basic Necessities Overload

Basic living necessities are no longer basic. Can you imagine the days when you didn't have cell phones, basic cable, Internet connections, or software upgrades? Now, can you imagine even functioning in your job or family life without many of these services? And how much are all those "basic necessities" adding to the other fixed costs in your monthly spending plan?

When you wonder why you can't seem to get ahead or make ends meet, often the problem is the increased volume of fixed expenses. Managing your money effectively may mean choosing to cut back on more of the discretionary spending to keep the expenses from spilling over onto the credit cards.

Now What?

So how does all this overload create obstacles to money management? More time and energy continues to seep out as you agonize over choices, hectic schedules, and unsatisfied wants, instead of spreading it over to important financial decisions, productive planning, and the implementation of a workable spending plan.

There is certainly no lack of information and help for getting out of debt and creating a spending plan. What *could* be lacking is the time or energy to evaluate the endless amount of information and determine what system would work best for your particular situation. You probably know inside what is best for you. To trigger your own insights, below are a few suggestions to help you get started.

- **Stop and regroup.** After 9/11, everyone had a wake-up call regarding their true priorities. Review your priority list again or create one. Which activities, responsibilities, or decisions can you let go of or pass on to someone else to free up more time to manage your money on a regular basis?
- **Pick and save.** Many money management systems already exist. Don't try to recreate the wheel or research and compare the choices to death. Choose one and start. Worrying about the best or easiest system or the least expensive one at this point is more about procrastination. Recognize that, move on, pick one system, and get started.

- **Manual or electronic?** If you are still more comfortable with the traditional pen and paper, start there. There are hundreds of books on the topic. To simplify your decision, go with a workbook that already has monthly forms set up. The better books will help you get organized, simplify the money management process, and save you thousands of dollars in the long run. Find a workbook that helps you manage your periodic expenses and monthly bills and tracks where the daily money is going. The same principles apply to electronic money management systems.
- **Simplify and streamline.** Have a weekly family "board meeting" with your children and spouse. Get input on ways to streamline events in the household. Discuss financial issues so more decisions are made ahead of time, rather than impulsively. Create space and time for staying current on a regular basis with managing your money. Reduce your number of accounts. Eliminate paying bills by check. Arrange for automatic withdrawal from your bank for monthly bills, pay bills online, or automatically charge monthly bills to your credit card if you are building up the miles. Of course, remember to pay off the credit card bill in full.

No matter what the cost of any system you use, by really using it, you will ultimately save at least 10 times more than you paid for it.

Take a moment to step back, look at your life, and make decisions that are proactive and rational, instead of reactive and emotional. Remember, the cost of financial peace of mind may be priceless.

ABOUT THE AUTHOR

Judy Lawrence is a financial counselor and coach in Silicon Valley and has been counseling individuals, couples, and small businesses for two decades. Her best-selling book, *The Budget Kit: Common Cents Money Management*, 4th edition, sold over 400,000 copies and has been in continuous print for 25 years. If you would like to sign up for Judy's free "Budgeting Without Tears" seven-week e-course or free monthly newsletter, or just find out more about her services and books, you can reach her at http://www.moneytracker.com, judy@moneytracker.com, or (408) 747–9589.

16

See It Happen! Visualization

Deborah Baker-Receniello

> Life does not consist mainly, or even largely, of facts
> and happenings. It consists mainly of the stream of
> thought that is forever flowing through one's head.
> –Mark Twain

As you become aware of the invisibility of creation, you can begin to understand how to make yourself more aware of your creative abilities. Science says you use knowledge and experience to build a larger, more expanded model of thought for greater experiences in life. You question, What if? What are the possibilities? How can I do that better or differently? How do I make miracles happen? What does it take to make the extraordinary common in my life? This is an internal reality that science explains through the process of brain function.

The frontal lobe of the brain is where pictures, in the form of electromagnetic energy, are stored as knowledge. The brain uses a process for generating and transforming energy into reality. You can think of a vision as a mental matrix, blueprint, or model. Take this blueprint and transform it with the aid of electrical stimuli (neurons firing in the brain). You need to charge or animate its form with energy (emotion), chemical constructs (hormones), and memory from the hypothalamus.

The more expanded the emotion or character of the vision, the more energy will be required to bring it into the physical world, using first the vision or intention, then concentrated focus to expand or charge the vision with energy. This brings forth more intense desire. With this desire comes the commitment, which transforms the emotion (energy) into physical force and action.

The truth is that our minds are tremendously powerful, and the pictures we focus on produce results in our lives, whether we like the results or not. The realm of ideas is the inner world of thought, imagination, intention, and feeling. Things, places, and circumstances make up the physical environment in which we live—actions, objects, and events.

Olympic athletes imagine themselves performing each move to perfection and then standing on the podium to receive the medal around their necks. Bruce Jenner, Nancy Kerrigan, and a host of others have publicly talked about the pivotal role visualization played in their achievements. If visualization techniques have such a powerful impact on the performance of these athletes, *imagine* what it will do for you and your personal and business success!

Have you ever daydreamed about being on a romantic Caribbean island, under the shade of a tree swaying gently in the ocean breeze? Have you pictured yourself having a conversation with Donald Trump or being interviewed by Oprah? Everyone daydreams at one time or another. What is the next step to taking a daydream to a reality?

You need to know your end result. If you want to be a great watercolor artist, see yourself as one. Visualize your work displayed in the best galleries around the world. Visualize raving reviews of your work by famous critics. Visualize yourself in your studio, creating works that are uniquely your own. Do not just see the picture, but hear it, feel it, live it, and be it! And make sure every single thing is what you really want, not something you think you have to do. Make it alive! Your subconscious will do the rest.

Visualize Forward

Visualize yourself doing whatever it is that you wish to do. Bring in great detail as if you have already arrived at your chosen destination. Want to start a new business? See yourself on opening day greeting new customers and making sales. One of the most legendary examples of actor Jim Carrey's devotion to visualization was when he made out a check to himself for $10 million for "acting services rendered." In 1990, when he was still a relative unknown, he had postdated the check for Thanksgiving 1995. It wasn't about money; rather, Carrey knew that if he were making that much, he'd be working with the best people on the best material. That was always his dream. The really amazing part is that just before Thanksgiving 1995, Jim Carrey signed a contract for $10 million.

Visualize Your Goals Already Completed

What would you be doing with your time? Who are your powerful clients and referrals?

How many? How often? How much money, satisfaction, gratitude, or treasures have you created for yourself? How much can you afford to give away to your favorite people or charity?

Visualize Any Forecasting

Use the same technique as above, except instead of a goal, begin to create a plush meeting room, several comfortable chairs, and a table. Invite prospects in, and have a conversation with them about their needs and desires. Invite leaders, experts, or friends in any field and ask questions.

Visualize Your Speech or Presentation, and Rehearse

Dr. John Gray, author of *Men Are from Mars, Women Are from Venus*, boldly used his visualizations. His subconscious mind could not tell the difference between the "reality" of having 70 people attend a seminar and the visualization Gray created of having 3,000 people show up to hear what he had to say. As a result, the subconscious mind, believing it to be true, acted on that belief and as if by magic, manifested the huge crowd!

- See yourself before the audience.
- Present yourself and your information with style and grace, or bodaciously and comically.
- See the heads in the audience nod in agreement.
- See the (*x* number of) smiling faces and the enthusiasm.
- Hear the applause.
- See the back end sales.
- See the new clients.
- See the next engagement.
- See the next product.

Visualize Your Successful Day

It's time to start your day—what time is it? You get dressed—what are you wearing? You open your door to business—where is it, and what does it look like? What do you do all day? See satisfied customers and clients. See yourself at the end of the day, knowing you did your best. When you retire for the day, you rest comfortably. Create your day—*this is a great exercise to do before you start each day.*

Commitment takes us across the bridge to action, planning, execution, and feedback. Commitment is the will to go for what you want and the willingness to let go of things that keep you from getting it. Then the action occurs—those steps you plan and initiate. Then you have the experience. After the experience you can build a better model. Take what is known about your experience and use that to make it better. Each time, you create a better model of your experiences and create a better world.

What are some ways that you can use visualization in your life or business?

ABOUT THE AUTHOR

Deborah Baker-Receniello is CEO of DBR Life Strategies & Business Coach, Inc. She is the author of *Why It Works! The Science Behind Manifesting Everything You Desire*, and her forthcoming book, *Play a Bigger Game! Proven Strategies to Design and Grow Your Successful Small Business*, premieres in 2006. Deborah is a noted speaker, author, workshop leader, and facilitator. If you are serious about playing a bigger game, contact Deborah to assist you in designing and growing yourself and your businesses, attracting more clients, and making more money. Visit her Web site at http://www.dbrlifecoach.com, or e-mail her at deborah@dbrlifecoach.com.

17

Finding the Work You Love!

Keri Coffman-Thiede

> The water pitcher cries out for water to carry, and the person cries out for work that is real.
>
> – Marge Piercy

Depending on the research you read, 40 to 60 percent of Americans are dissatisfied with their jobs. Perhaps this isn't surprising when you look at how most of us choose our careers. First, we go to school, gain skills, and get exposed to a variety of classes that leave us with a general sense of our relative likes and dislikes. From there we get familiar with the types of jobs in a certain field of interest and hedge our bets on which career will be the best fit for us.

So, we join the workforce, and after we've had our first job or two, our general sense of likes and dislikes becomes more honed. But there is still this pervasive feeling that you're not really sure what you want to do when you "grow up."

Culturally, a career seems to be defined as "a way to make money so that one can afford the quality of life one really wants." This perspective of career is focused on getting money so that you can have and do things when you're *not* working. The actual work of the career is overlooked or at best considered a tolerable necessity. Yet, for most of us, the hours spent working far outnumber the hours we have to enjoy our hard-earned "quality of life." Let's face it: we want to do more than tolerate our work. We want to enjoy it!

How Do You Find Work You Love?

Put down the classifieds and get clear on what you're looking for! To find work you love, you need to start by looking at your career from a different perspective . . . a perspective that recognizes that your satisfaction with the day-to-day activities of your work is vital for you to experience the quality of life you truly desire. *Work you love comes from engaging in work that cultivates your desired talents, honors your innate values, and serves to make the difference you truly want to make, while being both personally and financially rewarding.*

From this perspective you're looking for work that honors your natural way of being and puts it in service of others. Notice your natural tendencies of how you respond to others and create an impact on situations. Observe the features that consistently stand out in how you approach others and solve problems. Here are a few questions to consider as you look at your natural way of being. To get the most out of this, spend at least 10 minutes writing your answer to each question.

- What do people tend to consistently say about you? What do people praise about you?
- Describe three achievements that you are most proud of thus far in your lifetime. What's similar about the way you accomplished these achievements?
- What are you doing when you lose track of time? What are you doing when you feel most alive and fully engaged?
- Identify the various jobs you've had that were not a good fit. What value was stepped on or overlooked in each job? What beliefs were dishonored?
- Describe a time you were at your peak performance. Who were you being— what were you doing when you were most satisfied with yourself? What values were you honoring?

> You have a unique message to deliver, a unique song
> to sing, a unique act of love to bestow. This message,
> this song and this act of love have been entrusted
> exclusively to the one and only you.
> – John Powell, S.J.

Having knowledge and understanding of your natural way of being can help identify two main things: what you like to do and how you like to do it. For example, if you realize you consistently bring humor and camaraderie to group interactions and easily rally people around your ideas, you may find leading a team will be a natural aspect of work you'd love.

There is a third aspect of career that is perhaps the most important. Anyone can take his natural way of being and do a variety of jobs with it. But doing work you love isn't only about doing what you *can* do; it's about getting to do what you most *want* to do. What makes work fulfilling is when you put your natural qualities in service of what matters most to you. This requires discovering the difference you want to make—the impact you want to have.

When you think of doing work you love, *think big*! Think amazing possibilities! Think joy and fulfillment! Choosing a career becomes a reflection of your conscious choice to make a particular difference. Your career gives you the opportunity to get paid for the time and actions you take in effort to make your desired impact on others and the world.

Here are a few questions to consider when thinking about the difference you want to make. Again, to get the most out of this, spend at least 10 minutes writing your answer to each question.

- What is it you want to teach people? What desire do you have for creating a better way of doing something? What do you find yourself frequently talking passionately about?
- Where do you see potential for humanity to grow, change, and improve? What aspect of human potential inspires you most?
- What angers or saddens you about the world and humanity? What do you find yourself getting mad or sad about in the daily news?
- What's the legacy you want to leave? What do you want most for the people who come after you?
- Imagine for a moment that you are speaking before a large crowd. You deeply care for this particular group and speak passionately to them. What is the message you share? Who are the people in this crowd, and what is the impact of your message to them?

As your conviction becomes apparent, your vague sense of your likes and dislikes is replaced by a compelling drive to fulfill a specific purpose.

Doing work you love supports you to be who you want to be, to do what matters most to you, and to have more than you dreamed of. When you do work you love, you're doing your BEST work, work that:

- **B**rings you joy and abundance
- **E**mbraces your natural way of being
- **S**erves to make the difference you most want to make
- **T**ies your actions to what matters most to you.

> The highest reward for a person's work is not what they get for it, but what they become by it.
> – John Ruskin

As you know, your career life profoundly impacts your relationships, your finances, your health, your hopes, and your dreams—your whole life! What is possible if you commit to doing work you love? How will your life change if you do? How will it change if you don't?

ABOUT THE AUTHOR

Keri Coffman-Thiede, owner of Amaze Yourself Coaching, is a career coach who works with clients who are ready to go beyond making a living. She coaches her clients to make career choices that lead them to enjoying work that is personally meaningful and financially rewarding. Some of her clients include healthcare professionals, entrepreneurs, college students, and business professionals wanting more work satisfaction. Keri has a bachelor's degree in psychology and received her coaching training from the Coaches Training Institute. To schedule a complimentary coaching consultation, contact Keri at amazingu@merr.com. Also visit her Web site, http://www.amazeyourself.net.

Resource: Lynn A. Robinson, *Real Prosperity, Using the Power of Intuition to Create Financial and Spiritual Abundance* (Kansas City: Andrews McMeel Publishing, 2004).

18

CHANGE

Don't Resist: Cultivate Change!

Renée Canali

We spend much of our lives establishing routines. As children, routines were part of our daily lives. Eventually, routines become habits, and habits become patterns of behavior. We repeat them over and over without stopping to see if they are still effective. Once we establish a routine, it is a challenge to change. There are a few occasions for which we will change our routine temporarily, such as taking an alternate route to work. However, many times, changing our routines is a result of our wanting to avoid something. It is natural to resist change.

Interestingly enough, change itself is natural. Seasons change, bodies change, housing and economic needs change, even the airline industry experiences change. Change surrounds us every day, although we fail to notice it until the overall effects make it difficult to ignore. How often do we drive by the same vacant land, only to one day notice it is now developed into a new housing complex, and ask, "When did those go up?"

Your resistance to change is reduced or eliminated once you learn how to cultivate it instead. Resistance is an opportunity dressed in work clothes. By learning how to leverage changes around us, the experience of changing is less like sandpaper on silk.

> Change has a considerable psychological impact on the human mind. To the fearful it is threatening because it means that things may get worse. To the hopeful it is encouraging because things may get better. To the confident it is inspiring because the challenge exists to make things better.
>
> – King Whitney Jr.

Cultivating change allows you to deal with change one small step at a time, making times of unexpected hardship easier to navigate. Resisting change leaves you ill prepared for catastrophe. Do you refuse to go to the doctor for a checkup because you fear that something might be wrong? Acknowledge that you deserve health. Shift your mind-set to believe that knowing the truth about your health will provide many opportunities to have a more positive effect on your health. Choose to take a five minute "time-out" for yourself each day.

Welcoming change encourages you to take responsibility for creating your life in the way that works best for you. Begin to question why you choose certain behaviors. It may be that at some point early in life you tried something new, and maybe it didn't work out well. Did your parents make statements such as "you always seem to attract trouble"? Did you adopt the feeling that the world was against you? Years later, are you justifying things that didn't turn out as expected by repeating those same comments to yourself? Cultivate a change in attitude by listing every accomplishment that is evidence to the contrary. Acknowledge what you have learned or gained from those positive experiences.

Resisting change reinforces the victim mentality. Changing this pattern and refusing to accept that you attract everything negative provides the opportunity to move in a more productive direction.

Practicing the art of change allows you to take in more information, enabling you to make more informed decisions. Insisting that things remain the same results in stagnation and deprives you of growth and opportunities. When computers became more commonplace at work, much of the workforce resisted the change. "Computers are a passing fad; they won't last!" was a widely held belief. Workers who resisted the technological age spent valuable energy trying to convince others that computers were a waste of time and money. That energy could have been better spent learning computer skills and leveraging new knowledge to secure better employment.

When faced with a change, do you react or respond? *Reacting* is taking something at face value in the context of past experience. It can be a form of unconscious decision making, based on past experiences that "feel" or "sound" the same. *Responding* is openly accepting information with which to make a decision in the context of a current situation, and only within that specific context.

The ability to change your perspective makes you more attractive to others. Resisting change affects your relationships, career, health, and happiness. When you offer several solutions to a problem instead of giving advice on what you feel is best, is your input received more favorably? Try telling a teenager what to do, and you will experience resistance at full strength. Ask him what he believes is a good solution, and then listen. The more often you try this, the less resistance you will encounter. Changing your perspective from "I know" to "what do you think?" increases possibilities for better and deeper understanding.

Leveraging change by creating new habits provides new opportunities. Resisting change keeps you in a state of fear. Most of us remember our first job interview. Days before, you rehearsed answers to commonly asked questions, scoured your wardrobe for an outfit to make the right impression, and crafted questions to ask about the company and your specific position. How did you handle the first rejection? First, you may have vowed never to interview again. Then you tried again and resolved to learn how not to make the same mistakes. Most of us learned from that first experience and strengthened our interviewing skills.

Embracing change opens space for calm and purpose to expand in your life. Resisting change creates drama and uncertainty. Recently, a company lost a major contract, resulting in the anticipation of the layoff of thousands of employees. Most employees reacted by immediately calling job placement companies and recruiters. They started jumping ship before they knew if it was sinking. Some employees began gathering information about alternative jobs within the company or chose to investigate other interests they had been putting off for years.

> Learn wisdom from the ways of a seedling. A seedling which is never hardened off through stressful situations will never become a strong productive plant.
> – Stephen Sigmund

Cultivating change is a perception shift. By learning to respond to change instead of resisting or reacting to it, you can accept change for what it is, not for what it *does* to you. Cultivating change is identifying opportunities within a change that are inevitable, responding in ways that enrich your life, and seeking balance in the face of that change.

About the Author

Renée Canali is a life coach specializing in career transitions as well as life skills coaching for high school and college students. As a native of the Washington, D.C., area, she has over 20 years experience in retail management and is graduating from Coach University's ACP program. Her passion is to coach open minds toward defining, reaching, and sustaining a successful life. She offers group and individual coaching, workshops, and seminars. Her company, Cultivating Change, LLC, is dedicated to empowering others to create opportunity within the face of change. Visit http://www.landofpossibility.com, or contact her at Renee@landofpossibility.com.

19

CHOICES

What You Need to Know about Choosing

John R. Dempsey

Choosing is like breathing. You do it—*must* do it—all day, every day. Deliberate or habitual, in matters big or small, you are always choosing—what *next*, what *now*, what *if*, what *when*.

Like breathing, choosing can become so automatic that you are not certain how or why it works. You may not understand how or why it sometimes fails you.

Remember these ABCs of choosing, and you can breathe easier, become better at weighing your options in every situation, and become more effective in all your choosing—deliberate and habitual, big and small.

Two sides to every story

The story of choosing has two sides—perceiving and interpreting. To choose well, you must consider each side of the story independently of the other. You must consider the whole story, of course, and yet you must always distinguish clearly between what you perceive and what you interpret. The line between perceiving and interpreting can be very thin and very flexible. You can easily mistake one for the other.

Remember: You can only interpret what you can perceive—choosing requires both.

What is and what's possible

To choose well, you must consider *what is* that is relevant and meaningful for you. You must also consider *what's possible* that is relevant and meaningful for you. *What is* is the linear world of apparent cause and effect, *immanent reality*, and your physical senses perceive this world fully, accurately, and *consciously*. *What's possible* is the latent world, *transcendent reality*, and your intuitive senses perceive this world fully, accurately, and *unconsciously*. Your beliefs, preferences, and habits may limit your capacity to perceive fully and accurately, both consciously and unconsciously.

Remember: You perceive consciously and unconsciously—choosing requires both.

What you think and what you feel

To choose well, you must consider both the thoughts and the feelings that you generate in response to your perception of what is and what's possible. You interpret *logically* when you apply your mental awareness and intelligence—your thinking—to consider the meaning and relevance of what you perceive. In contrast, you interpret *nonlogically* when you apply your emotional awareness and intelligence—your feelings.

Remember: You interpret logically and nonlogically—choosing requires both.

Every choice affects both what is and what's possible

Choosing is a creative act, generating change in both the immanent and the latent worlds. Your choices lead you to action; your actions lead to outcomes. Your actions and outcomes create ripples that change both what is and what's possible.

You perceive the continuously changing landscapes of what is and what's possible. You may sometimes feel that the pace of change is impossible for you to keep up with, or you may feel paralyzed, unable to choose any action or outcome.

Remember: You choose what's possible to make what is—choosing changes both.

Risk and reward

As you perceive and interpret what's possible, you naturally find some actions and outcomes that appeal to you, some that repel you, and some that move you neither one way nor the other. An action or outcome that repels you is a risk; an action or outcome that appeals to you is a reward. Actions and outcomes that move you neither one way nor the other are less risky and also less rewarding. Actions that appeal to you may have outcomes that repel you. Outcomes that appeal to you may require actions that repel you.

Remember: Risk and reward are two sides of the same coin—choosing engages both.

Choosing takes time, energy, and attention (TEA)

You consume a brew of your own time, energy, and attention while perceiving and interpreting a situation and your options. You weigh the risks and the rewards. You perceive, you interpret, you perceive—back and forth—all the while consuming more and more of your precious TEA.

You may consume only a sip, or a cup, or even a full pot of your TEA. You may take your TEA in solitude, share it in quiet conversation, or serve it freely. Your time, energy, and attention are limited resources, continuously consumed by necessary perceiving, interpreting, and choosing. When you share your TEA with others, you perceive their interpretations, and they perceive your interpretations.

Remember: You put some time, energy, and attention into every choice—big or small.

Divergence and convergence

Perceiving determines how long choosing continues. You must perceive enough to complete the choosing, and yet you must interpret to know what is enough.

You delay choosing when you devote more time, energy, and attention to perceiving what is and what's possible and less to interpreting what you think and what you feel. Interpreting determines when choosing ends. You hasten choosing when you devote more time, energy, and attention to interpreting what you think and what you feel and less to perceiving what is and what's possible. You must know when to stop perceiving and when to start or continue interpreting.

Remember: You delay choosing when you focus on perceiving; you hasten choosing when you focus on interpreting.

TEA and possibility

The time, energy, and attention you devote to choosing vary with the amount of risk and reward that you perceive and interpret. Some choices need only a modest serving of TEA—you easily favor big-reward, small-risk options and ignore small-reward, big-risk options. You serve less TEA for small-reward, small-risk options. You may serve lots of TEA for big-reward, big-risk options. Your capacity for full and accurate perceiving determines how well you understand the risks and rewards involved when you are choosing.

Remember: You allot your time, energy, and attention to choosing according to the risks and rewards that you perceive and interpret.

TEA for two

Much choosing becomes routine, everyday, little sips and cups of TEA choosing. You create habits for everyday choosing, such as what you eat, how you dress, where you go, who you see. For these things you consume less and less TEA, perceiving what is and what's possible and interpreting what you think and what you feel.

A lot of your choosing is for special occasions, requiring you to bring out the good china for TEA. The frequency and quality of your special occasion choosing depends greatly on the amount of TEA you have spared from everyday choosing. The habitual choices that serve you well one day may not be suitable the next. "Big and scary" special occasion choices can seem bigger and scarier when you hardly ever entertain them.

Remember: You cultivate habitual choosing to free up time, energy, and attention for higher-stakes choosing.

ABOUT THE AUTHOR

Since 1979, John R. Dempsey has been a professional consultant in public and private sector organizations in the United States and Canada, developing and delivering effective educational and experiential workshops as well as consulting and coaching with groups and individuals. John offers e-books and e-courses and is available for personal consulting and coaching as well as telephone, Internet, and live seminars. His main Web site is http://www.optionist.com, and you can contact him via e-mail at JDempsey@optionist.com.

20

CONQUERING NEGATIVITY

Free Yourself from Negative Nelly and Billy Blamer: Three Easy and Effective Ways to Deal with Negative People

Shawn Driscoll

You know them. Maybe you work with them, live with them, or hang out with them. Negative is an understatement. They complain, they vent, they criticize, they blame. And you're tired of dealing with them.

Negative Nelly prefers complaining to finding a solution. Quick with the "buts" whenever a possible solution or new idea is offered, she sucks the energy out of a room within seconds.

Venting Victor likes to swoop in, dump his frustration all over anyone who will listen, and then go on his merry way. Venting Victor needs an outlet for every minor annoyance, frustration, and issue, and if you're his target, you're left feeling dumped on.

Billy Blamer is constantly critical, demanding, and berating and blames everyone and everything when things go wrong. He doesn't take responsibility; rather, he deflects it. Billy Blamers create a negative, guilt-ridden environment. It's usually them against the world, and you're left holding the bag.

While the most effective strategy for dealing with some of these people is to eliminate them from your life, in many cases, that's just not doable. You can't fire a coworker unless you're the boss. You can't, or don't want to, cut off ties with your family. And so you've learned to put up with their negativity.

But too much negativity can be toxic. It drains you, frustrates you, and sometimes it infects you. After being with Negative Nelly or Venting Victor, you find yourself going negative. You get sucked into their vortex, and your usually positive outlook starts getting dark. With Billy Blamer you walk away deflated, feeling as if you've let him down again.

You may wonder *why* they have to be this way and find yourself constantly wishing they were more positive, happy, or sensitive to others. The truth is that asking why usually doesn't change much. Unless the answer allows you to be more accepting—to come to love their negativity—knowing the "why" doesn't solve your problem. You need to know how to avoid the slippery slope of getting sucked in, frustrated, annoyed, and negative.

What can you do to stop the downslide short of cutting them out of your life or being rude? Here are three proven strategies you can implement immediately.

1. **The extinction strategy.** Extinction simply means to stop meeting their needs. Once their needs aren't being met by you, they'll move on to other ways of getting their needs met.

What attracts negative people to you is that you give them what they want or need. Not intentionally, of course. In fact, you are probably trying to be kind, patient, and friendly. But the truth is that if they weren't getting some need met by spewing their negativity all over you, they wouldn't be doing it. Negative people need one of two things from you. They are either looking for someone to commiserate with, or they want someone who will provide lots of cheerleading. Commiserating gives them affirmation. "You can do it" support gives them energy (by taking it from you).

Become a no whining zone. How? Simply refuse to engage. If you've been caught up in the "ain't it awfuls," it's time to stop. If you've been relentlessly cheerleading, stop. Have a simple phrase that you can repeat in a "charge-neutral" tone (without anger, frustration, or reaction, as if you were saying something as simple as "the sky is blue"), such as "isn't that interesting." Say nothing more, nothing less. After hearing that (and nothing else) three times, they'll start to get the hint that you're not going there with them.

2. **Set limits.** You can't afford to spend 20, 30, or more minutes listening to someone rattle on about everything that's wrong in the world. It's far too costly to your peace of mind and productivity. With Billy Blamers you need a zero tolerance policy. Get to a place where you simply won't tolerate the rant (abuse). With Negative Nellys or Venting Victors, set a time limit, and stick to it—somewhere between three to seven minutes, maximum.

Once Negative Nelly or Venting Victor has hit the three-minute mark, cut off the conversation. If you're at work, say something like "I really have to get back to my project now." If they continue (they will), be ready to get stronger. Stand up, create more space between you, and begin to move away. Say "I'm going to get back to work now." It can be easier on the phone. Make your "I've got to go" statement, and insist on hanging up within the minute.

3. **Be unconditionally constructive.** You may have tried being positive, but positive doesn't work. When you're positive, you are trying to build the other person up (a form of cheerleading). This can be very draining because you are trying to move someone from extreme negativity to extreme satisfaction or happiness. That's like pushing a large rock uphill. Alternatively, when you're unconditionally constructive, you're helping the other person build something for himself.

Instead of saying "You can do it! Here's what I think you should do . . . ," you could say "I'd really like to hear how you solve that." Or instead of saying "I'm really tired of hearing your criticisms all the time," you could say "I'd enjoy hearing your ideas about what would work." By consistently doing this, you can teach the person that you will only engage with them when they are unconditionally constructive, too. You only have room in your life for people willing to bring solutions, ideas, and energy.

These strategies can and do work as long as you are consistent and clear. If you waiver, the negative people in your life will sense the opening and pounce. You have to stick with it. Expect that they will test you. You will likely see an escalation of the negativity, drama, venting, or blaming at first. This is when holding strong to your time limits, charge-neutral tone, and higher standards is a *must*. Once you've passed the test, usually after three to five incidents, you'll see dramatic change.

Billy Blamer or Negative Nelly will move on to other sources of energy. Venting Victor will vent less or seek out a new dumping ground. And you'll feel lighter and more energetic. Most importantly, you will start to attract people just like you—unconditionally constructive, with healthy limits and a passion for what's possible.

ABOUT THE AUTHOR

Shawn Driscoll, owner of Succeed Coaching & Development, is a professional coach, speaker, and author who specializes in teaching people how to master change, create work-life balance, and achieve career satisfaction. She guides her clients to make strategic career choices that lead to a well-balanced life so they struggle less and enjoy more. As a recognized expert on career trends, the firm can teach you how to take control of your work and life to drive your own success. Are you ready to chart your course to career success and fulfillment? Get your Career Success Toolkit today at http://www.succeedcoaching.com.

21

COURAGEOUS VISION

Harness the Power of Vision

Margie Warrell

I'm sure you are busy. Who isn't? The question is, What are you so busy about? Too often, we get so caught up with our everyday responsibilities that we don't take the time to ask ourselves what all this running about is for. Regardless of what work you do each day, what matters most is that what you are working toward is truly meaningful and inspiring to you—that you have a vision that leaves you feeling purposeful and powerful in every aspect of your life.

Why? Because a vision can unleash enormous power. Not only does a vision act as a compass to guide your choices and allow you to see opportunities you might otherwise miss, but it brings greater meaning to your present circumstances, and it empowers you to deal more effectively and courageously with the future challenges life presents to you.

Helen Keller once said, "The most pathetic person is one who has sight but no vision." The fact is that in any aspect of your life where you have no vision, you also have no power. Without a vision to work toward, you can end up being like a rudderless ship sailing aimlessly through life, settling for less than you'd *really* like and moving in whatever direction requires the least toil and short-term discomfort—mental, emotional, or physical. Accordingly, people who have no vision often find themselves:

- spending years doing things they don't truly enjoy
- making choices that are driven by self-doubt and fear
- saying yes to near every request, offer, or opportunity that comes along because they can't think of any better way to fill their days
- blaming their lack of success or happiness on external factors rather than taking responsibility for their experience of life

- failing to fulfill their full potential and ultimately living a much smaller and less fulfilling life than they could have.

If you think of people who have achieved something truly great in the world—for instance, Mother Theresa, Mandela, Gandhi, and Martin Luther King—you will note that what distinguished them from others was the size of their vision. They were born ordinary people, but by having the courage to dream big dreams, dreams that propelled them into powerful action, they became *extra*-ordinary. Ultimately, a great vision brings out the greatness in he who holds it.

So what vision do you have for your life? What difference would you like to make in the lives of those you care about and in the world in general? What could you do with your time, energy, and talents each day over the next 10, 20, or 50 years which, when you arrived in the twilight of your life, would leave you feeling a deep sense of fulfillment? The fact is that you have no choice in the matter of your death, but you do have a choice in the matter of how you live. The rest of your life will pass by regardless of what you choose to do with your time each day, so why not spend it doing something that would immeasurably enrich your experience of being alive (not to mention the lives of those around you)?

No matter how great or "ungreat" your life is right now, I challenge you to ask for more out of life and to give more to it. However much you have accomplished or failed to accomplish up until now, you are capable of much more than you think. Don't let your doubts keep you playing small, don't let your fears stop you from aiming high, and don't let your feelings of inadequacy about your ability to turn your vision into a reality deter you from getting started. Once you have connected with something that inspires you deeply, you will find within you all the courage you need to step boldly into action and to stay the course toward that which tugs on your heart and beckons you forward. After all, courage is not the absence of fear, but action in the presence of it.

Michelangelo once said, "The greater danger is not that our hopes are too high and we fail to reach them, it is that they are too low and we do." Life is short. Dare to dream bigger dreams, and trust in the wisdom that created you that whatever direction they may take you, you have both the courage and ability to travel. In the end, it matters not whether you manage to achieve your vision, but that you had the courage to pursue it in the first place. For at the end of the day it is the vision, if reached or not, that makes great the life.

Four Steps to Harnessing the Power of Vision

1. **Write it down.** On a clean sheet of paper, write the heading "(YOUR NAME) DREAMS BIGGER!" Then for each of the areas of your life listed below, write your answers to the questions that follow.

Career/Business, Relationships, Financial, Health/Well-being, Recreation/Leisure, Home, Environment, and Community Service

o Casting yourself ahead 10 years from now (you can make it more or less if you'd prefer), describe how this aspect of your life would be for you to feel extremely good about yourself?
o How would this be an improvement to how you feel about this aspect of your life now?
o What would need to change for this part of your life the way you wanted it to be?
o How will you feel 10 years from now if you take no action in this area of your life (and so, by default, it continues on the way it has up until now)? Describe the personal cost on your senses of well-being, happiness, and peace of mind?

2. **Create an action plan.** List the first few actions you can take (however small) that will move you closer toward your vision in each of these aspects of your life. Then put a date beside each one indicating when you will have it done.
3. **Design a supportive environment.** Write down what you can do to create an environment around you that will support you and hold you accountable to staying in action toward your vision. For example, share your vision with a friend, find a mentor, hire a coach, join an association or group of individuals with a similar vision, attend seminars that empower and inform, or read great books (like this one!).
4. **Schedule time-outs.** Regularly allocate time to reconnect with your vision (and to update it in whatever way inspires you most deeply) as well as to update your action plan. Then honor your commitment to yourself as you would any other.

> The only place where your dreams become
> impossible is in your own thinking.
> – Robert H. Schuller

ABOUT THE AUTHOR

Margie Warrell is a coach, an internationally syndicated columnist, and author of *Find Your Courage!* (due out early 2007). Margie is also a professional speaker who does keynote presentations and runs workshops for organizations and associations internationally. Originally from Melbourne, Australia, Margie has lived, worked, and traveled all over the world and had her four children along the way. Margie is passionate about helping people find the courage to live bigger lives and to pursue goals that inspire them—personally and professionally—with greater success and balance . . . less the stress! To subscribe to her free e-newsletter or for more information, please visit http://www.margiewarrell.com or e-mail info@margiewarrell.com.

22

DATING

When to Take That Leap of Faith into Marriage

Amy Schoen

Putting yourself out there to meet marriage-minded singles can be a lot of work. If you are dating people you know only from the Internet or a phone conversation, this can be frustrating. But just remember, you are able to exert all this effort because you believe it's going to work and that before long, you are going to meet that special someone. I'm here to tell you that yes, it does happen. On the other hand, what if you are in an exclusive relationship with someone and wondering if he or she is the Right One? And how can you tell when it is happening to you? What are the signs that he or she is the Right One?

There are signs that a relationship has lasting value. There is more to it than simply "being in love." You are committing yourself to a lifelong relationship, so you will want to think about where you will be in 10 years, in 20, in 50. Think about how you feel about your partner now, and imagine how you might feel when you are taking the grandchildren to Disney World 30 years from now. You may want to ask yourself the following questions about the relationship you are now in.

- **Chemistry.** Do you get a lift by just seeing this person? Do you desire to be with this person a lot?
- **Love.** Do you have genuine concern for this person and deep caring about his or her comfort and well-being? Do you believe in this person and what he or she stands for?
- **Common Goals.** Do you share the same dreams with this person for 10 years from now and beyond?
- **Shared Values.** Do you share similar emphasis on what matters most to you in life? Do you care about the same things?

In my interviewing I have found that there are six criteria that married couples most often cite as the reasons they took the leap of faith and got married.

Six Signs That You Have Found the Right One!

There is a feeling of "home"

There is a sense of comfort. The person you are dating feels so naturally right that it seems preordained. You just know that this person is the one. It's like you have known each other your whole life because it's so easy to talk to one another. You feel familiarity with your partner. You can be sitting on the beach with nothing else going on, and just being together is enough.

There is a flow

The relationship has ease. Time just flies when you are with the right person. Yes, relationships take work, but this is joyous work. The concept of flow is true both in and out of the bedroom! For instance, at dinner in a cute Italian restaurant, instead of ordering two entrées, you order two appetizers and one entrée to share your choices. You have a spirited discussion about which wine to order. He wins, but you are pleasantly surprised that you adore his choice. Without a big effort, things just move along.

You are able to laugh together, have fun, and enjoy each other's company

You enjoy each other's sense of humor, even though you may not have exactly the same humor, and you do crack a smile. On our second date my husband and I were sitting in a restaurant booth and both blew straw wrappings at each other— like kids! We both had a good laugh. It's okay to be silly with the right person.

You are each other's best friend

There is a sense of trust and loyalty. You know your partner will be there for you through thick and thin. Your partner can be counted on to give you the benefit of the doubt when others find fault with you. You want to share everything with this person—the good stuff *and* the bad stuff. If the boss doesn't appreciate her work, you are the one who encourages her to apply for a transfer and assures her that others will see her strengths—just as you do.

You are passionately fond of one another

You arrive from the airport after midnight, exhausted. He has been waiting up and leaps to the door and throws his arms around you. You know he's genuinely happy you're back. It's not an act. He really wants to be right next to you because he's missed you so much the past three days.

You both act in a "we" way rather than in a "me" way

She loves scuba diving, and you love hiking. Instead of heading for either the Caribbean for her or the Appalachian Trail for you, you research options until you find that resort in Costa Rica where she can dive and you can hike. Even better, the resort has golfing facilities that you can enjoy together. Whether for long- or short-term goals you make decisions that benefit the relationship instead of only the individual. You share life goals and work together toward them. You care about how your actions affect the other person. You are willing to work out your differences to keep your partnership going.

When all these signs are in place, then it is natural to want to take the relationship to the next step, which is marriage. Sometimes, though, several of these signs are missing in your current relationship. At this point you must decide if you want to give it more time to see what develops or to move on to find someone who could be better suited to you for marriage. This isn't an effortless path for it's too easy to hope things will change with your partner. The probability is that your partner will not change his or her personality. It is what it is. Those who are determined not to settle for anyone less and stay focused in order to achieve their goal of finding the right marriage partner are truly Motivated to Marry™!

My mom has an expression: "Fish or cut bait!" Either you want to get married to that person, or you don't. If you are not sure, listen very carefully to your gut— because I will bet you that this person is most likely not the Right One. I have seen time and time again with couples over 30 years old that when there is aligned synergy between them, the couple gets engaged in six to eight months and married within a year or two at most.

When all the ingredients are in place and there are no outside influences or beliefs standing in your way, you will surely be impelled to take that leap of faith into marriage and embrace your precious and fortunate union.

ABOUT THE AUTHOR

Amy Schoen, MBA, CPCC, is a certified professional life coach and a dating-relationship expert. Her speeches to professional organizations and social groups have been quoted in publications such as *The Washington Post* and the *Washington Business Journal.* In her coaching business Amy specializes in helping singles to discover what they need and want in relationships and how to find their desired romantic partner. Amy is the author and creator of "The Motivated to Marry™ Method." For down-to-earth tips and helpful hints on dating and relationships, you can subscribe to her popular e-zine or her tele-classes at http://www.heartmindconnection.com.

23

DEBT

Get Out of Debt Now

Vicky Spring Love

Although it may be necessary to go into debt to make major purchases, such as a car or home, I do not believe we should make debt a lifestyle. And even when we do have to borrow money, we should make it our goal to pay off those debts as quickly as possible.

There are three types of people when it comes to debt. The first type of person is someone who pays all their bills on time each month and thinks that debt is okay because it's convenient and they are current on all accounts. The second type of person is struggling to pay their bills each month, living from paycheck to paycheck, and trying to cope in a constant state of frustration and anxiety. The third type of person has given up on paying their bills; they are thinking of or may have already filed bankruptcy and are allowing accounts to get further behind while the creditors are trying to track them down.

It doesn't matter which one of the above scenarios represents you, this chapter is written for you. I believe that excessive debt brings a curse on your finances that prevents financial blessings from flowing freely in your life. It's up to you to make the decision, however, that you will turn away from debt as a lifestyle. This chapter will give you concrete ideas for getting out of debt and a specific plan of action that you can implement to make it happen.

Make Getting Out of Debt Your Top Priority

Although it is extremely easy to get into massive amounts of debt very quickly, it takes time, discipline, and commitment to get out of debt. You have to make a life-changing decision that you no longer wish to be in debt because getting out of debt is going to affect every area of your life.

The first thing you need to do is to complete a spending inventory to find out where you are right now. A spending inventory is simply a list of everything you spend for an entire month, whether by check, charge, or cash. The purpose of this exercise is to help you locate the waste in your budget. I believe that everyone can find $100 to $200 a month in wasteful spending that can be cut. You will use this additional money in your plan to get out of debt.

When you make getting out of debt your top priority, it affects your thinking, decision making, and habits. If you usually walk around the mall at lunchtime and end up compulsively buying things, then you will no longer go to the mall. Instead, you will take a brown bag lunch to work or eat in the company's cafeteria. You will begin to analyze every purchase to decide if it is really necessary. You will cut unnecessary expenses and learn to live frugally. It's important, as you start your plan of action, that you do not incur any new debt. Begin to only purchase things that you can pay for in cash.

Call All Your Creditors and Contact the Credit Bureaus

One of the first things you should do when you decide to become debt-free is to obtain a copy of your credit report. By getting your credit report from each of the bureaus, you will know all the debts that you have outstanding, including any collection accounts or charge-offs that you've forgotten about. You can obtain one free copy of your credit report from all three bureaus, Experian, Trans Union, and Equifax, at http://www.AnnualCreditReport.com. After reviewing your credit report and your current account statements you should contact your creditors if you are currently behind in your bills to let them know you intend to pay them off. When you call your creditors first, they will be more willing to work with you than if they have to track you down. Talk to them about how much you can reasonably afford to pay each month to see if they are willing to negotiate lower monthly payments. If a creditor does negotiate a deal with you, make sure you keep your word and send them the agreed upon amount every month, faithfully.

If you are current on all your accounts, especially if you have a good payment history, you should contact your creditors to ask for lower interest rates.

Get Out of Debt Plan of Action

If you follow these 10 steps, you will develop your plan of action and implement it to become debt-free.

1. Make a commitment to get out of debt, and stick with the plan. Set a deadline date for completion.
2. List all debts, including loans from family members.
3. Find an extra $100 to $200 per month in your budget using the spending inventory.
4. Put debts in order of priority to pay them off. Put them in order by highest interest rate to lowest, or by lowest balance to highest.
5. Separate debts into categories, in this order: credit cards and lines of credit, student loans, personal debts, car loans, mortgage debt.
6. Start with bill number 1 as your targeted bill. On the targeted bill you are going to pay the minimum due plus the extra $100 to $200 you located in your budget. Pay only the minimum due on all other debts.
7. Once bill number 1 is paid off, target bill number 2. Take everything you were paying on bill number 1 plus the minimum you were paying on bill number 2 and begin paying it all on bill number 2 each month.
8. Once bill number 2 is paid off, repeat step 7 with bill number 3. Continue this process until all your debts are paid.
9. Close credit card accounts as they are paid off. Keep one MasterCard or Visa account for emergency purposes only. Write a letter to close each account and to tell them not to have their telemarketers call. If you call to request the account closed, the creditor will offer you something tempting to convince you to keep it open.
10. During this process you must pay cash for all purchases and not incur any new debt.

The Benefits of Being Debt-Free

After you pay off your bills you can begin to target your money toward worthwhile financial goals, such as saving for retirement, your children's college education, starting a business venture, or simply taking a well-deserved vacation. One of the biggest benefits of being debt-free, however, is peace of mind. You will no longer have to be stressed out about money.

ABOUT THE AUTHOR

Vicky Spring Love is President of Victory Financial Corporation, a residential mortgage company. In addition, she frequently teaches seminars and workshops at churches, businesses, and community groups on topics related to money management. This article is an excerpt from her book, *Stop Robbing Peter to Pay Paul*, a Bible-based book on managing money, getting out of debt, and cleaning up your credit. She can be contacted at http://www.StopRobbingPeter.com.

24

The Art of Decision Making:
Make Powerful Choices and Take Control of
Your Life When You ACT

Talia Mana

Do you have trouble making decisions? Are you stuck in a situation that is causing you stress, and don't know how to fix it?

The ACT methodology is a tool that you can use to help you sort out your options and arrive at a decision. At the heart of each issue, challenge, or decision are three choices. You can choose to Accept, Change, or Terminate the situation. At each step you consider the energetic and logical consequences of your actions until you reach the best outcome.

Remember, it's better to make a wrong decision and learn from your mistakes than to endlessly weigh up pros and cons. Successful people are decisive. The ability to make decisions will set you apart from others. If you're not taking action or are putting off making decisions, then you won't feel as good about yourself as you will if you are taking control of your life and achieving your goals and dreams. With practice, decision making will become easier!

Accept

Psychologist Carl Rogers suggested that it is impossible to change yourself or your life until you first accept yourself and your situation in its entirety. At a spiritual level, no decision or change is possible until you have accepted your starting position.

A major benefit of acceptance is that once you accept the situation, the next step becomes clear. It's also important to understand that you don't have to agree with something to accept it. You may have heard the expression "let's agree to disagree." When this happens, you are asserting your right to have a different opinion, without being upset that others don't agree with you. When you belong to teams or committees—or even in your own family—there may be conflicting views, but you can remain composed if you have accepted that there will be differences.

Other times, in accepting a situation, you may realize that changing it is beyond your control. At the most extreme end of the spectrum is death. You cannot bring someone back from the dead, so in grieving and reaching acceptance you arrive at the best solution for your own emotional well-being.

A common annoyance many of us face is driving during rush hour. It can be both frustrating and time consuming. After investigating your options you may decide that you will still travel during the busiest time of the day, despite the fact that it is slower. Because you have made a conscious decision to accept the situation, you can travel without feeling irritated by other drivers, red lights, or slow traveling times. You take it all in stride. Acceptance isn't always passive: to help you cope with the stress of rush hour traveling, you may introduce other tools, such as playing your favorite music to make the journey more pleasant. The key to acceptance is in your mind-set and the inner peace that comes when you cease to struggle against something you cannot change.

Change

If you've decided the situation is unacceptable, then you need to canvas ways to improve, challenge, or change it. The circumstances may seem to be out of your control, or you may struggle to see an alternative, but there are usually steps you can take to arrive at a decision you are happy with.

When you feel stuck and you don't see any options opening up, grab a piece of paper and start writing. If you are a left-brained "list" person, then brainstorm 20 possible solutions, no matter how crazy or impossible they may seem. If you are right-brained, then write a story for a minimum of 20 minutes about how you could creatively solve the problem.

Now ask yourself whether any of the solutions seem workable. Often, the best decisions combine facts with intuition. Consider the logical impact of each option in tandem with your own intuition or energy. Do you feel your energy moving toward or away from the option being considered? If your energy feels strong and positive, then this is a clue that your intuition is guiding you.

Let's say your mother phones you every night, and it is interfering with your life. You aren't prepared to let the situation continue, but you do want to keep in touch with your mother. Your options might be to:

- install caller ID on the telephone and only answer calls from your mother when it is convenient for you
- set a schedule of times or days when your mother can call
- sit down with your mother to identify the reasons for her calls and find other ways for her to resolve problems without calling you
- find other family members or friends that will telephone your mother
- hold a weekly family dinner to keep in touch
- use a combination of the above.

In a situation like this it may be difficult for you to learn to say no to your mother, but by doing something different, you can minimize or eliminate the phone calls and free yourself to do other things. You need to be willing to change the things that you know are causing you stress—often the fear is worse than taking action—and with the ACT methodology you know that you always have other options.

Terminate

Terminating or ending a situation can sometimes be the best outcome, especially when the situation is untenable or when all other useful options have been dismissed. If your job is harming your health or destroying your spirit, leaving may be your best option.

One way to check that terminating the situation is the right approach is to use the energy test again. Sit quietly, and think about the situation, issue, or decision. How does it feel to let go and move on from the situation? Does it fill you with a sense of calmness or an inner knowing that this is the right approach?

If you find it impossible to live with the situation, then you may need to walk away. If you hate your job and can't accept it as it is or make changes, then find yourself a new job. If the person you love is never going to make a commitment to you or agree to have children, and these are burning desires for you, then act. You can't change other people, so find someone whose goals match yours.

It isn't easy to walk away from something, but there are times when it is the only remaining solution.

ABOUT THE AUTHOR

Talia Mana is a health psychologist, inspirational speaker, and author who *specializes* in personal growth and wellness. Her first book, Romancing the Frogs: A Singles Guide to Love and Happiness, helps people find love. Her second book, The Art of Calm: Freedom from Stress and Worry, offers more than 100 tips on stress management and is based on her own experiences with stress-related illness. Talia is currently researching emotional eating and mental health issues. She can be contacted through her Web site: http://www.taliamana.com.

25

Visualize and Affirm Your Desired Outcomes

Jack Canfield

You have within you an awesome power that most of us have never been taught to use. Elite athletes use it. The super rich use it. And peak performers in all fields are now starting to use it. That power is called visualization. The daily practice of visualizing your dreams as already complete can rapidly accelerate your achievement of those dreams. Visualization of your goals and desires accomplishes four very important things.

1. It activates your creative subconscious which will start generating creative ideas to achieve your goal.
2. It programs your brain to more readily perceive and recognize the resources you will need to achieve your dreams.
3. It activates the law of attraction, thereby drawing into your life the people, resources, and circumstances you will need to achieve your goals.
4. It builds your internal motivation to take the necessary actions to achieve your dreams.

Visualization is really quite simple. You sit in a comfortable position, close your eyes, and imagine—in as vivid detail as you can—what you would be looking at if the dream you have were already realized. Imagine being inside of yourself, looking out through your eyes at the ideal result.

Mental Rehearsal

Athletes call this visualization process "mental rehearsal," and they have been using it since the 1960s when we learned about it from the Russians.

All you have to do is set aside a few minutes a day. The best times are when you first wake up, after meditation or prayer, and right before you go to bed. These are the times you are most relaxed. Go through the following three steps.

1. Imagine sitting in a movie theater: the lights dim, and then the movie starts. It is a movie of you doing perfectly whatever it is that you want to do better. See as much detail as you can create, including your clothing, the expression on your face, small body movements, the environment, and any other people that might be around. Add in any sounds you would be hearing—traffic, music, other people talking, cheering. And finally, recreate in your body any feelings you think you would be experiencing as you engage in this activity.

2. Get out of your chair, walk up to the screen, open a door in the screen, and enter into the movie. Now experience the whole thing again from inside of yourself, looking out through your eyes. This is called an "embodied image" rather than a "distant image." It will deepen the impact of the experience. Again, see everything in vivid detail, hear the sounds you would hear, and feel the feelings you would feel.

3. Finally, walk back out of the screen that is still showing the picture of you performing perfectly, return to your seat in the theater, reach out and grab the screen, and shrink it down to the size of a cracker. Then bring this miniature screen up to your mouth, chew it up, and swallow it. Imagine that each tiny piece—just like a hologram—contains the full picture of you performing well. Imagine all these little screens traveling down into your stomach and out through the bloodstream into every cell of your body. Then imagine that every cell of your body is lit up with a movie of you performing perfectly. It's like one of those appliance store windows where 50 televisions are all tuned to the same channel.

When you have finished this process—it should take less than five minutes—you can open your eyes and go about your business. If you make this part of your daily routine, you will be amazed at how much improvement you will see in your life.

Create Goal Pictures

Another powerful technique is to create a photograph or picture of yourself with your goal, as if it were already completed. If one of your goals is to own a new car, take your camera down to your local auto dealer and have a picture taken of yourself sitting behind the wheel of your dream car. If your goal is to visit Paris, find a picture or poster of the Eiffel Tower and cut out a picture of yourself and place it into the picture. With today's technology, you could probably make an even more convincing image using your computer.

Create a Visual Picture and an Affirmation for Each Goal

We recommend that you find or create a picture of every aspect of your dream life. Create a picture or a visual representation for every goal you have— financial, career, recreation, new skills and abilities, things you want to purchase, and so on. When we were writing the very first Chicken Soup for the Soul® book, we took a copy of the *New York Times* best-seller list, scanned it into our computer, and using the same font as the newspaper, typed Chicken Soup for the Soul into the number one position in the "Paperback Advice, How-To and Miscellaneous" category. We printed several copies and hung them up around the office. Less than two years later, our book was the number one book in that category and stayed there for over a year!

Index Cards

We practice a similar discipline every day. We each have a list of about 30 to 40 goals we are currently working on. We write each goal on a 3 × 5 index card and keep those cards near our beds and take them with us when we travel. Each morning and each night, we go through the stack of cards, one at a time, read the card, close our eyes, see the completion of that goal in its perfect desired state for about 15 seconds, open our eyes, and repeat the process with the next card.

Use Affirmations to Support Your Visualization

An affirmation is a statement that evokes not only a picture, but the experience of already having what you want. Here's an example of an affirmation:

> I am happily vacationing two months out of the year in a tropical paradise,
> and working just four days a week owning my own business.

Repeating an affirmation several times a day keeps you focused on your goal, strengthens your motivation, and programs your subconscious by sending an order to your crew to do whatever it takes to make that goal happen.

Expect Results

Through writing down your goals, using the power of visualization, and repeating your affirmations, you can achieve amazing results. Visualization and affirmations allow you to change your beliefs, assumptions, and opinions about the most important person in your life—*you*! They allow you to harness the 18 billion brain cells in your brain and get them all working in a singular and purposeful direction.

Your subconscious will become engaged in a process that transforms you forever. The process is invisible and doesn't take a long time. It just happens over time, as long as you put in the time to visualize and affirm, surround yourself with positive people, read uplifting books, and listen to audio programs that flood your mind with positive, life-affirming messages.

Repeat your affirmations every morning and night for a month, and they will become an automatic part of your thinking—they will become woven into the very fabric of your being.

ABOUT THE AUTHOR

Jack Canfield is the founder and cocreator of the billion-dollar book brand Chicken Soup for the Soul. Jack has spent the last 30 years showing literally millions of people how to up-level everything they do.

If you're ready to jump-start your life, make more money, and have more fun and joy in all that you do, get your *free* success tips now at http://www.JackCanfield.com.

26

DETERMINATION

Persistence

Bob Proctor

If you were to choose just one part of your personality to develop that would virtually guarantee your success, I'd like to suggest that you place persistence at the top of your list.

Napoleon Hill, in his classic *Think and Grow Rich,* felt so strongly about this subject, he devoted an entire chapter to it. Hill suggested, "There may be no heroic connotation to the word persistence but the quality is to your character what carbon is to steel."

Think about it. If you took a quick mental walk down memory lane and reviewed some of your accomplishments in the past—large and small—you would have to agree that persistence played an important role in your success.

Napoleon Hill studied many of the world's most successful people. He pointed out the only quality he could find in Henry Ford, Thomas Edison, or a host of other notable greats that he could not find in everyone else was persistence. What I found even more intriguing was the fact that Hill made comment of the fact that these individuals were often misunderstood to be ruthless or cold-blooded and that this misconception grew out of their habit of following through in all of their plans with persistence.

It's both interesting and sadly amusing to me that as a society, we would be quick to criticize people for realizing they had an unshakeable power within them and were capable of overcoming any obstacle outside of them. This power would ultimately move them toward a greater chance of achieving any goal they set for themselves!

Milt Campbell is a good friend of mine. He and I have shared many hours together . . . discussing the very topic of persistence. Milt was a Decathlete in the Olympic Games held in Helsinki, Finland, in 1952. His goal was to capture gold for the U.S. Unfortunately, another fierce competitor who had taken home the gold four years previous in London wasn't satisfied with one gold. Bob Mathias wanted two; Milt had to settle for silver. That did not deter Milt one bit. He had formed the habit of persistence, and four years later in Melbourne, Australia, Milt won the gold medal, earning him the title of the greatest athlete in the world.

On numerous occasions, Milt has said, "There were many guys in school who were far better athletes than me, but they quit." I can recount story after story about individuals who overcame obstacles so great, but only did so because they dared persist. These individuals are no different than you and I.

Ultimately, persistence becomes a way of life, but that is not where it begins. To develop the mental strength—persistence—you must first want something. You have to *want* something so much that it becomes a heated desire . . . a passion in your belly. You must fall in love with that idea. Yes, literally fall in love with the idea, and magnetize yourself to every part of the idea. At that point, persistence will be virtually automatic.

Persistence is a subject I have studied all of my adult life, and I can tell you one thing I know for certain: very few people ever, mentally or verbally, say to themselves, "This is what I really want, and I am prepared to give my life for it," and thus they never develop the persistence to achieve it.

Persistence is a unique mental strength; a strength that is essential to combat the fierce power of the repeated rejections and numerous other obstacles that sit in waiting and are all part of winning in a fast-moving, ever-changing world. As Napoleon Hill found out, there are hundreds of highly successful men and women who have cut a path for others to follow, while leaving their mark on the scrolls of history. And every one of these great individuals was persistent. In many cases, it was the only quality that separated them from everyone else.

It is generally believed that a lack of persistence is a consequence of a weak willpower. That is not true. A person could have a highly evolved willpower and still lack the persistence required to keep moving forward in life. In more cases than not, if a person lacks persistence, he or she does not have a goal that is worthy of him or her, a desirable goal that excites him or her to the very core.

Though willpower is important in moving a person toward his or her goal, if there is ever a war between the will and the imagination, the imagination will win every time. What that means is that you're powered by desire and fuelled by the dream you hold. Once you start to use your imagination to help you build a bigger picture of your dream, to define and refine it until you get it just right in your mind, the emotion that is triggered by that desire far outweighs any force that may be caused by sheer will alone. I am not suggesting the will does not have to be developed, it does. It must become highly developed in order to direct you toward the image with which you are emotionally involved.

Your intellectual factors hold the potential for enormous good when they are properly employed. However, you must remember that everything has an opposite, and any of your intellectual factors can turn, without warning, into destructive lethal enemies when they are directed toward results that are not wanted. It is easy to find individuals who are persistently doing what they don't want to do and achieving results that they do not want. A lack of persistence is not their problem; that person is persisting to his or her own detriment. Ignorance and paradigms are the enemy that we must defeat. Everyone is persistent. Our objective must be to put persistence to work for us rather than against us.

Vision and desire have to be the focus of your attention if you're going to develop persistence into the great ally it can become.

Another excellent example of persistence was demonstrated when, in 1953, a beekeeper from Auckland, N.Z., Edmund Hillary, and his native guide, Tenzing Norguay, became the first two people to climb Mt. Everest and return, after having tried and failed the two previous years.

Hillary had two obvious character strengths that took him to the very top—vision and desire. Even despite the seemingly insurmountable challenges, he had no trouble persisting with the strenuous acts that were required because every act was hooked into the image of him standing on top of the mountain. They were expressed because of his persistence, but he was persistent because he was emotionally involved with the image. Without persistence, all his skills would have meant nothing.

Persistence is an expression of the mental strength that is essential in almost every profession where repeated rejection and obstacles are part of a daily routine.

In closing, let me give you four relatively simple steps that will help you to turn persistence into a habit. These steps can be followed by virtually anyone.

1. Have a clearly defined goal. The goal must be something you are emotionally involved with, something you want very much. (In the beginning, you may not even believe that you can accomplish it—the belief will come.)
2. Have a clearly established plan that you can begin working on immediately. (Your plan will very likely only cover the first and possibly the second stage of the journey to your goal. As you begin executing your plan, other steps required to complete your journey will be revealed at the right time.)
3. Make an irrevocable decision to reject any and all negative suggestions that come from friends, relatives, or neighbors. Do not give any conscious attention to conditions or circumstances that appear to indicate the goal cannot be accomplished.
4. Establish a mastermind group of one or more people who will encourage, support, and assist you wherever possible.

What do you dream of doing with your life? Do it. Begin right now, and never quit. There is greatness in you. Let it out. Be persistent.

ABOUT THE AUTHOR

For 40 years, Bob Proctor has focused his entire life and agenda around helping people create lives of prosperity, rewarding relationships, and spiritual awareness. To order any or all of Bob Proctor's extensive library of success products, including *The Goal Achiever*, *The Born Rich Learning System*, *Your Mission in Commission*, *The Success Puzzle*, *The Science of Getting Rich*, and *The Success Series*, go to BobProctor.com or call (800) 871-9715.

27

DIFFICULT PEOPLE

Putting Your Best Foot Forward Instead of in Your Mouth: 10 Keys to Successful Communication with Difficult People

Jeanne-Marie Grumet

We all have to deal with them at one time or another: difficult people. What is it that makes someone difficult? Why do some people push our buttons more than others? And how can you handle them in a way that feels better, reduces conflict, and produces the outcome you want?

There is an important thing to consider. Is what you're doing or saying contributing to the difficulty? Taking responsibility—for yourself and for the way you communicate—is an important step to reducing conflict.

Here are some key tips.

1. **Are they *truly* difficult or just different from you?** Sometimes when people have different ways of handling things than we do, we label them as difficult. Responding with an approach of "that's interesting" instead of concluding that they're "wrong" or "annoying" can help you find value in the differences. You may learn something new about yourself or about them.
2. **Mirror, mirror. . . .** Often we react because the other person reflects something in ourselves that we don't like . . . or don't want to look at. It helps to first take an honest look at ourselves. You might ask, "Is there any part of me that is like her? Is there something I'm seeing in her that I find distasteful in myself? Maybe I need to have more acceptance and compassion for myself."
3. **Be aware that there are different styles.** People have natural differences in their behavioral styles. Some people's styles are brief and to the point. They

are more task-oriented. Other people are more talkative and social and place a higher emphasis on relationships. Then there are people who tend to be more analytical. They focus on analysis, data, and order. Still others place a high priority on steadiness and security. If you communicate in a way that mirrors a person's style, you will be speaking his or her language. This builds rapport quickly, and you are very likely to have a successful communication—and less conflict.

4. **Actively listen.** Give the person your full attention. It's easy to miss things he or she is saying when you react emotionally. In this busy world, most of us listen while we are "multitasking." Try this approach:

   - Put yourself in the person's shoes as best you can.
   - Ask questions to clarify.
   - Summarize or paraphrase—restate in your own words—what he or she has said.
   - Finally, acknowledge the person's point of view, even if you don't agree. For example, you might say, "It seems that this is very important to you" or "I can hear that you're angry about this." While you're listening, keep the focus on him or her, rather than bringing it back to you. Ask yourself, "Am I *really* listening or just waiting for my turn to speak?"

5. **Notice when your emotional "buttons" get pushed.** Take responsibility for your reactions; after all, a person may have pushed your buttons, but he probably didn't install them. Take a break until you're less reactive. Interacting when emotions are high can be risky. Taking a walk or doing some other physical exercise can help to blow off steam.

6. **Watch your "yes . . . buts."** When you use "but" (or "however") after supposedly agreeing with someone ("I understand, but . . .") or after giving him a compliment ("You did a great job, but . . ."), you are really dismissing or devaluing what the person has said or done. Instead, use the "yes . . . and" approach. For example, say "I understand your perspective, *and* I'd like to share mine with you."

7. **Use "I" statements.** "You" statements tend to create defensive reactions. For example, instead of "you're always late," say "I need for you to be on time." "I" statements are more powerful and productive. Be careful about "you" statements in disguise. "I think you're a jerk" is not an "I" statement.

8. **Be aware of your body language and voice.** So much of what we say is communicated through our body language and our voices. They speak a language all their own. It's often not what we say; it's how we say it. If your body language is closed (for example, arms and legs crossed), you are

sending a strong message that you are closed off. Even though you may be comfortable in that position, it's important to be aware that you're sending a message—a strong message. Open body language sends an important message about your receptivity. Keeping your arms unfolded and open gestures are examples of using open body language.

For the general population in this country, if you don't look someone directly in the eye, there's a perception that you are hiding something or being less than truthful. Eye communication, such as rolling your eyes (in disgust, for example), also can speak volumes.

Is your tone of voice adding to the conflict? Some people aren't aware how terse or edgy they might sound. Try listening to yourself on an audiotape or voice mail. It can be helpful and enlightening!

9. **Focus on and state the positives!** When frustrated or irritated, so much of what gets said is negative. For example, instead of "why don't you ever clean your room," you can say "I really love it when your room is clean!" When you ask for a positive outcome, you are much more likely to have success.

10. **Use the 4F model ©.** Here is a model I've created that will help you handle difficult communication.

- **Step 1: Foundation valuing statement.** Identify and state the genuine value in the other person or situation.

  "What I appreciate about you is. . . ."

  "Our relationship is important to me *and there's* something important I'd like to talk about with you."

  If you're going to say it, make sure it is authentic and sincere! If not, start with step 2. And remember to leave out the "but" following an appreciation or acknowledgment.

- **Step 2: Facts.** Make sure you state observable facts—not assumptions.

  "I notice you've been late for our last three meetings."

When you state "the facts" as you see them, it gives you an opportunity to check if the other person has the same understanding.

- **Step 3: Feelings or results.** Let the person know how you're feeling about it.

  "How I feel about this is. . . ."

  "As a result, I'm feeling (irritated, frustrated, sad, etc.)."

- **Step 4: Future action.** Ask for the change you want.

  "What I would like in the future is. . . ."

While you may want others to change because they seem difficult, the only person you can really change is yourself. Using these 10 key tips will lead to more successful and satisfying communication—even with those difficult people in your life.

About the Author

Jeanne-Marie Grumet, President of Communication Catalysts in northern California, is nationally and internationally respected as a dynamic speaker, author, coach, and facilitator of leading-edge communication training. For over 20 years she has engaged participants in powerful programs that produce lasting, positive results. Backed by her years of experience and proven success working in sales, training, and management, she delivers customized speeches and courses. Programs include interpersonal communications, presentation skills, team building, customer service, sales, conflict resolution, and leadership. For other information and insightful communication tips, visit her Web site at http://www.jmgrumet.com.

28

DRAMA

Deciding to Drop the Drama

Deanna Davis

I had spent the better part of a week in a sleep-deprived delirium brought on by a vicious little souvenir (aka respiratory infection) I had carted home from a recent vacation. I had tried every known natural remedy to stave it off—from homeopathic elixirs to Chinese herbal tonics and from aromatherapy immersion to megadoses of vitamin *everything*, all to no avail.

I graduated to nightly Nyquil benders and holed up in the guest bedroom to spare my husband from the incessant hacking. I moved into the psychological realm to attack the little lung invaders from the inside out, resorting to positive psychology, then to reverse psychology, and then to what I can only describe as disturbingly *abnormal* psychology to convince my mind to heal my lungs. When none of that worked, I succumbed to anger, resentment, and extreme bouts of dramatic self-pity, none of which seemed to make a difference in my situation (go figure).

So, on my husband's sane advice, I dragged myself into my physician's office the next day, fatigued beyond recognition and ready for Western medicine to free me from my immune-compromised prison. But, of course, during the height of cold and flu season, everyone else had the same idea. As such, I sat in the waiting room for the better part of 45 minutes and did what everyone does in a waiting room: I waited. And coughed. And waited. And coughed. And . . . well, you get the picture. . .

I sat there, sleep-deprived, rationality-impaired, and most uncomfortable due to the unfortunate dislodging of major body organs from my hacking cough. I was completely overcome by frustration. I imagined the assertive manner (read: menacing and aggressive) in which I could share my disdain with the physician who had kept me waiting while my very life hung in the balance. I scripted a compelling and colorful response to the long wait, certain that he would nod in agreement, pound his fist on the exam table, and shout with conviction, "Things have got to change around here so we can heal the sick and comfort the downtrodden . . . and quickly!"

What actually happened when the door opened was that I lost every nuance of my thoughtfully planned "waiting room efficiency" speech and lapsed into uncontrollable sobs interspersed with incoherent babble, such as "so tired . . . haven't slept in a week . . . broke all the capillaries in my face . . . think I'm going to have an aneurysm." The doctor looked at me with compassion and gently said, "Well, actually, if you already *had* an aneurism, maybe you would have *burst* it."

His comment stopped me in my tracks. I was flabbergasted. I mean, here I am, looking like hell, blithering like a lunatic, and somehow it's important for him to correct my description of my self-diagnosed, potentially fatal maladies? Who cares if I said I would *have* an aneurysm or *burst* an aneurysm? Isn't it all just related to the fact that I have a rip-roaring headache and an out-of-control cough and need *help*? He smiled a sheepish grin, and we both laughed (well, he laughed, and I alternately giggled and gasped for oxygen). "Now," he said, "let's talk about what the problem is and see if we can fix it."

What I later realized is that this is exactly what I *needed* him to do—diffuse my frustration and help me step out of my self-imposed drama long enough to take some practical steps to improve my situation. What a novel concept! With an unexpected comment and a gentle dose of humor, that physician reprogrammed our entire experience and, fortunately, saved himself an earful of caustic remarks that bordered on both literary genius and verbal abuse. Lucky man. Even more importantly, though, he directed our mutual efforts toward the *outcome* I wanted to achieve—quite simply, to get healthier and feel better. I left his office armed with the medication and the renewed attitude I needed to do just that.

As with most incidents like this, it got me thinking that the simple act of dropping the drama is a strategy we can and should be practicing on a regular basis, whether with ourselves, our partners, our children, or anyone else. When we do this, problems are solved, frustration is lessened, and everyone wins. Consider these suggestions.

1. **With yourself.** Sometimes people allow their negative thinking to spin out of control like a blindfolded child whacking aimlessly at a runaway piñata. My experience with piñatas is that they're a really inefficient way of securing treats, and they're usually hazardous to everyone involved. The same holds true with irrational and unproductive thinking. Make the choice to remove your "awareness blindfold" and ask yourself what is *really* happening. Often, when you step back and look at a situation from a different angle, you see that it is far less dire than you originally thought. Then ask yourself, rather than just lamenting about it, what you can do to *influence* the situation, either through your thoughts or your actions. Both these questions will help you divert your attention *away* from the drama and *toward* constructive action. This is a modified version of Martin Seligman's widely researched approach to Learned Optimism. By consciously choosing optimism and rationality over pessimism and helplessness, you'll be amazed at how much you can accomplish.

2. **With your partner.** The foremost researchers in marital success, John and Julie Gottman, have found that one of the most important things you can do during a conflict with your partner is to *avoid escalating it.* One of the most effective ways to diffuse conflict and come to rational decisions or mutual understanding is to very simply *choose* to drop the drama. You can do this by taking a deep breath, committing yourself to simply listen without judgment for a period of time, or agreeing to take a break and come back to the conversation when you have both calmed down. By boycotting escalation, you will escape the drama long enough to focus on *solutions* rather than defensiveness or aggression.

3. **With your children.** Anyone who has lived with a toddler or a teenager (sometimes they feel like the same developmental stage) knows how hard it can be at times to drop the drama when you are dealing with kids. Jane Nelsen, author of *Positive Discipline*, suggests that at times you can divert the drama by letting your children know that you want to listen to them and to help them feel better. Take a break from the push-pull cycle long enough to offer a hug, a moment of quiet reflection together, or an opportunity to listen to their emotions for a few moments in order to reduce tension. Then get back to working *with* them to come up with mutual solutions to whatever issue is at hand. As you empower them to express themselves and to be a part of resolving a concern, you effectively remove one element of the drama (the desire for control) that can undermine your best intentions.

These strategies offer a simple rule of thumb—*choose drama when you want entertainment and rationality when you want results*. When in doubt, decide to drop the drama!

ABOUT THE AUTHOR

Deanna Davis, PhD, is the author of *Living with Intention: Designing a Wildly Fulfilling and Remarkably Successful Life*. She is a professional speaker focusing on topics such as peak performance, balance and resilience, laughter, and cultivating powerful perspectives. Deanna is an admitted laughaholic and a strong proponent of adding chocolate as a key category of the USDA Food Pyramid. Visit Deanna online at http://www.deannadavis.net, where you can also subscribe to her free monthly e-zine (online newsletter), also called "Living with Intention."

29

EMBRACING OPPORTUNITIES

Affirming Opportunities:
The "Yes, and . . ." Principle

Suzanne Blake

For years I have been involved with comedy improvisation, where performers create scenes with each other spontaneously. As demonstrated in the popular television show, "Whose Line Is It Anyway?," the group is usually given a topic from the audience, and then they create a scene without a script. This process forces one to be spontaneous and to practice teamwork. My first comedy improvisation teacher taught me that "good improvisation is good life."

In order for the unique process of improvisation to work, several important guidelines need to be followed. These guidelines can also help to create a more dynamic, vibrant, and collaborative life.

1. Commitment is all important. Give your all and give your best, without back doors or thinking about other agendas.
2. Listen to your partners. Respond to what they are saying, without denying what they want from you. Work to support the group, avoiding individual agendas and attempts to control outcomes.
3. When offered an opportunity, say, "Yes, and . . ." instead of an automatic, "No, but. . . ."

Although all the principles above can benefit your life, I'd like to focus on the "Yes, and . . ." aspect. All too often, we get interesting "offers" or opportunities that seem too big, too scary, and too strange. Our first instinct is to deny them, to negate them, or to stick to our own agendas or paths. The universe is constantly sending us offers that we can choose to adopt or reject. These offers often come from our souls' inner longings. Our souls will often work together with the universe to bring to us that which we truly desire. Our egos want to reject what might really be good for us to maintain the status quo.

Here is a great example of a soul working to create a great opportunity and an ego wanting to push it away: A marketing executive in his early fifties longs to leave Corporate America. He holds a dream deep in his heart of teaching and publishing. He has already published one book and has taken on some part-time teaching at a local community college on top of his full-time marketing job. When he is unexpectedly laid off, he initially experiences fear and worry about finances.

His ego warns him that it was foolish of him to take time off and that he should be looking for a job right away. His inner critic says that he will lead his family down a path of poverty and despair. However, after gaining some perspective, he sees that it is the perfect time to begin teaching more and to work on making a living from his writing. He consults a financial planner and confirms that the severance package and unemployment he will receive will carry him through for many months if he is frugal.

The real growth and depth in life comes from saying "Yes, and . . ." to new and creative ideas, to different solutions, or to our partners, families, and friends. It's important to look for the gift in every opportunity and to embrace it instead of misinterpreting or rejecting the offer. Especially in romantic relationships, if we accept ideas and offers, we enrich ourselves and our relationships. If we say "No, but . . . ," we create a barrier to intimacy and the concept of teamwork. The relationship stays stuck in the individual mode, rather than becoming a dynamic partnership.

Saying "No, but . . ." cuts off the flow of relationships, ideas, and processes. Instead of doors opening, they slam shut. Our inner critics will come up with new and creative ways to convince us that the new opportunity isn't good for us. Look beyond your ego and into your heart and soul for ways to embrace these offers that aren't part of your picture of the way you perceive you want your life to go.

It's especially important to say "Yes, and . . ." to compliments as they are wonderful sources of positive energy and encouragement. When we say yes to them and really take in what someone is saying, it can increase our motivation and self-esteem tremendously. Instead of denying the compliment ("Oh, no, I really don't look good"), work on embracing those affirming messages.

By opening our minds with a "Yes, and . . ." attitude, we walk through doors to huge possibilities, to partnerships, and to expanded outcomes. The "Yes, and . . ." principle is important in harnessing the power of the universe. The more we say yes to the offers and opportunities the universe sends us, the more we will increase the flow of positive energy coming our way.

Moving Forward

Take a moment to ask yourself these questions to create more positive energy and experiences for yourself and others.

1. What offers or opportunities have you said "No, but . . ." to lately that you could have said "Yes, and . . ." to? What was/is the cost of saying no to these opportunities?
2. What offers or opportunities that you have been given recently could you say "Yes, and . . ." to? What benefits and results would you receive by saying "Yes, and . . .?"
3. This week, practice saying "Yes, and . . ." to all that is offered to you, except dangerous situations. Notice what difference this makes in your life after you do say yes. What other offers would you like to say "Yes, and . . ." to?

ABOUT THE AUTHOR

Suzanne Blake, PCC, works with individual and corporate clients across the globe to achieve their professional and personal goals. Clients receive structure, accountability, and encouragement so they move past barriers to living the life they desire! A noted speaker, facilitator, and spokesperson, Suzanne's coaching work has been featured in numerous media venues, including *The New York Times*, *The Boston Globe*, *Smart Money* magazine, Boston WBZ "Television News," and Boston Channel 5's award-winning *Chronicle* magazine. This article is an excerpt from Suzanne's book, *Great News for Dating and Mating: Winning Strategies That Work*, which is available through her Web site at http://www.suzanneblake.com.

30

Holding the Key to Your Emotions

Lesley Moore

Many times, when you're having a great day, one unexpected turn can turn that perfect day into a horrible one. Maybe it's your coworker who sees everything as negative, the slow driver holding up traffic, or your teenager's hormones going wild, but in that instant the positive outlook you've had all day is gone—just like that. Suddenly, you find yourself in the same negative space your coworker is in or with the same raging hormones your son or daughter now has. But what if you could continue holding the key to your emotions, regardless of how others around you were feeling?

The truth is that you do have the ability to control your mood and that if you choose to have a day that is upbeat and positive, you will have it. While I am simplifying it now, it really isn't that difficult but is more a simple matter of understanding that you are the one who is, in fact, controlling the emotions you have. That is the good news. The bad news is that you will have to stop blaming all the other people who have not chosen to have a positive day.

I am not suggesting that you won't be affected by other people's behavior; rather, I am suggesting that the behavior of others will only affect you if you *choose* to let it do so. Although it is not easy and will take some work on your part, you can opt to stay in your positive state of mind, regardless of what is going on around you.

- First, take a careful look at what is actually occurring. Try to remove the emotions and look intently at what is going on.

Let's use the example of your son coming home from school in a very bad mood. He comes in slamming his backpack to the ground and throwing his shoes across the room. Within an instant he is picking an argument with his brother, who has come into the house peacefully, and when you intervene, the belligerent son begins to yell at you for siding with his brother. After the pleasant day you've had you immediately feel your heart racing and your anger brewing. As you begin to yell back at him, you also begin to take on the exact mood your son has brought in the door.

Take a deep breath, and acknowledge only the facts. *The fact is that your son has had a bad day and does not know what to do with his emotions.* He is dealing with his emotions in an inappropriate way, and he needs to know that.

• Create a visualization that allows you to focus on yourself and on *your* emotions only.

Take another deep breath, and concentrate on yourself and on the space you were in before your angry son walked in the door. Remind yourself what made your day a good day just seconds ago.

Now, pretend that you are standing in a clear box (with air holes, of course!). This box represents your good mood of the day. I like to call it your *happy space*. Visualize that no matter what, no one can get in (unless they're happy too), and no one can pull you out. It is your emotion today, and you have created it. Remind yourself that the angry emotions you see in front of you, outside your happy space, are not yours but are, in fact, your son's. So let him have them. You can offer assistance ("Do you want to talk about your day?") or set consequences ("Maybe you need to go to your room until you are ready to talk about it or let it go.").

Remember that we have been conditioned to take on the moods of others around us, so this exercise is not an easy one. It is something that really works, though, and allows you to really have control over your day and what mood you choose to be in. The best part, surprisingly, is that when you don't engage in the emotions of others, they may find it easier to let go of the anger they're having and join you in your happy space as well!

You'll be amazed at how much more often you're able to maintain a sense of peace and happiness within yourself. You will see that if the happiness comes from within yourself, it is not dependent on the variables around you. The emotions you have are truly *yours*, and you certainly do hold the key to them. So, the next time you feel yourself sliding into someone else's day, stop, take a breath, and unlock the emotion you want to have . . . with a smile on your face!

ABOUT THE AUTHOR

Lesley Moore is president and owner of LifeScope, Life Coaching. She specializes in working with individuals in transition, empowering them to create lives they love. She is also a personal fitness trainer and a freelance writer. Lesley graduated from the University of Maryland with a degree in journalism and has studied coaching through the Mentor Coach Program, which is recognized by the International Coach Federation. LifeScope, Life Coaching can be contacted at (609) 730–1540, lessmore4@comcast.net, or http://www.lifescopecoach.com.

31

Road Trip to Empowerment

Kay Richardson & Sarah Fuelling

Sarah and I pulled into Yellowstone's north entrance at 2:00 A.M. and were greeted by the official National Park warning: "Beware of Bison!" The bright yellow flyer had a comic, yet equally horrifying black sketch: a bison, head down, horns forward, tossing a flailing human into the air, his camera flying. On this dark, moonless night, with no other human being in sight, we were thrilled to arrive, but uncertain whether to proceed.

The Power of Facing Our Fears

There was no one to collect our entrance fee, no one to tell us if we were safe to continue, and no one to help us if needed. We each heard the voice of caution familiar to many women—am I taking too great a risk? There are times to heed that voice by not continuing and times to simply hear it, recognize the possible dangers, and trust your instinct to move ahead.

Road trips provide multiple opportunities for empowerment, beginning with the chance to face our fears. Each time we push past what's comfortable and succeed, we gain confidence in our power of discernment. This frees us to live an adventurous life!

That night in Yellowstone, we embraced just such an opportunity. With adrenaline pumping, we drove on into the park for one of the most exciting and beautifully eerie experiences we've ever had. Everywhere we looked, there seemed to be eyes—little dots of light in the night looking back at us—a set of two here, a group of many there. We drove slowly, taking it all in.

The Power of Spontaneity

After an hour or so we parked our trusty Saturn on the paved shoulder. It was very late; we'd covered many miles that day. It's surprising how comfortable you can get with reclined seats, a pillow, and a sleeping bag.

On that trip we simply stayed wherever was convenient. Ironically, we'd planned it that way. Our day-to-day lives were filled with deadlines, decisions, and goals to reach. This road trip was an opportunity to step outside that and simply do whatever we wanted, whenever we wanted—a unique chance to let the children in us play and the adults rest.

By 4:00 A.M., we just wanted sleep. So we got comfortable in the car, giggling at ourselves for selecting the one spot in front of a pay phone. You know, just in case one of those bison got ideas. . . .

The Power of Others

One of the things you discover on road trips is how many interesting, kind, and caring people there are in the world. There were the folks who gave us gas when we realized our tank was nearly empty in a huge national park with the nearest gas station miles away. There was the camp host who brought extra firewood and doted on us like a grandfather. There were the countless smiles and moments of small talk.

It's easy to become wary of strangers, particularly with the barrage of tragic stories in the media. Road trips are a chance to experience firsthand the larger community we live in and feel support outside our usual world of friends, family, and colleagues. The power of that knowing includes a sense of greater security in our day-to-day lives and a feeling of connection rather than isolation from others.

The Power of Self-Knowledge

Yellowstone Park was one of many destinations on that luxuriously long road trip, and through our journey together we got to know ourselves in a new way. We were open to such learning because we had fewer distractions and time to consider our experiences. Unlike many life lessons that require big change for us to stop and notice, the things we learned were, for the most part, fun and easy.

Many of these lessons were practical nuggets of wisdom about what we really need to be comfortable. You can live without a hair dryer—but not without toothbrush and toothpaste. Moist wipes can clean hands, clean spills, clean the car, and clean your body in a pinch. A hot shower is one of life's greatest sensual pleasures. Clothes that "feel like you" are essential and empowering. Having gear that keeps you cozy in any weather frees you to enjoy the outdoors. Less is more; being able to find what you need because your space isn't cluttered is freeing.

The Power of Creating Your Dreams

As we got to know our essential selves in a new way, our real dreams for our lives had room to surface. Around late-night campfires we rediscovered some of our childhood dreams and explored others we wanted to pursue. We decided to act on them by writing down "My Five Dreams." We began: "I co-create with the universe . . ." and then listed five of our most significant life dreams. This brought them right into the present, as we took responsibility and claimed support from the spiritual realm to attract our dreams into our lives. The expansiveness of the road was echoed in our dreams—rather than being limited to one, we had five to expand on. This helped us develop an exciting life vision to take home, inspiring us to continue on our highest path.

The Power of Forgiving Yourself

Another tool we hit on in our travels was the power of giving ourselves a break. We did some soul searching by writing things from the past we were carrying guilt or regret about. Then, from a spiritually connected place, we simply said, "I forgive myself for _____." The joy of being spontaneous on the road was magnified by the lightness of being that comes from truly forgiving oneself.

The Power of Being

The ultimate power of any road trip is the opportunity to be a "human being," rather than a "human doing." Most of us live such hectic daily lives that we don't realize we are whole and complete just by being ourselves. Instead, we are constantly in motion, our focus on the next thing to be done or on the list we haven't gotten to. As a result, we can become disconnected from our experiences, unaware of who we are or what we need because we are too busy to notice. We become unable to adjust our lives to better suit our dreams and passions because we don't have enough time to do so or the self-knowledge to make good choices.

There is incredible power in stepping outside our typical selves and venturing into the unknown.

Leaving behind the familiar can be frightening, even intimidating, and we often engineer our lives to avoid such situations. But the joy of travel and being with friends can push us to venture into those places, with the added bonus of it being our choice to do so rather than circumstances making the choice for us. The resulting learning and life experience are bonuses over and above the simple pleasures of a road trip.

So take the chance to face your fears. To be spontaneous. To reach out to others and be touched by them. To know yourself. To create your highest dreams. To forgive yourself, and to simply be. And if your road trip takes you to Yellowstone, watch out for those bison!

About the Authors

Kay Richardson, MFT, is a Certified Life Coach whose gentle spirituality and collaborative style invite clients to step into their true selves and create their highest dreams, bringing head and heart together in purposeful, compassionate action.

Sarah Fuelling has a master's degree in psychology, has been working in computer software usability for the last 10 years, and facilitates empowering workshops for women of all ages. She lives in Seattle with her son, husband, and their two dogs and four cats.

Road Trip to Empowerment workshops and individual Life Coaching sessions are available from any location by teleconference. More at http://www.kayrichardson.com.

32

Failure Can Catapult Your Success

J. Victor Eagan

For every successful venture, I have yet to see complete, undaunting achievement without accompanying failure. Oftentimes, we think of failure as a tragedy; it's true that it can be a temporary setback. Nevertheless, every great endeavor has a degree of darkness in its past, often masked in the clothing of risk. Call it calculated or uncalculated risk: some failure is inevitable.

Most people are trained to view failure as defeat. It shatters self-esteem as opposed to being a bridge to success. Consequently, failure is not embraced as a tool for learning.

Failure Is the Mother of Invention and Innovation

I'm reminded of a story I heard about Joe Dudley, the inventor, owner, and distributor of Dudley Hair Care Products, a multimillion-dollar company. He failed first grade and was labeled retarded. He had learning disabilities, struggled with his grades throughout school, and was written off as a failure. It devastated him, but he converted his failure into his greatest success. He went back to his grammar books and learned how to read. His career took off, he married a wonderful woman, and by 1995, he was awarded the prestigious Horatio Alger Award after achieving tremendous success.

I look at modern day icons like Donald Trump, touted as one of America's most successful billionaire real estate magnets, yet he has filed bankruptcy two times and restructured over $2.8 billion dollars of debt. At first the look of failure was devastating; however, he bounced back stronger both times. Moreover, what about Walt Disney, who had failed ventures before the colossal success of Disneyland theme park and Disney motion pictures? Or people like MC

Hammer, Henry Heinz, Henry Ford, and a host of other luminaries who have had bankruptcy as a part of their resumes? Great achievements are often surrounded by high risks that can sometimes result in failed outcomes.

Dictionary.com defines failure as receiving an unintended result. If we receive unintended results, all we have to do is learn from them, change our strategy, and do something different to achieve the intended outcome. Thomas Edison, after hundreds of failed attempts to invent the incandescent electric light, said each time, "I am not discouraged because every wrong attempt discarded is another step forward."

Have the Courage to "Do Something Different"

Sometimes we need to take a different route to achieve success. Most of his college professors probably dubbed Bill Gates a failure for dropping out of Harvard in his junior year, but today, according to *Forbes Magazine*, he is the richest American, with a net worth of $46.5 billion, and loving it. He is also significantly philanthropic, with a foundation of over $32 million. With a passion for developing computer software programs, Gates decided to do something different. Oftentimes, doing something different requires you to take a risk. Whether calculated or not, taking a risk can potentially result in failure. Generally, the greater the risk, the greater the reward. It is far better to take the risk and shoot for the stars than to not risk at all. Perhaps you are the next world changer.

Failure is a Part of the Learning Curve

Thomas Edison once said, "Many of life's failures are men who did not realize how close they were to success when they gave up." Once you realize that failure is a part of the learning process, you can recognize it as instructional, move on to accomplish your goals, and achieve your dreams. Press through the hard places and achieve your success.

Be Proactive: Take Action to Get Past a Failure

The following actions will ensure the proper response and provide a stimulus for growth, development, and self-improvement.

- Recognize that now you know more than you did before.
  - You know what not to do, and thereby you increase the probability of success.
  - "Remember the two benefits of failure. First, if you do fail, you learn what doesn't work; and second, the failure gives you the opportunity to try a new approach." – Roger von Oech, author of *A Whack on the Side of the Head*
- Change your assumptions and look for new opportunities.
  - Donald Trump got partners to help share the risk and to attack the problems.
  - "When one door closes another door opens; but we often look so long and so regretfully upon the closed door, that we do not see the ones which open for us." – Alexander Graham Bell, inventor of the telephone
- Don't give up.
  - Thomas Edison kept trying new approaches to obtain success, and he succeeded with over 1,090 inventions. After 10,000 unsuccessful attempts to develop his electric light bulb over one and a half years, Thomas said, "I have not failed. I've just found 10,000 ways that won't work." Edison discovered that men do not fail; they give up trying. Success means not giving up.
  - "Don't fear failure so much that you refuse to try new things. The saddest summary of a life contains three descriptions: could have, might have, and should have." – Louis E. Boone, author of *Contemporary Business*
- Reinvent yourself or the project.
  - Take a fresh look at the challenge and have the courage and creativity to strategize a different approach. Toss the problem up in the air and look at it from all angles.
  - "Because a fellow has failed once or twice, or a dozen times, you don't want to set him down as a failure till he's dead or loses his courage—and that's the same thing." – George Horace Lorimer, former editor of the *Saturday Evening Post*
- Encourage yourself.
  - A failed project does not mean you are a failure. Never give up hope. Failure is an event. If you have 10 failures, you are a person who has had 10 failed events. You are not defined by your failures. List 10 amazing things about yourself daily.

- o "History has demonstrated that the most notable winners usually encountered heartbreaking obstacles before they triumphed. They won because they refused to become discouraged by their defeats." – B. C. Forbes, founder of *Forbes Magazine*
- Evaluate and make adjustments.
  - o Take time to identify the unexpected outcome and do what it takes to be successful. Evaluation is a continuous part of the success equation. Always evaluate, and then make the necessary adjustments—don't be afraid to change your plans.
  - o "The majority of men meet with failure because of their lack of persistence in creating new plans to take the place of those which fail." – Napoleon Hill, author of *Think and Grow Rich*
- Take the risk.
  - o I once heard someone say that there are three types of people: those who make it happen, those who watch it happen, and those who ask "what happened?" In order to experience success, take the risk.
  - o "Forget past mistakes. Forget failures. Forget about everything except what you're going to do now—and do it." – William Durant, founder of General Motors

When you recognize that failure is part of the process, you can use it to catapult yourself to your next level of success. An old proverb says that a wise man falls seven times, but he gets back up. Failure is not an option.

ABOUT THE AUTHOR

Dr. J. Victor Eagan is a highly successful entrepreneur and achieved his wealth in the area of orthodontics. He is a teacher and speaker in demand worldwide. A graduate of the University of Michigan, Dr. Eagan has achieved prestigious awards and recognition for his work in teaching people how to develop excellent business systems and achieve business success. He and his wife, Catherine B. Eagan, coauthored *Dominating Money* and *How to Discover Your Purpose in 10 Days* (both books are available at http://www.eaganbooks.com). Dr. Eagan is a business coach who uses time-tested principles to prepare his clients to be more successful in business and experience an extraordinary life. To sign up for Dr. Eagan's monthly e-newsletter, "The Eagan Report," visit http://www.eaganbooks.com.

33

FAITH

Believe and You Will See

Peggy McColl

Many years ago, my husband and I decided to divorce. We listed our house for sale. At the time it was a downward market, and houses were not selling.

Patiently, I waited. While the house was listed, I began a search for a new home, but we were losing equity in our home every day. Our house was listed for less than what we paid for it, and we had decreased the listing price twice. I had no money to buy a new home.

But I was dead set on my goal—I clearly described my dream home on a goal card that I carried with me. My goal statement was as follows: "I, Peggy McColl, am enjoying living in my gorgeous, four-bedroom home, beautifully decorated, fully furnished, double-car garage, in a modern subdivision on a nice lot, in a neighborhood with lots of trails and parks for Michel and I to go cycling."

Michel is my son, and at the time he was two and a half years old. It was important for me to have a nice home for my son and to raise him in an area where there were other small children and where we were surrounded by nature.

While I was in the process of looking for a home, I heard of an interesting lottery in our city. It was called the "Dream of a Lifetime." In exchange for a $100 ticket, you had the opportunity to win the grand prize: a large, four-bedroom home, completely furnished, professionally decorated, professionally landscaped, complete with two new cars, groceries for a year, all legal costs included, and moving expenses and cleaning services paid.

This was a great solution to my problem.

The Dream Home, as they called it, was open for visiting during the day. I drove out to the home, passing several parks and nature trails, and arrived at a home fitting perfectly the description on my goal card.

I walked in the front door and fell in love with the house. I immediately started to visualize living there as I sat in all the rooms. Upstairs, I decided which bedroom would be Michel's. I visualized sleeping on the bed in the master bedroom. I got in the extra large bathtub and imagined what it would be like to have a wonderful, warm bubble bath in the great tub.

I visited the house several times after that as it remained open right up until the day of the draw. When I visited the house, I would go for walks around the neighborhood. I would drive to the house and imagine I was driving home from work. I also changed my goal card to include the address of the home along with the description I had already written on it.

On December 7 the Dream of a Lifetime draw was held. A local doctor won the house. What did I do? I changed my goal card and simply removed the address. I did not lose sight of my goal.

Several months passed. The home Charles and I owned together was still not sold. I asked my husband if he would be willing to keep the house if I left and took nothing. He agreed. We determined an appropriate shared custody schedule for Michel and set a date for when we would part ways as husband and wife.

I decided to take a drive past the Dream of a Lifetime home. As I drove up to the house, I noticed a "For Sale" sign. I figured it was a "sign" for me. I called the real estate agent and said, "I want to make an offer on that house."

Within 30 minutes the agent had arrived. We sat at the dining room table (the doctor was selling the house along with all the furniture). I wrote up an offer that allowed me to move into the home and occupy it for a period of time and close at a later date. This idea just came to me. When I called the agent, I had no idea how I would pay for it, but I knew I would find a way. I do know that when we are committed, there is always a way.

Two months later, Michel and I moved into our new home. We loved it! It was absolutely perfect.

At the time we moved in I was an "occupant," with an agreement to purchase and a firm close date. Then I had to come up with the money. Honestly, in my heart I knew I would do it, but I did not know how. I had to believe it before I could see it and believe with all my heart.

Interestingly enough, I worked for a company that was about to go public. The IPO (initial public offering) was set. I had saved some money for the close of my house, and I put every dollar on the IPO and bought shares—a very risky move. The IPO was set for November 26, and my house was to close on December 1. All the money that I had raised was now tied up in a stock, and I had no idea which direction the stock would go.

Was I nervous? You bet. But I refused to give up. I maintained my high level of certainty, continued to believe in the outcome of my desire, and replaced negative thoughts with positive and supportive ones. I had clearly defined my goal, and I was focused on making it happen. I developed an unwavering faith.

On November 26 the company went public, and the stock shot up like a rocket. I sold the shares immediately, and on December 1, I closed the deal on my home. I owned the Dream of a Lifetime home and lived there with my son for eight years, until we sold it for a very healthy profit and bought another home.

Buying that house impacted me in more ways than I had realized at the time.

I realized that we need to remind ourselves of some valuable lessons because it is highly unlikely anyone else will. Sometimes we need to be our own strongest supporters. The most empowering beliefs that strengthened me during this period were:

- even though there is no evidence of the desired outcome becoming a reality, you must remain connected to the feeling (joy, happiness, elation, gratitude) of already having it (the "act as if" philosophy)
- if others (your friends, family, coworkers, colleagues) will not support you, keep your thoughts, ideas, and goals to yourself
- you do not have to know *how* the goal will materialize—just believe it will, and it will
- pursuing a goal does not mean that you will be without fear, but when the fear comes, be ready to deal with it—combat it and break it down with unwavering faith. Faith is the only solution to fear.

It is my desire that my own experience of pursuing a dream will inspire you in some way to go for yours. And as much as we know all this, it is sometimes a little more challenging to follow through, but I have found that when I follow through, the rewards are enormous.

ABOUT THE AUTHOR

Peggy McColl is an internationally recognized expert in the area of goal achievement, inspiring individuals to realize their goals and reach their maximum potential for the past 25 years. She is President and Founder of Dynamic Destinies, Inc., an organization that trains authors, entrepreneurs, corporate leaders, and employees in some of the most compelling and strategic goal-setting technologies of our time. She is the author of numerous books, including a Hay House Publication (to be released May 2007) called *Your Destiny Switch: Master Your Four Keys Emotions and Attract the Life of Your Dreams!* Visit http://www.destinies.com, or e-mail Peggy at peggy@destinies.com.

34

Eight Success Lessons from My Mom

Michael G. Rayel

As my mom receives treatment for a lingering illness, I can't help but think about what she has done for me and our family. As a young boy, my father used to remind me that without Mom, our family would have crumbled. "In every good family, there's always a good mother behind it," he emphasized.

I can't forget those words coming from my dad, but my young brain couldn't fully appreciate it at that time. While I was growing up, Mom never talked about any success principle. However, through her attitude and actions over the years I have realized that Mom is indeed the strength and foundation of the family. In fact, she has instilled in me life lessons important to success.

Be Enthusiastic

My mom has always been enthusiastic. She was enthusiastic as a teacher, as a businesswoman, and as a mother. You could feel her presence because her positive attitude was infectious. Her smile, speech, and gestures showed a woman full of confidence in doing her tasks.

A relative once commented that my mom was "a woman in a hurry" and "always busy." And yet you could always find a smile on her face, even during stressful times. She would tackle her task with ease and gladness. It was her positive attitude and enthusiasm that helped her develop long-term friendships and business relationships all through the years.

Pursue Your Priorities

When she got married, she committed to raise her family the best way she could. Mom was always there for us, always willing to provide her precious time. We prayed, went to church, and had fun together as a family. Moreover, she gave us the necessary tools to do well in school. Many times, she had to swallow her pride just to borrow or rent Boy Scout uniforms or formal attire so we could participate in school programs.

Early on, she made us aware of her mission. Her priority was to provide each of us with a college education regardless of her financial circumstances. She considered education as the only way to prepare us for the future.

When the family business was thriving, she used the additional income to buy properties as investments. Her intention was to save for her children's future needs. So when I was in medical school and money was tight, she never hesitated to sell them just so I could pay my tuition fees and other school expenses.

Develop a Strong Focus

My mom worked hard. She used to wake up early (around 5:00 A.M.), despite going to bed late (around 1:00 or 2:00 A.M.), to prepare the store for the day. Aside from her day job as a teacher, she was a full-time businesswoman in the evenings. She took care of her small restaurant and barbershop after work. During the day she would bring products to sell in a school store. I saw her rush to school not just with a lesson plan but also with products in tow. On weekends she spent her free time with the customers and buying supplies, such as flour, bread, and meat, in nearby cities. Through hard work and focus Mom and Dad expanded their farm and grew their small business.

Establish Your Integrity

My mom's coworkers and friends have always talked about Mom's integrity. Her words were consistently followed by appropriate actions. In short, her words were her actions, and vice versa. No wonder she gained the trust of her friends, relatives, and customers.

Even lenders trusted her with their money. Each time she needed money, lenders would not hesitate to give her what she needed. Because of her integrity, some friends and relatives had asked her to borrow funds for them from "difficult" lenders or to serve as a guarantor. She had helped many families through these unselfish actions.

Believe in Your Abilities

Mom has always made us believe that we're capable of achieving our goals. I was only 10 years old when she would announce to everyone how "intelligent" my siblings and I were. To prove her point, she would even ask me or my older siblings for suggestions about family or personal matters.

My mom has always been proud of us. She values us. She focuses on our strengths and appreciates our efforts. She frequently reminds us that we each have a bright future. Because of her praise and positive expectations, we have confidence and strong belief in ourselves.

Practice Self-Reflection

As a teenager, I was rebellious. I used to share with her my unconventional ideas about morality, religion, and politics. Instead of making comments, she would listen intently and made sure she understood me. Even during those times when I made mistakes, she never argued nor gave advice. Her infrequent and minimal comments would instead focus on the fact that I was "smart enough" to know what was good and appropriate.

But I realized later that her "quiet" response was more powerful than any argument or advice in the world. Her unexpected response allowed me to analyze and criticize my own thoughts and behavior during my quiet moments. Likewise, it allowed me to learn from my mistakes through self-reflection.

Be Generous

All her life, my mom has always been generous. She gives even if she has little. I remember as a young boy when she had to borrow money so she could give to a relative or a close friend who required urgent assistance. In addition, she sent some of our poor relatives' kids to school. She liked to help because she experienced the harsh reality of poverty when she was young. Her intention was to help stop the cycle of lack in those families through education.

Moreover, she never hesitated to help a friend or a relative in need of basic necessities such as food and clothing. Her mind-set was to serve others even if it meant sacrificing her own comfortable existence. It was, however, this profound sensitivity that endeared her to the hearts of others.

Have Faith

Like any woman who has had to deal with an unfaithful husband, she suffered from sleepless nights and emotional pain. When my dad eventually left her for a younger woman, her only refuge was prayer. I saw her endure from that ordeal. She wept. She lost weight and had some restless nights. And yet, through constant prayer, she maintained her equanimity and survived the worst storm in her life.

Her faith was tested yet again when my grandmother was suffering from the complications of dementia. For at least 10 years she was the only caregiver who was in my grandma's presence to meet her needs 24 hours a day, seven days a week. Through her unceasing faith she faced the challenges of caregiving and provided for her mother's care without complaint.

Now that she faces another adversity—her own serious medical illness—she will remain strong as she has always been. For sure, her character and her faith will once again shine. Life has handed Mom its wonders and hardships, its opportunities and challenges, and its surprises and disappointments. No doubt, she has embraced them all with acceptance and firm resolve. My mom, who rarely gave direct advice, has proven that role modeling is crucial in teaching young minds the life lessons of success.

ABOUT THE AUTHOR

Michael Rayel, MD, CEO of Oikos Global—the maker of emotional intelligence games and educational products—has helped others learn emotional intelligence through his award-winning invention, the Oikos Game Series. Recently, he has published award-winning self-help literature for youth: *A 31-Day Success Principles and Positive Affirmations for Kids and Teens*. In his book, *First Aid to Mental Illness*, he introduced the CARE Approach as a first aid methodology for mental health. Dr. Rayel also serves as the Editor of *Oikos' Insights! A Family and Self-Improvement Journal*. For details, visit http://www.oikosglobal.com, http://www.soardime.com, and http://www.oikosinsights.com.

35

FATE

Embrace Positive Fatalism

Samuel Okoro

> In doing so, he had simply obeyed the laws of his
> nature, and we have good reason to believe that he
> was, to some extent, a fatalist, but of an orthodox
> school of fatalism withal, that led him to rely upon
> himself and even upon Providence.
>
> – Jules Verne, *Five Weeks in a Balloon*

We usually associate fatalism with a passive, do-nothing attitude toward life. However, the sense in which I mean to use it here is captured in the above quotation. Fatalism in this more positive and active sense is a gut-level belief in an ultimate outcome.

In general, no great and successful life could have been all planned from beginning to end. What does happen is that the man has a burning hunger, a vision, promptings, and intuitions of what is possible and gives himself wholly in pursuit of it. And believes—this is where fatalism comes in—that it will turn out as dreamed, no matter what current circumstances seem to suggest. Without such a fatalist approach, no great achievement is possible.

The odds, at first glance, of good triumphing over evil, enlightenment over ignorance, order over chaos, accommodation and understanding over prejudice, or abundance over extreme and widespread poverty seem laughable at best. The effort required to bring about such a victory seems, on the basis of fact and logic, so titanic that we might just want to be realistic and remain content with more attainable, humdrum pursuits. And those who insist on being vanguards in such impossible struggles appear suicidal to many. But time and again, these Davids trounce their Goliaths very convincingly.

History and contemporary life are replete with examples of such fatalists. Recall Winston Churchill's unshakable belief in final victory during World War II, or Edison's confidence that the solution to puzzles in invention would be found, or Mandela's battle and final victory against the vastly superior forces of apartheid, or Helen Keller's miraculous rise above personal circumstances that should have deprived her of her very humanity.

To acquire the sort of fatalism we are discussing here, you must believe that the universe is ordered. It doesn't hurt to accept that some power—God, the universal mind—is in control or has at least loaded the dice of life in favor of good, justice, light, and truth.

It also helps if you align your purposes, thoughts, and actions with eternal verities and principles. That way, you come to believe that your cause is just. This belief gives you the sort of boldness that, in Goethe's words, "has genius, power and magic in it."

You must believe that you have a specific purpose for being here and a special contribution to make to advancing life in some way. And your whole life must be dedicated to fulfilling your mission, starting right where you are and with what tools you have.

Whether the effects are wholly psychological, or mystical, or both, they are very real. These gut-level beliefs drive everything you experience (or at least, your interpretation of what you experience), become, and achieve.

Developing the Fatalistic Mind-Set

Observe nature. Perhaps nothing so impresses on your mind the idea of inexorable progress as an observance of nature at work: mostly patient and unyielding, like winds that wear down rocks over the course of long years, and sometimes sudden and cataclysmic, like a volcanic eruption.

Recall the march of history. The universe keeps unfolding and the course of human history with it. The general direction of progress through the ages is toward greater freedom, knowledge, and truth. Accept the same as true for you personally, that the course of your life will unfold as it should.

Develop a rich inner life. Spend time alone to connect with God and with your inner self. That way, you develop a peaceful core that can withstand the vagaries of events. You also develop insights and intuitions about the direction your life should take.

Read the lives of great people. Read about great people, and notice how their personal determination seems to unleash forces that aid them toward the achievement of their dreams.

Effects of a Fatalistic Mind-Set

By developing positive fatalism, you become patient and persistent. You become focused on long-term results and are confident in the inevitability of ultimate success. You also combine an infectious and persuasive optimism with humility that is unfeigned.

ABOUT THE AUTHOR

Samuel Okoro is the CEO of Leapfrog Alliance Ltd., a management training and consulting firm that helps organizations to reduce costs and improve quality through better business processes. His vision is to use the company as a platform for taking African and Third World businesses to world-class levels. For further details, please visit http://www.leapfrogalliance.com. Sam lives in Lagos, Nigeria, with his wife Tayo and their sons Dede and Ama.

36

FEARLESS LIVING

Live Like Your Nail Color!

Mary Foley

Wild Berry. That's the name of my favorite nail color. To me, it says fun, bold, sexy, and just simply makes my fingers and hands look so good. It's a funny name for a nail polish, but then, so many women's cosmetics have funny names. There's Mango Spice lipstick, Roaring Red blush, and Whispering Mist eye shadow.

Just saying these words makes me think of walking along the beach on a tropical island wearing a flowered sarong, matching top, and the perfect makeup to highlight my features against the setting sun . . . while George Clooney comes running toward me!

Oh, how the mind gets going! I so very much want to live like my nail color—full-up on passion and feeling alive! Take me away, Wild Berry!

Now I know that painting my nails Wild Berry, or any color, for that matter, won't magically create this alive sensation. To feel that way has to come from within. Only after I've connected with, nurtured, and allowed myself to release my passion for life can I truly be Wild Berry. Starting on the inside is the starting point for living up to my nail color.

Who knew there was so much to learn from a nail color?! Who knew that when I started my young adult life as an $8-an-hour customer service representative at America Online, I would rise through the ranks, get married along the way, and discover in myself the desire to be much more like my nail color than I ever expected?

My internal good girl was aghast! But my inner Bodacious Woman was starting to push her way to the forefront. Good thing, too, because personally and professionally, life would knock me around a bit and test just how much I wanted to be "wild" about taking care of myself as well as my future.

And I'm not alone. Many women struggle to feel good about themselves and their lives. Perhaps you're one of them. You've wanted to feel like your nail color, but you've had fears or guilt or pressure in your life to stay put and not cause waves. Been there, done that, and it's not a fun time!

In my own struggle, there were times when I wanted to feel like Wild Berry, but I felt more like Wet Leaves. In time, though, I found another way, a way that affirmed my existing internal strength and enabled me to get stronger, wiser, healthier, and be a whole lot more fun! I call it the Bodacious Way.

What does *bodacious* really mean? I love asking that question! I've heard everything—wild, colorful, spontaneous, energetic, strong, fearless, courageous, assertive, open, free, gutsy, tenacious, confident, and positive. Being bodacious became a personal rallying cry during my demanding "decade of adrenaline" when I worked for AOL and tried to create a healthy marriage. Being bodacious gave me courage to make choices, small and large, that were *good for me*. Being bodacious gave me the courage to take risks. And on hard days, being bodacious gave me the courage to put one foot in front of the other.

Out of this experience, I came up with my own definition of bodacious: the courage to be in charge of your life! Being in charge of your life starts with being authentic with yourself, about who you are and what you want. It then takes courage to follow through. Courage is something that never goes out of style because contrary to what the media says, ultimately, life isn't a fashion show. Shocker, I know.

To help women wrap their heads around what it looks like to live bodaciously, I created my easy to remember Bodacious Woman Mantra. I like to think of it as four phrases that can change your life!

Look Within.
Think Strategically.
Act Bodaciously.
Love Every Minute of It.

141

Bodacious Women know that all the skills, techniques, and savvy in the world won't stick until you improve the quality of your inner messages. What you say to yourself *is* a major tool in building a fabulous life. That's why the Bodacious Woman Mantra starts by looking within.

Looking within means trusting your inner voice and means that you first have to listen to what's going on inside you. If you listen carefully, your inner voice will help you determine how you feel about yourself and what you want. Looking within also means protecting yourself from self-esteem busters. Unfortunately, our culture tends to confuse self-esteem with self-absorption or just plain selfishness, and this confusion leads women to be discouraged about taking care of themselves

Part two of the Bodacious Mantra is to think strategically. You can't decide how to get where you're going until you decide where you are going and why. Well, duh. But how many times do we race off in the morning going from one thing to another until we drop? Those days turn into weeks, and weeks turn into months or years. So, here's the big question: Do you know what you want? Or are you simply moving in the direction you believe you were supposed to? Good girls don't ask themselves such questions and just go along for the ride. Bodacious Women consider the messages they received growing up and then determine what's right for them.

There's no doubt in my mind that living bodaciously starts on the inside by looking within and thinking strategically. But at some point, you need to go public! It's time to act bodaciously for all the world to see. Acting bodaciously involves saying what you want and taking risks, which is often something good girls aren't comfortable doing. Maybe you're thinking that it's not "nice" to say so directly what you want. It feels a bit harsh. Consider this: It's not "nice" to so muffle your communication that others don't know what you want and don't have a chance to positively respond, which leaves the both of you frustrated and full of blame. Bodacious Women know you're doing everyone involved a favor.

When it comes to taking risks, Bodacious Women know that to get anywhere in life takes risk. They also know that the biggest risk is not taking one at all. I'm not talking reckless risks. I'm talking the kinds of things you need to do to reach your goals. And remember, giving something a shot that doesn't work out as planned doesn't mean you're a failure; it means you're a Bodacious Woman demonstrating her guts and courage.

As you continue to live the Bodacious Woman Mantra, I've got one last piece of advice: love every minute of it! Learn to love the ups and the downs. Laugh and play along the way, and life will never get boring. Hold on to your hats, Bodacious Women, the ride has just begun! Personally, I don't think the sky is falling, but life is definitely changing dramatically, and that can increase our feelings of insecurity and chaos. To stay energized and engaged, you've got to be serious about not being so serious! Be play-full. Laugh as much as possible, and find the humor that's begging to be discovered.

So, there you have it, the Bodacious Woman Mantra. By practicing this Mantra, you've decided to face your internal good girl. You've started trying new behaviors. And you're feeling more authentic, more powerful, and more alive because of it. Don't let it stop there! Keep growing in your bodaciousness, and remember to do what we all need to do—bring others along!

ABOUT THE AUTHOR

During a successful, demanding rise through the ranks of a 10-year career with America Online, Mary learned that the only way to thrive in today's world is to be bold, positive, and courageous—bodacious! Today, Mary, author of *Bodacious! Woman: Outrageously in Charge of Your Life and Lovin' It*, inspires women everywhere to be bodacious in their lives, careers, and businesses. You can be inspired, too! Get a free copy of Mary's e-book *How to Be Courageously in Charge of Your Life and Lovin' It* at http://www.gobodacious.com!

37

FINANCES

How the Financial Markets Can Grow More than Just Your Bank Account

John Forman

The financial markets provide us with the opportunity to grow in ways that most people probably do not even think about. We all know of the gains in wealth to be had buying and selling stocks, bonds, commodities, currencies, and other instruments. One need not look far to find stories about the riches to be had. Successful traders, investors, and portfolio managers, like George Soros, Peter Lynch, and Warren Buffet, have become household names. What is less commonly talked about is the personal development that takes place along the way.

Trading and investing, like any worthwhile pursuit, provides more rewards than just the obvious accomplishments. To paraphrase the old saying, the destination is not always as important as the path taken to get there and the things seen along the way. While it is true that the expansion of one's portfolio is what ultimately indicates success or failure in the markets, how those gains are achieved can provide outstanding opportunities to learn important lessons about ourselves with far-reaching value. These lessons reach across all areas of our lives.

Playing to Your Strengths

We all have our strengths and weaknesses and a kind of structure in which we operate based on the demands on our time, education, experience, and an array of other factors. In the markets we need to make assessments about these things to help us decide what to trade, the time frame in which to operate, and how to make our trading and investing decisions. Why? Because it is unlikely that we will achieve our objectives if we do not honestly judge ourselves and how we can best operate. For example, I am unlikely to be a good day trader if I cannot dedicate my days to watching the markets for long stretches and frequently buying and selling. I must either choose another course or alter my schedule to accommodate the demands of being a day trader.

It is the same in the rest of life. We must constantly consider our personal inventories and life situations. They dictate what we can do and how we can do it. That said, these are not static things. Just as I could alter my schedule to allow for day trading, so, too, can we change things to expand our options. Education, in all its forms, is part of that equation. So is seeking out new experiences, meeting new people, and even consciously changing our attitudes toward things. If a goal is important enough, there are things we can do to make achieving it possible. Part of that is knowing what we have to work with and how to most efficiently apply it. The other part is knowing how to open up new avenues.

Knowing Who to Listen To

In the markets, there is a vast array of information available. It comes in every form imaginable, from data released by the government to commentary by analysts to tips from Uncle Joe. Some of this information is useful to us. Some is not. A great deal of what came out in the aftermath of the stock markets collapsing in 2000 and after was the number of conflicts of interest those who provided "expert" opinions had. These people did not have the interests of those they spoke to about this stock or that at heart, but rather their own interests, or their firm's. Many, many people listened to these pundits to their detriment. Clearly, a hugely important element of successful trading is knowing what information is of value, which sources can be trusted, and what should be taken with a grain of salt.

The same holds true in all other areas of our life. All of us are constantly provided with information and advice. Some is solicited. Much is not. Before we can decide whether to make use of it all we must be able to assess the veracity of the source. Some people are trustworthy and wise. We can depend on what they say. Others do not have our best interests in mind. We must carefully consider what they say and the motivations behind it before deciding whether it is worthwhile or should be ignored altogether. Being able to effectively judge the input we receive from sources such as our family, friends, and peers is a priceless skill.

Being Disciplined

Success in the markets is achieved by doing what we know is the right thing to do. The single biggest reason people fail to consistently produce the returns they seek is that they fail to maintain a disciplined approach. Sound familiar? It is the same as anything else we do. Want to lose weight? You must be disciplined about diet and exercise. Want to learn how to play guitar? You must exercise the discipline required to practice the hours required to attain the skill.

Understanding Why You Fail, Knowing How to Succeed

Perhaps the single greatest thing about trading and investing in a meaningful fashion is that it provides a fantastic opportunity to see what you do which causes you to fail and what leads to success. The conscientious trader/investor has a plan and thereby a way to make evaluations. Whether things go according to plan and profits accrue, or whether they do not go well, he or she knows what needs to be done going forward and why.

Achievement in life requires that one follow a similar course. No matter the objective or pursuit, we must understand what it takes to succeed and have ways we can judge whether we are doing those things or not. To do otherwise is to act in a random fashion, never sure if we are doing what is right and necessary.

These are just some of the valuable life lessons that trading and investing can provide. There are plenty more just as worthwhile, to go along with the more commonly thought of value in understanding how the markets can be used to improve your financial well-being. And these lessons need not come at great expense either since modern trading and investing can be done with very small amounts of money—even none at all in the case of demo accounts. All the more reason to make the markets a source of both financial and personal growth.

ABOUT THE AUTHOR

John Forman is author of *The Essentials of Trading*
(http://www.TheEssentialsOfTrading.com). He is a near-20-year veteran of analyzing and trading a wide array of markets. John has written literally dozens of articles on trading and analytic methods and has taught the same topics to students in the classroom for the last several years.

38

Goodbye Grudges, Hello Love: How Forgiveness Allows You to Attract Your True Match

Nancy Pina

We all draw relationship partners in accordance with our core beliefs. If you consistently attract emotionally unhealthy relationship partners, there is a pattern that you must break in order to recognize a balanced and devoted relationship.

During my years of matchmaking I have found that relationship struggles are twofold: a psychological challenge to break free of controlling beliefs formed in childhood and a spiritual battle over negative thoughts concerning unresolved past issues.

In essence you are a compilation of your past experiences, the choices you made, and the paths you followed. The larger question you need to honestly assess is "do I allow my past mistakes, circumstances, and pain to define who I am?" Are you holding on to sorrow and becoming a person who is identified by that grief? It is through forgiveness that you can overcome your sorrow and release yourself from the burden of carrying resentment in your heart.

When you resolve to forgive someone, you choose to live in the present. Forgiving does not mean forgetting but rather releasing the damaging emotions and moving toward an emotionally stable life. Forgiveness does not mean you condone the actions of others.

It is up to you to decide not to be controlled by your circumstances and to take the initiative to forgive those who do not know better. People tend to hurt others out of their own fear and pain. Forgiveness allows love to enter your life. By clinging to anger, you permit your ego to relive the wrongs of your past. Continuously reliving past anguish in your mind and verbally describing your situation to others gives life to your sorrow.

Most of us go through a period of mourning, especially after the end of a relationship, as we try to figure out what happened to the life we knew. The danger here is remaining in this phase and incorporating this stage into your essence. By concentrating on fear—anxiety, sadness, anger, and pain—you block the very thing you want to attract, which is love. If you lead your life with your injuries, you cannot properly grieve, recover, and move ahead with life. It takes a conscious effort to let go of the temptation to be cynical, pessimistic, judgmental, and resentful about the end of a relationship or any other event or situation you feel is unforgivable.

Am I Sabotaging My New Relationship?

If you do not release built-up resentment and anger from previous relationships, you will carry those feelings over into the next one, as Jeremy did.

> After being married for over eleven years and divorcing because we drifted apart, I found myself in a love relationship five months later. In the beginning, it was nothing but excitement. Just the thrill of talking to each other was more than any two months put together of my previous marriage.
>
> We had a definite physical attraction from the get go, and as I got to know her, I really became interested. We had similar ways of thinking and upbringing, which made me feel understood. Now after being together, living together and proposing to her, it seems all I can do is look for her flaws. She is still the strong, beautiful, sexy, and caring person I met, but I can't seem to stop thinking about what I don't like.
>
> Is this because of my fear of being hurt again, or is it that I've reached a point in the relationship that I am actually weighing what matters most to me in a life partner? Either way it doesn't make me feel good because I do love her.

Jeremy's fear of vulnerability emerges as his relationship goes from physical attraction to an emotional attachment. His fear of being hurt again is magnified primarily because he has not taken the time to forgive what happened in his relationship with his ex-wife. He is fearful of being vulnerable in another committed relationship that runs the risk of emotional pain. Unconsciously, he will repeat the same relationship pattern if he does not resolve the core beliefs that led to the end of his marriage.

Through forgiveness you are giving yourself permission to love yourself. You are acknowledging that you are worthy of love. You are designed to give and receive, not to hold on to anger, revenge, bitterness, and resentment. You open the door to physical illness, psychological damage, and soul despair by clinging to negativity.

How do you forgive those who have hurt you earlier and shed the sorrow, anger, and loneliness that encumber you today? Where do you start in order to give yourself permission to heal? Following are five steps I encourage you to take to release resentment.

Step 1: Acknowledge Your Pain

To truly forgive, the first step involves admitting what is bothering you and how it makes you feel. Suppressing your grief will not make it disappear. Until you go through this process, the pain will only resurface in future relationships.

One way to accomplish this step is to journal in detail any past actions you can't forgive yourself for and any wrongs done to you that you cannot release. Once you have finished, read the list and take comfort in the wisdom that you did the best you could with the information you had at the time.

Step 2: Allow Yourself Time to Grieve

Facing heartache can be frightening, but by fully experiencing the sadness, you will keep it from dominating your life. Many people are taught to suppress their negative feelings toward others because those emotions are viewed as wrong. Being stoic will not free you from distress.

Do not deny yourself the opportunity to grieve. Forgive yourself and free the anger and hurt around this person and situation. Liberty from a distressing event will be achieved when a discussion concerning what happened does not create anguish or agony in your heart. Your sorrow is very real, so do not minimize it or try to bypass the mourning period. You must go through this grieving stage in order to release your pain.

Step 3: Examine Your Perceptions

Making sweeping judgments can keep you in a cycle of replicating dysfunctional patterns. When emotional upheavals happen in your life, it is an opportunity to examine why you journeyed down that path. It is not the time to form negative core beliefs in a stage of anger.

Step 4: Empathize

For genuine forgiveness to happen it is necessary for you to place yourself in the shoes of the offender. If you do not forgive, you will automatically respond out of your own pain and fears and will ultimately hurt others.

Step 5: You Are Free When You Forgive

You can forgive and still maintain your integrity. The key is to absolve others for their actions. Grace is not a license to sin. Forgiveness is full of compassion but demands a change in conduct.

Forgiveness is not for the benefit of the person who wronged you. It is your key to happiness and emotional freedom.

ABOUT THE AUTHOR

Relationship advisor, author, and former matchmaker Nancy Pina offers spiritual advice based on her extensive experience over the past 20 years. She helps individuals worldwide define, visualize, and actualize their relationship goals by conquering their fears and overcoming negative core beliefs. Her books include *The Right Relationship Can Happen: How to Create Relationship Success* and *Goodbye Mr. Wrong: A Matchmaker Reveals How to Find "The Right One."* Her books illustrate how to emotionally and spiritually prepare for a lasting and loving commitment. Please visit her Web site for information on personal relationship coaching, books, counseling, and complementary weekly newsletter subscriptions: http://www.yourtruematch.com.

39

GIVING

Gifting from the Soul:
Personal Development Skills through Gifting

Janlia Chong

What does gifting have to do with your self-development? Plenty. We are all a part of this abundant universe that revolves around giving. Abundance *is* truly all around us. At times you may not feel like it, but if you take a moment to see what you have all around you every single day, you will agree that you are abundant in many ways. Just take a look at nature and the way God has designed it.

When you need something, you must give back first. That is one of the principal laws of our universe. You see, when you give back, you detach from materialistic objects or feelings that hold you back from having more. And when one is too attached to something, it creates a negative energy. You must trust in the universe to provide for you and *do* all in your power to make unselfish acts every day.

Gifting is sharing, loving, letting go, becoming free from oppression, and becoming one with yourself as well as with the universe.

Everybody and anybody can gift at any time. We all have something to give and share. Sometimes we may not recognize the fortunes we all have that we can give nor see how we can make any difference at all to anybody else. Becoming aware of all your abilities and all the gifts you were born with is vital for personal success, wealth, and health.

Gifting can come in many different forms. You can gift with your self (with your spirit), with your mind, or with your actions.

Gift Your Self (Spirit)

Smile, laugh, listen, speak kind words, take care of yourself, and present a good example. This is a form of gifting that you can practice with anyone that you come into contact with. You are giving and projecting positivity to those close to you as well as to strangers. Imagine your loved ones feeling more and more drawn to you or being able to make someone's day a brighter place just by your presence. I think the world can do with a lot more people practicing giving by their spirit.

We can all easily do this in every moment of our lives. Become conscious of this, and make it a good habit to do so in every moment that you have. For example, if you are waiting for something during your day, you can practice this by smiling and projecting good vibes. You do not have to be in the presence of others for the effect to take place.

Even sales meetings or negotiations should be spent in giving to each other and not in battle. For example, listen to what the other party has to say—he or she will be grateful for your attentiveness, and your company will benefit from a winning deal.

Always make it a habit to take good care of yourself. You will be pleasant to others and uplift all those around you. Do so by taking time out to look after yourself, by maintaining a healthy diet, and by exercising regularly.

Don't be fooled into thinking that you shouldn't care what others see or think. What the outside projects is often a result of what we first project.

Gift Your Mind

Teach, and share your knowledge, experiences, and wisdom. Don't be afraid to share ideas and what you know—you will always have more to gain from teaching others. This can be anyone at all. Be aware that we are all individuals with different experiences and that anyone we come into contact with can gain some knowledge from us.

When you teach, you confirm your knowledge, and you might just be able to teach yourself a thing or two in the process. Teach when you have the opportunity, but be careful to not force it on someone. Become aware of all the situations in your life now that you can possibly use to share your knowledge. Share your story today.

Gift Your Actions

Your deliberate and conscious acts of gifting are evident during the holiday seasons. This is when you have the opportunity to give something to someone in the form of a present or gift. What a great time to show your love and affection! Think of these times as a bonus in your life, and don't let these opportunities go to waste. Meet each holiday or occasion as if it will be the last, and maximize your acts of love toward someone else.

This is not to say that you must spend more and try to outdo yourself each year. You should be thoughtful in the process and only give something deep from your heart. Always think of the recipient's interests and favorite things and how you can surprise him or her. We live in a very materialistic world, but gesture will always outdo any price tag.

Here are some critical things to remember when gifting.

1. **Do not pick and choose giftees.** When you have the opportunity to share with someone, you should take full advantage of it and give freely. Do not judge and choose your giftees based on the past or on negative emotions. It is just as important to give to those you love as to anyone else. Try to cut the negativity in gifting by thinking of others outside of your immediate circle.
2. **Never expect anything back.** Gifting is from the heart and not from the head. You should never gift only because you know you will get something in return. Gift because you care. Gift because you love. Gift because you are just being you. You *will* be given something back in different wondrous ways if you practice this. Gift unconditionally, every time.
3. **Gifting is not deliberate.** Do not gift only because it's the holiday season and you feel obliged to do so. Gift at all times and on any occasion possible (or on no occasion at all).
4. **Do not gift for self-interest only.** This is similar to expecting something in return. Be careful not to gift only because you feel that you are doing yourself justice. Do not gift because it makes you feel superior, creative, or because you are doing a kind justice to the world.

Take a good moment alone to think about all the ways that you can gift today. Start gifting from anywhere and at any time. Do not let physical boundaries stop you. Send a card, phone someone, e-mail a photo of your smiling face, send a thank you note, make and send a gift "just because," or even just send a quick, happy e-mail to someone.

True gifts don't die—they will last a lifetime. Your gestures remain effective even if repeated every day and all the time. It's the act itself that counts. And the people around you will always appreciate and remember it, even if they don't show it. Just keep gifting, no matter what. Start giving today. Start giving right now. Start by a thought. Then by an act. Practice good positive gifting, and you will be a better person for others as well as for yourself.

ABOUT THE AUTHOR

Janlia Chong is the author and owner of numerous positive lifestyle Web sites. She shares with the world her fresh, inspirational tools and innovative creations in practical ways for improving our lives every day. For more information to get started today, visit http://www.janliachong.com for practical information on what all teams and individuals need to achieve great results today.

40

GRACE

Being Graceful Makes Your Life Happen

Guru Kaur

It is hard to put into words how much the guidance that I received from Yogi Bhajan changed my life. It all seemed so very simple. He fixed me with those eyes, full of love, and said, "All you have to be is regally graceful."

I had no idea what that meant. Graceful—what was that? At the time my life looked pretty good from the outside: I had a great job, a wonderful husband, and a beautiful house. Something was missing, though, deep on the inside. And now, Yogi Bhajan had given me the clue: grace.

Looking around me at the women with whom I came into contact through my high-powered job, so many of them seemed, like me, to feel dissatisfied deep down within. They were working in a male-oriented world and had adopted male values and attitudes in order to succeed in it. They had denied and suppressed their innate femininity, killing off what was most precious in them. Worst of all, they had lost not only their own self-respect, but also that of those with whom they worked.

I realized the answer was not for women to leave the workplace. Instead, we needed to regain those qualities that make us womanly and integrate them into our daily domestic and working lives.

Around this time I met a very powerful woman in Indian politics. She commanded respect in a way no other woman whom I had previously met did. She was successful on her own terms and never compromised, used, or abused her femininity. Each time I met her, she would tell me stories about how she got things done.

As a young woman in politics, she was given the unenviable role of arranging water to be piped to a very remote village in the Himalayas. Each of the previous (male) incumbents of her post had failed. Some had tried bribery, some had tried bullying, and some had not even bothered to start this mammoth project. When she visited the village, she saw how hard life was for the women, who had to carry water across the valley. She gave her word that the piped water would come. She would not let them down, but she had absolutely no idea what to do to make it happen. She thought about it for many days and then came up with a plan. Despite the impossibility of the task, she succeeded.

Her solution was a graceful one and one that I have varied again and again over the years. She telephoned the (male) Chief Minister to invite him to come and officially open the new water pipe and got a date set in his planner for it. After that it was plain sailing. The Chief Minister's staff was so enthused by all the positive PR he would get for the project that they saw to it that the budget was approved, the money sent, the contractors paid, and so on. To this day, the women in that valley call her "the lady of the water."

What I love about this story is that she found a way to work that was creative and that honored all the people involved. Now, that's what I call grace.

In my own life, though, I just didn't know where to start. I decided to take it one day at a time. It began to dawn on me that grace was a state of being which came when I opened up to all the wonders in life. It was when I felt at peace with and within myself so much so that I didn't react to what was going on around me. It was when I included everybody in the picture.

Being graceful was not an esoteric concept either. It was highly practical and affected my behavior at a very deep level. I noticed that it became a virtuous circle. When I wasn't needy or pushy, people responded to me differently so that I became their calm reference point. The atmosphere changed to one in which people wanted to be. They became more relaxed; I became more relaxed. Nagging and begging became things of the past. We now had a win-win situation.

Being graceful opened up opportunities, and my life took on a magical quality. I discovered that it was true what Yogi Bhajan had said: "When a woman maintains her grace, everything is possible."

156

If you want to see how much more is possible in your life when you are graceful, here are four areas of your life with which to start.

1. **Manners.** Don't just be polite for the sake of it. Please, say it with a genuine smile. Listen with your full attention to what the other person is saying, without putting your own story into the picture. A key aspect to work on is how much your behavior is based on the insecurities you felt as a child. The benchmark is, Did I just make today more wonderful for that person?
2. **Morals.** From the ancient yogic scriptures to all the world's religions, there are codes of conduct that give a moral backdrop to our lives. It is not a question of whether you can do something without getting caught or how far you can push the boundary. The moral code is within you. The benchmark is, Can I sleep peacefully tonight?
3. **Standards.** For what do you stand? What do you represent to the outside world? Standards create the structure of your life, and standards are built on that to which you are committed. Integrity is the foundation. The benchmark is, How much can I be trusted?
4. **Style.** We each have our own ways of expressing our identities in this world. Our styles are a discreet language that impacts our surroundings subliminally. The beauty of your own style reflects how comfortable you are within yourself. How do you describe your style? Is your style noisy, untidy, trashy, or crude? Straighten this up, and start being graceful. Do you dress to display your sexuality and sensuality, or to radiate your grace? A quick test is to ask yourself, "What do people remember about me: what I was wearing or who I am?" The benchmark is, How much does my life flow with ease?

ABOUT THE AUTHOR

Guru Kaur is a KRI certified teacher trainer of Kundalini Yoga as taught by Yogi Bhajan and a Sikh minister. Before founding Amritvela Limited, she spent 14 years working in London. During the last seven years she has developed Amritvela Limited's Regally Graceful © design and consultancy. Guru Kaur offers Regally Graceful for men and women, both as individual counseling and life design and as corporate consultancy. She is married to the photographer Nick Fleming, and they are based in London. For more information, please visit http://www.amritvela.com. For more information on Yogi Bhajan and his teachings, please visit http://www.3HO.org.

41

Living in Gratitude

Jackie Bredl-Dietrich

> Gratitude unlocks the fullness of life. . . . It turns
> what we have into enough, and more. It turns denial
> into acceptance, chaos to order, confusion to clarity.
> It can turn a meal into a feast, a house into a home, a
> stranger into a friend. Gratitude makes sense of our
> past, brings peace for today, and creates a vision for
> tomorrow.
>
> – Melody Beattie

A glimmer of something to be grateful for can be found in nearly every situation we experience. It is a rare circumstance that can't be turned around—even slightly—when it is looked at through the lens of grateful eyes. Admittedly, it takes a conscious choice to be grateful instead of focusing on negative events or emotions.

One of the greatest gifts of gratitude is that it is impossible to feel both positive and negative emotions at the same time. Gratitude brings about only positive feelings, such as love, joy, and hope. When we focus on being thankful, fear, worry, and anxiety miraculously melt away with little effort.

But living in gratitude is really more than just thinking positively. When a person concentrates on being grateful, it gives him something to actually look for and pay attention to. Amazing things are revealed when we are aware, and this can provide much inspiration.

One of the best ways to improve your life is to make the choice to focus on what you are grateful for.

Being Grateful Makes Us Better People

Research indicates that being grateful makes us better people, both personally and professionally. Consider what recent academic studies have shown.

1. People who describe themselves as feeling grateful tend to have higher vitality and more optimism, suffer less stress, and experience fewer episodes of clinical depression.
2. Grateful people tend to be less materialistic.
3. Those who keep a "gratitude journal" achieve better physical health, are more optimistic, exercise more regularly, and describe themselves as happier.
4. Grateful people are more likely to appreciate the interconnectedness of all life.

Enhancing Gratitude

It's easy to be grateful when life hums—when money is in the bank, when romance is divine, and when you are healthy. But when you don't know how the bills will be paid, he says he doesn't love you, or you're reeling from a devastating diagnosis, "thank you" usually isn't the phrase that immediately comes to mind.

Here are the keys to enhancing your perception of gratitude.

Make a conscious **choice** *to be aware of things that touch your heart*

In other words, take responsibility for how you view your life and your experience of it. It's your choice to "see" the things that touch your heart. In any challenge, there's a critical point when you choose to begin walking the path of gratitude and stop focusing on what's not working. In early conversations with coaching clients, they typically share what they're not happy about in their lives, and that is where their vision is focused. As a result of the coaching experience, they make a conscious choice to focus on being grateful.

Pay attention *to whatever gives you energy and amazes you*

At some level you're aware of the many things to be grateful for, even on the worst of days. Are you paying attention?

Stillness + Awareness = Intuition and Synchronicity

Being still and being aware are at the core of a person's intuition bubbling to the surface and allowing the synchronicities to happen. Having a daily practice of sitting for one minute of silence and committing to turning off the television are two examples of how you can quiet your mind.

Seek out the meaningful coincidences *in life*

These are referred to as the "ah-ha moments," when, for no explainable reason, the stars and planets align to send you a message or to give you a much-needed sign.

After a long hike in Sedona, Arizona, often referred to as the Mystical Disneyland, I checked in to my hotel room. I called my husband to let him know I had arrived and to give him the number of the hotel. As I read out the list of numbers, we both gasped because we realized that the last four digits of my office phone number were exactly the same: 4700. He said, "I guess you were meant to be there." These types of things happen all the time.

Capture *the moments in writing*

Writing about your gratitude is another very important step to putting gratitude into practical use. Once a person makes the choice to be aware, pay attention, and seek out coincidences, there's no time to waste. Write it down, or it will be forgotten.

A few years ago, I personally began what I refer to as "grati-toodling"—I record random acts of gratitude in a notebook throughout the day. The more I look for, the more I find! Sometimes I jot down one word and other times many words. I carry the notebook with me wherever I go. I look back at those tidbits, and they are a constant source of inspiration in my life—which is full of connections, ah-ha moments, and synchronicities.

With a commitment to writing about what you are grateful for, you will increase your awareness of all the amazing things that happen each and every day. This has the ability to shift your mind-set into daily gratitude.

Be* inspired *by gratitude and* share *your gifts with others

Living in gratitude is a source of inspiration to yourself and others. Find your unique way of sharing the gift of gratitude with the world. Tell the stories that inspire and empower. The more grateful energy you send out, the more you will attract.

The Devil Car

You have responsibility to enhance the gratitude level in your life. However, sometimes gratitude is revealed through the eyes of someone else.

Toward the end of college, I drove a blue, four-door Pontiac Grand Am that was fondly referred to by friends, family, and even myself as "the Devil Car." In a period of three years I was involved in not one, but five car accidents, including one hit-and-run. It seemed that every few months, I was making the series of phone calls and annoying repair arrangements. My insurance agent and I talked regularly and were on a first-name basis.

After the fifth accident I decided it was time to sell, with the hope that the next vehicle would mark an improved driving record. While we waited for the new owners to drive the car away, my husband-to-be and I reminisced about all the places that "the Devil Car" had taken us. He asked me, "Did you ever get injured in any of the accidents?" I said, "No." He looked at me and without hesitation said, "Then your car isn't 'the Devil Car.' It's really 'the Angel Car.' It has protected you and saved your precious life!" I was very grateful to him for offering me a new perspective on this accident-prone car.

What's "the Devil Car" in your own life? How can you see it as "the Angel Car"? How do you express your gratitude each day to the people who surround you at work and at home—your customers and colleagues, friends and family, and even complete strangers? It's important to communicate two simple words that can speak volumes and make people feel appreciated. And above all, be sincere.

Have fun making gratitude a part of your everyday life, and watch the greatness unfold!

ABOUT THE AUTHOR

As a life and business coach, Jackie empowers entrepreneurs and those wondering what to do with their lives, both personally and professionally. People learn who they are, overcome fears, and create the mind-set to take action. Jackie also presents to service and community-minded audiences, including women, associations, and entrepreneurs. She is the perfect choice for women's events and staff retreats. Her topics focus on mind-body-spirit wellness, communication, intuition, and gratitude. She is a Certified Health Education Specialist (CHES), a Certified Newfield Coach, and a Professional Certified Coach (PCC) through the ICF. Visit her Web site at http://www.WholeLifeVisions.com, e-mail her at Jackie@WholeLifeVisions.com, or call her at (715) 421–4700.

42

Mastering Eyesight and Expanding Insight: Three Tips to Help You See Better and Better, Every Day

Jeannie "Viveka" Fitzsimmons

Tip 1: Be Open, Imagine the Possibilities and Explore the Cause of Good Sight

Our eyesight can improve and our insight can expand at any time in our lives. It is natural to see with our own eyes. Most of us have memory of seeing well, even if we are wearing glasses or contacts now. In that remembrance is often a longing, confusion, and a wistful wishing that we could return to that sharp sight we once had.

Most of us went through the proper stages of early childhood development, and most of us had perfect sight as children. So, what happened, and what can we do to reverse this "curse" of a visual blur? The good news is that genetics is not the cause of "blurring"; instead vision-habits, ignorance, and emotional and mental distress over a period of time cause us, in vision training terms, to "throw a blur."

This might sound radical to some people since there isn't a lot currently written on the subject. We "throw a blur"? That sounds preposterous, doesn't it? Let's accept the concept for now and see what happens. See if anything I describe resonates with you. By the time I have led you back into some inner wisdom for your eyes, you will see for yourself, although skepticism is certainly allowed and welcomed. We will take a brief inward journey, but first, we will start with an outward picture.

163

Tip 2: Go Out and Play! It is the movement that releases and frees our sight!

A few decades ago, when glasses were more of a rarity, we used our eyes and developed the natural "seeing skills." As children, we learned to crawl, then to walk, developed eye-hand coordination, we could see straight ahead and peripherally, and we learned to identify colors and shapes and to become digitally adept. What used to help us? Tinker toys, erector sets, Hot Wheels, balsa wood ships, Lincoln Logs, Mr. Potato Head, card games, Chutes 'n Ladders, building bricks like Legos, and many other fun and detailed games were commonplace in every home closet across America.

What did these games have to do with eyesight? Everything! Focus, detail, eyes working together, and *play*! We played with blocks, pointed to what caught our attention, looked directly at things that interested us, learned to open doors, to reach for items and succeed, and to play ball. We ran with our pets, played with friends, rode our bikes, and played sports for fun rather than within the framework of the stressful competition play has become for children today.

All childhood physical activities are "vision games." They teach our eye-brain connection to become vibrant and healthy, while developing an effective physical navigation system. By two, three, or four, we are seeing well and playfully using our eyes, and the ability for our sight to function for us has been set in place and is working perfectly. Grown-up activities are also vision games and keep our vision sharp. Examples are baseball, basketball, golf, riding bicycles, playing Ping-Pong, throwing a Frisbee, playing tennis, and skiing. All of these require action, flexibility, playfulness, and a lot of head movement, without a lot of thinking, strain, or staring.

Now what do kids do? They sit and stare at a screen and get strained thumbs from video games; they never breathe, get out into the sunshine, drink enough water, eat food with high nutritional value, throw a paper route, or do puzzles or games that are interactive. Of course vision is going to suffer—there is no movement. Now what do adults do? They live in front of the computer, most often stressed, on deadline, hours at a time without moving, eating, breathing, or having water. Technology is wonderful, but only if we balance it with healthy movement.

The good news is that eyesight is tremendously forgiving and resilient. It isn't too late for our eyesight to get better, regardless of how long we may have worn glasses or how severe our dependency on them. Vision can be gently reversed and improved—who knows how far?

Tip 3: Relax into the Visual Blur,
Rather Than Fighting It—Getting Out of the Way

This will sound strange to many people. The reason I wear glasses is to see clearly—why would I want to see blurry without them? Well, the answer is to give your eyes a break and to leave room for improvement by taking that strong optical trick away from the brain for a while. Of course, you should do this in a safe environment.

I used to take my students on walks around the block or have them bounce big, colorful beach balls without their glasses. Eventually, their eyes began to trust, let go, and move again. They got more relaxed, and their eyes started seeing better, often with "flashes of clarity" flickering in and out. Their muscles began to relax, and their eyes started to play. Go ahead and try it. Remove your glasses and relax into the blur and let it become your friend. This suggestion may sound funny, but you will see what happens. Remember that sight naturally fluctuates, too.

Many approaches to vision improvement can be made, and most have a series of exercises as their foundation. I am grateful that I was not put into an exercise program in order to see and for my eyes to do what they already know how to do naturally. To be fair and balanced, as they say, I did learn *what to do properly* to relax my tightly wound system, which had previously caused an ever-increasing blur and the need for a stronger prescription.

I gave my eyes a break and tossed my pretty blue lenses, trading them for glasses that I could easily remove when unnecessary. This gave my eyes even more rest and encouraged them to become happier, move more, and relax because that "disc of distortion," a phrase I coined in the 1990s, could stay off my brain. I learned to return to childlike playfulness with my eyes. I started paying attention to my straining habits. After a few weeks the *poor vision habits* faded away and were replaced with good ones; I reduced the strength of my glasses, and my vision gently returned. Now as promised, the brief inward journey and the underlying stress factor that affects and diminishes vision.

What most people don't realize is that the eyes are the only organ directly connected, through the optic nerve, to the brain, and perception or "seeing" actually occurs in the brain at the back of the head. The delicate muscles around our eyes, which affect the eye's ability to make fluid accommodations, which allow our eyes to enjoy the natural ability to see near and far through the fluctuation of those muscles, are immediately responsive to our thoughts and feelings. It is all connected, and the mystery of visual blur and eye strain is available for reversal to a great degree. The more relaxed and "softened the mind," the "softer and more flexible the eyes"—they are fully connected and reflect that in our visual/emotional clarity. Our "feelings" about what we see affect *how* we see, and strain results from our lack of presence and our interpretation of our world—for near-sighted, far-sighted, astigmatism, lazy-eye, and more.

So, the more *we* strain, the more strained our vision becomes. The more we become used to "how poorly our eyes see for us," the more anguished we become inside. The habit of strain, resistance, rebellion, and anguish is then set into the cellular and muscular areas within and surrounding the eyes, and the result is a visual blur, and we are locked behind ever-strengthening optical devices, i.e., glasses or contacts, getting used to seeing clearly through those "discs of distortion."

At this point it is important to inform you that seeing better again is also a healing, from the inside out. At times we can feel more disgruntled or be more exhausted because "disgruntled feelings or exhaustion" is flushing up and out of our cellular system. Not to worry: emotions, memories, and even tiredness is naturally let go of as our vision gets more and more clear. The eyes are not only "the windows to the Soul," but being our navigational devices, they are the recipients of information, and our interpretation of that information impacts how we see. As we gently back-step out of our strong glasses, vision naturally improves. Vision improvement is "winding back out of this subconscious, visually stressful journey" and gently and lovingly returning to relaxation for inner and outer clarity. Relaxation is the key to clear seeing, and this is the healing process.

Master your vision by letting go of inner stress . . . and going out to play!

ABOUT THE AUTHOR

Master vision trainer, author, non-dual teacher, and frequent TV/radio guest on "the art of seeing and letting go," Jeannie "Viveka" Fitzsimmons, CNVI, LCT, is a passionate global pioneer for positive change. A specialist in natural vision work and in letting go, she developed hybrid vision training, a spiritual path through "releasing for improved eyesight and expanded insight" and a Vision PopQuiz (http://www.visionlady.com). Bringing The Sedona Method® for letting go of unconscious, underlying stress to Los Angeles 25 years ago, her transformational "inner and outer seeing" seminars and spiritual retreats are dedicated to Self-Realization. She founded http://www.awakenedheart.com for HeartWisdom™ Seminars and is writing a book *30 Days of Vision Games to Improve Your Eyesight—For the Rest of Your Life.* She is also the author of *Beloved Reflections ... A Spiritual Odyssey,* a poetic/prose journey on liberation,and love.

43

The Secret Hidden in Your Favorite Pastime

Leah Grant

Sailing. Reading. Biking. Sewing. Cooking. Singing. Golfing. Everyone has something other than work and tending to home responsibilities that they love to do.

Think of your favorite pastime, but not quickly—slow down and really put yourself in the moment of teeing off on an ideal course, or hitting that high note, or adding just the right touch of oregano.

Are you there? Do you feel the rush of endorphins flooding your system as you imagine doing something that brings you joy? If you're like me, you lose track of time, you wish the experience would go on forever, and you have the feeling that you are exactly where you're supposed to be.

There's a reason for this feeling of contentment that accompanies participating in your hobby. It's an amazing secret that your pastime has been keeping for you.

How I Learned My Pastime's Secret

In 1994 I left my corporate job to enter the freelance jungle. I tried several different things. I succeeded at a few and I failed at a few before landing in the coaching profession in 1997. My business started off with a bang, and I was satisfied with my career choice. It allowed me to use almost all of my skills and talents. It provided me with my social circle. It met all of my needs. I couldn't have chosen something more perfect.

But there was a problem. I had this little niggling in the back of my mind.

"Isn't there more?" a disembodied voice would ask.

On more than one occasion I investigated the question. I took career assessments, discussed options with my coach, changed my target market, added new products, and even took some side jobs to "try on" a different profession. No matter what I did to change the way I made my income, the voice kept asking the same question.

After a few years I just stopped listening. I was happy as a coach.

Then something profound happened. I belonged to a writing critique group of four women, and we had traveled to several conferences together and had even held our own retreat. At these events we had taken pictures. I decided that a nice gift would be to make a scrapbook for each person. Since I'd never scrapbooked in my life, I'm not even sure where the idea came from, but it sounded like a good one.

Although my parents owned two art galleries when I was growing up and I had minored in art in college, I hadn't spent any time in my adult life doing art that wasn't on the computer as part of my short-lived job as a graphic designer. However, I knew the hiatus from creating with my hands and using my artistic talent was over when I spent three plus hours in the craft store selecting the items I needed and oohing and aaahing over many others. If asked, I would've sworn I'd been there less than an hour. I emerged feeling refreshed.

Over the next three months I spent every available moment working on the scrapbooks. I hadn't realized what I was getting into when I decided to create not one, but four identical scrapbooks. It was a lot of work, and I loved every minute of it.

Something else happened also. The voice was silent.

When I had completed the gift-making project, I felt a little sadness that I wouldn't be scrapbooking anymore, but I shoved that feeling aside and returned to my rewarding coaching work of helping other people. I even used my creativity to design a new logo.

"Isn't there more?" the voice asked. It was back. And it wanted to tell me the secret.

I semi-ignored the incessant questioning for a few months, until one day, while journaling, I realized the voice had disappeared during the time I was scrapbooking. This phenomenon fascinated me. Scrapbooking wasn't something I could do to make a living. It was a hobby—a pastime, like golf or hiking or writing poetry.

That was when the secret was revealed to me.

Pastimes stem from your values, and therefore pursuing them reconnects you with your innermost self and brings you fulfillment. The question "is there more?" was really asking "is there more than just feeling satisfied?" The answer is yes—there is feeling fulfilled.

My career provides huge amounts of satisfaction, and the pastime provides fulfillment. They are both necessary for living a balanced life. I now spend at least one full day a week scrapbooking, and I'm voice-free.

Needs and Values

Everyone has a set of core needs and core values within them. All humans share Maslov's hierarchy of needs for food, water, and shelter, but after that, everyone has a set of core emotional needs unique to him or her. Psychologists usually connect these items back to needs that weren't met during the formative stages. They can include things like attention, acknowledgment, safety, security, and guarantees. Most people choose partners or careers that meet these needs.

Your personal core values are different from cultural, religious, or even family values, although there can be some crossover. These three to five primary values per person are items you must have in your life in order to feel fulfilled. You can have what you want and need but still not feel fulfilled because your values aren't represented strongly enough in your life.

Values can be anything from accomplishment and control to teaching and serenity. They are unique from individual to individual.

Hearing Your Secret

To determine what values reside in your pastime, you'll need to explore why you enjoy it. For me, scrapbooking is about interacting kinesthetically and bringing many different components—the photographs, title, frames, paper, embellishments, journaling—into a cohesive and attractive creation. Therefore creation, collaboration, beauty, building, designing, and assembling could all be possible values revealed by my hobby.

When I read the list aloud, two stand out: creating and designing. Since I have the ability to be creative in my career and creativity is a trait I possess, I determined that designing is the value that is revealed by my love of scrapbooking. I confirmed this by recalling other times I was able to design and how I felt. A few years ago, when I was designing the interior for my home, I felt the same sense of fulfillment.

Let's take another popular hobby to see the secret it could be revealing. Golf is a widely played sport that people engage in for different reasons. Some of the values golf could represent are precision, nature, skill, solitude, socializing, competition, and challenge. If you will only play on the best courses with the most expensive equipment, it could also reveal values of prestige and wealth.

Now take your favorite pastime. What is it about for you? Why is it enjoyable? What possible values could it represent? Make a list of possible values, then read them aloud and choose the ones that resonate with you. Next, confirm them by recalling other times that value was represented in your life. How did you feel?

No matter what your pastime, it has a secret to tell you about your innermost self. Lean in and listen to reveal your core values and provide the pathway to fulfillment.

ABOUT THE AUTHOR

Leah Grant is a business and marketing strategist for small home-based business owners, a Master Certified Coach, and an avid scrapbooker. For nine years, in her consulting and coaching, she has used a three-pronged approach: Leah addresses *who* the business owner needs to be to be successful; *what* she needs to do in terms of the nuts and bolts of her business; and *how* she needs to market herself. She is the author of "Overnight MBA"—a home study program for the new business owner. Visit her Web site at http://www.leahgrant.com for free business tips, monthly specials, resource recommendations, and to purchase "Overnight MBA."

44

HUMOR

Making Today's Problem Tomorrow's Joke: Finding Humor and Peace in Life's Minor Crises

Richard Carlson

My daughters bought me a rock that says "Today's crisis is tomorrow's joke" engraved on it. I absolutely love it, and it's displayed prominently in my home office. I look at it several times a day to remind me that while it's certainly true that life is chock-full of dramas, it's also true that dramas come and go, and come and go. They always have, and they always will.

Before I go on, please know that when I say "today's crisis is tomorrow's joke," I'm obviously not referring to any of the hundreds of "life-changing" events that can be categorized as a true "crisis." Instead, I'm referring to the virtually unlimited number of relatively minor events that most of us tend to stew about that, in retrospect, really aren't that big a deal.

Have you ever gone to a family or high school reunion and listened to the conversations? It's fun, in part, because the conversations sometimes tie into this bit of wisdom. So many things that used to be seen as "big, giant, huge emergencies" are now the topics of great jokes. They are funny because they are seen with a bit of distance. We may have been furious at someone, for example, for God knows what . . . and now it seems so silly and insignificant. So, while we used to get really uptight about it, we now laugh about the very same set of facts.

And I'm not sure about you, but when I think about the way I was behaving just yesterday—running around like a chicken with my head cut off, as if there were not enough time—it seems funny to me now. I see how absurd it was. The trick to getting to the point where life doesn't seem like just one crisis after another is when we can see it as funny, not after the fact, but actually while we're acting a little crazy and taking life a bit too seriously. I've obviously got a way to go, but I'm working on it!

One of my favorite spiritual teachers has a great line. He said, "If you don't have a sense of humor, it just isn't funny." I think that says it all. Without a sense of humor, you're in for a tough ride, no doubt about it. You're going to be superserious. So lighten up, especially regarding taking yourself and others too seriously. Try to see yourself and everyone else not as people who should be trouble-free or perfect, but rather as "characters" on the stage of life. When people act strangely, or when you do, rather than take it personally, try to see the humor in it.

The world is a big, confusing place, and most of us are doing the best we can. It's far easier to develop the perspective that people don't have to be perfect or live up to some made-up set of standards than it is to get all uptight when things don't go according to plan, or when life isn't living up to our expectations.

Lighten up and live a little. It's a heck of a lot more fun and an easier way to live.

Often, though, you might find it difficult to see the humorous side in certain aspects of life—particularly during times when you're feeling harried, frustrated, or angry due to events beyond your control.

One of the most memorable self-help seminars I ever attended was way back when I was a teenager. Since I'm 44 years old now, that was about 30 years ago. One of the main topics the trainer covered was obnoxious drivers.

I'll never forget the conversation because I've rarely been frustrated by bad drivers ever since—particularly those who tailgate and who are aggressive, two of the main components of road rage.

In the seminar, the trainer posed the following question: What would you do if you were being tailgated?

The answers were all over the map, but two that stood out were "I'd put on my taillights so the person behind me would think I was putting on my brakes" and "I'd put on my brakes so that the bad driver behind me would have to slow down."

Both of these answers are terrible ideas in today's world.

As we all know, road rage is a very real thing, and it's very dangerous. The last thing we want to do is make an angry driver even angrier.

Actually, this is one of the simplest strategies I can offer you and one of the easiest ways to get rid of angry drivers who are tailgating you or putting you in danger.

All you have to do is this: simply pull over and let the jerk pass you by. Allow him or her to go and have an accident somewhere else. It's that simple.

You'll be safe, and chances are you'll never see him again. Then let it go, and don't spend another minute thinking about it the rest of the day. Be grateful it's all over.

The best thing to do is to try and remember that while it's true that there are many bad drivers and, in fact, many bad people, it's important to keep it in perspective. I have no idea on the actual percentages, but I'd guess that for every angry, horrible driver on the road, there are probably 50 perfectly courteous and safe ones.

The same applies to people in general. True, there are jerks. But there are so many more nice people.

Try to focus on that instead. When you're driving, notice the thousands and thousands of people who are following the rules and doing the best they can, given the circumstances.

Notice the people who do let others into lanes of traffic or move aside, even when it's not convenient for them.

There will always be road rage, and there will always be jerks. However, there's no rule that says any of that has to bother us one little bit.

So let the jerks—and all of those minor events—pass you by, and you'll have a great day.

ABOUT THE AUTHOR

Richard Carlson, PhD, is considered one of the world's foremost experts on happiness and stress reduction. His 20 popular books appear in over 100 countries. Dr. Carlson's book, *Don't Sweat the Small Stuff . . . and It's All Small Stuff*, was the #1 best-selling book in America for two straight years.

The Big Book of Small Stuff, a 10th anniversary compilation of the don't sweat series, and his newest book, *Don't Get Scrooged: How to Thrive in a World Full of Obnoxious, Incompetent, Arrogant and Downright Mean-spirited People*, will both be published in the fall of 2006. Visit Richard's inspirational and informative website at www.dontsweat.com for more.

Richard lives in California with his wife and two daughters.

45

IDEAL LIFE

Seven Behaviors for Creating the Life You Want

Ronald Finklestein

The key to success lies in how well you create an "attitude of success." My studies have shown that combined with the correct attitude, there are seven behaviors that all successful people exhibit.

Selfishness

When I talk about successful people being selfish, I am not referring to the childish behavior where everything is "mine, mine, mine." I am referring to a mature selfishness that allows them to make decisions based on the outcomes they want to experience.

Being selfish asks, How do I protect my time, energy, and money so I am only spending them on those things that will take me closer to my goals? Until you can define the type of life you want to create, it is very hard to be selfish. You can define this life through the creation of a personal vision and mission statements. After your personal vision and mission statements are complete you can create well-defined goals. After your goals are defined you can go through a barrier-busting process that will help you understand how to achieve these goals. When you complete this step, you can start being selfish. You have your personal goals defined, you know the kind of life you want, and you are ready to seek out and meet the people who can take you there.

Focus

It is very hard to be focused if you don't know where you are going. The dictionary defines focus as "close or narrow attention; concentration." Without a clear perspective you cannot focus on the desired outcome. It is too easy to become distracted, unorganized, and inconsistent. When you understand what it is you are to be selfish about, you generate a clear focus—a sense of purpose.

Discipline

Discipline is controlled behavior resulting from training and self-control. You are selfish and focused, and you now have a new weapon in your arsenal: discipline. Your mind is made up. You have decided to achieve your goals.

Being disciplined means you will not abandon your goals. Since you are creating the life you want, discipline is another tool of your success. Discipline has taught you that life is not smooth and that there are rough spots. Experience has taught you that by being disciplined, you can get through the tough spots. Your eye is on the target, and you have the discipline of a laser-guided missile; you seek out your objectives, and your focus never falters.

Persistence

Persistence can be defined as the continuance of an effect after the cause is removed. The defining moment that caused you to create your ideal life is behind you. Your goals are clear; you are focused, disciplined, and selfish. You encounter unplanned obstacles. Your persistence allows you to see these obstacles not as problems, but as opportunities. After all, if it was easy, anyone could accomplish what you are accomplishing. But not everyone is on the field of battle with you. They see obstacles and stop. You see obstacles and see opportunities.

You keep your eyes clearly fixed on your objectives; you try different things to overcome these obstacles. You know where you are going. You know you can't be stopped. You know that your persistence is what drives you forward. You will find a way around any obstacle.

Ownership

Ownership is the state of being an owner. It is taking the legal right to the possession of a thing. These are your dreams, your goals, and your life; if you do not take ownership for achieving your dreams, who will? As Jesse Livermore said, "There are only two emotions in the market—hope and fear. The problem is, you hope when you should fear, and you fear when you should hope."

But not you. Your fear is motivation to move you forward because you learned that when you take action, you get results. You always hope for the best and plan for the worst. You are ready for what life throws at you. You have to be. Taking ownership is about change—making change to move forward, changing behaviors that are not working, possibly changing your friends who don't understand, dealing with the world as it is and not as you want it to be.

You own the outcome because you are clear where you want to go, and you take ownership for it. With ownership you know that if you are not getting your desired results, you can take action and change the outcome. Ownership is so very empowering. You know that if you do not have the skills, you can learn or hire someone to teach you.

Orientation toward Results

Results mean to end in a particular way. You defined your goals—the outcome you want to achieve. You defined how you want things to end, and because you took ownership, you now have the power to create your desired outcomes. You can create the results.

When you don't get the results you want, you fall back on persistence, ownership, focus, and discipline and know that you have the skills, the drive, the desire, the knowledge, and the road map that will take you where you want to go. Results are simply a way of measuring your success. You either get the job done, or you don't. If you don't, because of your ownership, you go back and try something different. No excuses. No remorse. Only results. You understand, as Yoda once said, that "there is no trying, only doing."

Focus on People

Every successful person understands that his success comes with and through other people. A successful person will recognize these individuals and appreciate them for their contribution to the results. He will also assume complete responsibility for things not working. He must—there is no other course of action when you are the owner and take ownership.

ABOUT THE AUTHOR

Ronald Finklestein, President of AKRIS, LLC, small business success expert, business coach, consultant, speaker, author, and trainer, has published two books: *Celebrating Success! Fourteen Ways to a Successful Company* and *The Platinum Rule to Small Business Success*. He founded the Business Leadership Association and cofounded Celebrating Success! NEO Business Innovation Conference (formerly the Greater Akron Business Conference). Finklestein is available for coaching and consulting and for speaking engagements, workshops, and seminars. You can contact him at info@yourbusinesscoach.net or reach him at (330) 990–0788. Sign up for his newsletter at http://www.yourbusinesscoach.net.

46

INNER CHANGE

---

24 Hours:
A Day in the Life of Mary

Colleen Hoffman Smith

History:	Born March 1966. Mother: disappointed, withdrawn, depressed. Father: angry, controlling, with drinking problem. Mary never felt good enough.
Bio:	Assistant editor for a major home magazine. Husband Mike, advertising executive. Married 15 years, with two kids: Maggie, age 12, Neil, age 10. Lives in town house, suburbs of Boston.

Tuesday, March 10, 2006—Mary's talking mind. . . .

6:00 A.M.	The alarm clock triggers the morning, and anxieties close my heart.
6:30 A.M.	My husband Mike rolls out of bed with no warmth or acknowledgment. He heads right to his computer . . . I say good morning, and I feel negativity in my heart. We don't talk anymore. . .
7:00 A.M.	No time to be with the kids . . . they get their own cereal. I hurry them out of the house, yelling from the top of the stairs.

7:45 A.M.	Driving them to the bus stop, I feel agitation building as the kids argue about nothing important. I lose it, sharing my disappointment in them. They jump out at the bus stop.
8:00 A.M.	While feeling guilt about my projection of anger, I find my way to the racetrack highway that sucks me into the morning road rage. Stress builds as I listen to news of gang violence on the radio.
8:30 A.M.	As I take the elevator to my office, I feel uncomfortable with the people around me . . . they all feel like strangers . . . silence speaks.

My life is sad . . . I have anger and resentment in me. Passion for living is gone.

As I walk to my office, I feel my fear of the day ahead of me. I am late, and my boss gives me a look of disapproval. He is angry and controlling, and his intimidation takes up a lot of space.

I sit at my desk and feel my self-doubt knocking on the door.

9:00 A.M.	Out of nowhere, my boss pounces in and criticizes a project that I had put my heart and soul into. I feel disrespected and overwhelmed . . . I promise him a revised package in 24 hours.
9:30 A.M.–12:30 P.M.	I take out my conflict on my assistant and become critical. Disregarding her lunch, I push her all day to accomplish the deadline.
12:30 P.M.	My lunch is a venting session with my girlfriend, releasing my rage about my boss.
1:30–6:30 P.M.	I don't have time for a drink of water, let alone to breathe!

6:30 P.M.	Carrying my full briefcase home, I pick up some fast food, telling the kids to fend for themselves . . . they love eating in front of the TV.
7:30 P.M.	When my daughter asks for help with homework, I snap at her. My son needs a hug, but I brush him off quickly, saying, "I have so much work to do."
9:00 P.M.	My husband comes home . . . late as usual, drinking again . . . . . . he is no help to me and speaks rudely when I greet him with a closed heart.
9:30 P.M.	Tucking the kids in . . . they are already asleep. I grab a bag of chips and fill my emptiness as I finish the project with resentment.
11:00 P.M.	I fall into bed exhausted. Before my eyes close, a tear releases pain from my heart. I am sick and tired of my life struggles . . . I feel lonely. How can I find happiness?

11:00 P.M.–6:00 A.M.—**Mary's dream. . . .**

Sleep came in on the wings of peace. I opened to a world I have dreamed of. The air had a calmness, and I could breathe fully into the present moment. I was drawn to a woman who had an inner strength about her. I couldn't make out her face . . . such warmth and peace. Every insight she spoke moved through me as truth. In silence I felt acceptance and had no fear. Her eyes were of love.

I could feel heaviness in my heart. Reaching out to me, she placed a gift in my hand. I rested it on my heart. I felt like a sponge as I absorbed truth that changed my perception. It was like a switch was turned on in me, and I was different. We sat under a blossoming tree while she shared a process called the Inner Workout that would keep me emotionally fit. The gift showed me how to take responsibility for my feelings and release my anger, resentment, and fear on my own, without blaming others. Freedom in my heart opened me to self-discovery and truth, giving me the power to make healthy choices in my life. This goddess inspired me with my purpose, career, family, and relationships. I released my emotional pain . . . information moved into my veins like a blood transfusion. I could feel my self-worth strengthen.

I entered a doorway, looking over my shoulder . . . the light shone bright on the woman's face... she was me. *The opening took me back to relive the past day...*

March 10, 2006

6:00 A.M.

The alarm clock triggered the morning. I took the time to feel my anxieties, and I greeted the beautiful sunrise. I reached over to my husband and kissed him good morning. As I showered and dressed, I felt the challenges of my day and then remembered the gift . . . seeing the opportunities ahead.

6:30 A.M.

My husband shared with me his worries about his job. I held the space as he felt his fear. I looked at him with eyes of love and told him that I respected his choices.

Family breakfast was great . . . I felt so present with everyone's plans and chatter.

I encouraged the kids to get moving, and our drive to the bus stop included Neil's jokes and solving a girlfriend issue with Maggie.

8:00 A.M.

I could feel love for my children as I drove off. The busy highway afforded a great time to listen to a new CD . . . I loved the trip as I made my way through the traffic.

8:30 A.M.

In the elevator I greeted my coworkers, interested in getting to know them. As I walked to my office, I could feel my fears . . . I put my hand on my heart. When my boss gave me his piercing look, I smiled calmly, feeling my self-worth strongly.

9:00 A.M.

My boss opened my door with his critical voice. I said, "I appreciate your feedback, but I don't like how you project your anger." For the first time I felt my boss respected me, and we had a productive meeting.

184

9:30 A.M.–12:30 P.M.   *I could see that my boss was under pressure, and I had compassion. I told him that I would revamp the project within the week. We were open to each other's ideas. It felt good!*

12:30 P.M.   *At lunch I invited my assistant to join me, and we discussed the new deadline. I wanted her to know how much I appreciated her.*

1:30 P.M.   *I felt so connected, and my afternoon flowed . . . accomplishing so much, I didn't have to bring work home and compromise family time.*

5:30 P.M.   *I had time to go to the gym and pick up healthy groceries for dinner. While I was driving home, my husband called and said he would pick up the kids.*

6:30 P.M.   *Mike and I made dinner together, and we enjoyed family time. Neil talked about a conflict at school. I asked him how he felt. He felt angry, and his dad shared with him an experience just like his, involving a bully. I shared how I don't see my boss that way any longer . . . I stood up for myself today, feeling respected.*

9:00 P.M.   *Mike and I tucked the kids in together, telling them how proud we were of both of them.*

9:30 P.M.   *I lit some candles in our room, and Mike and I opened our hearts, intimately talking about the struggles and successes of our day. Our relationship deepened as we held each other in our arms, feeling gratitude.*

10:00 P.M.   *While in the bath, I took time to feel any anxieties of the day . . . I put my hand on my heart and felt the gift. . . .*

11:00 P.M.   *Comfortable in my bed . . . I fall asleep peacefully with a happy heart.*

Wednesday, March 11, 2006

6:00 A.M.   Mary woke up to a life worth living!

ABOUT THE AUTHOR

Colleen Hoffman Smith is a Toronto-based author, inspirational guide, facilitator, and relationship expert and coach. Twelve years ago, her life crashed . . . physically, emotionally, and financially. From this place she had nowhere else to go but inside, and this inward journey inspired her to create the most important life tool we could ever need to feel comfortable in our lives. The effectiveness of the Inner Workout™ program has changed the lives of thousands of people across North America, and through her books, audio programs, seminars, and workshops, Colleen continues to share how anyone can significantly improve his or her life . . . even in 24 hours! Visit http://www.theinnerworkout.com.

47

INNER VOICE

Barbie Doesn't Live Here Anymore!

Mary Jo Kurtz

There I was, with only a week to go, and I was no closer to finishing the assignment, a final requirement for my coach training and certification. The assignment was to present to my peers a physical representation of the "voice" inside my head, otherwise known as my Gremlin. "Everyone has one," they told me in class. The goal of the exercise was to disempower our Gremlins and transform them into supportive "new friends."

For months the class was frenzied as we tackled our demons. Some prepared life-size monsters, pictures, and paintings; some wrote and performed songs. Others created depictions of friends and family who had long ago imprinted negative messages in their heads. Everyone else seemed happy and eager to share their inner thoughts, but time was running out for me. I had spent hours talking about it with anyone "safe" that would listen. I tried drawing, listening to songs, searching magazines and books, but I was blocked. How would I really show this to my class? The bigger question was, *could* I really show this to my class? Could I really admit that I had a voice inside of me that constantly beat me up? The voice taunted me, "Come on, you're supposed to be a coach. You're supposed to have all the answers. You shouldn't have a *Gremlin*!" No wonder I was struggling.

I sat at my desk in my basement office, a safe place, out of the way. I got up to stretch and walked into the kids' playroom. There they were, covering the floor: Barbies, Ken, a load of babies, assorted children, even the Volvo station wagon! I knew it instantly. It was as if they were all lying there laughing at me. Malibu Barbie and all her friends were barely clothed, and their hair was tangled and matted. Yet it didn't matter. They all had smiles on their faces and still looked *perfect*! I sat on the floor and looked around.

Barbie was "the voice." She lay on the floor, beautiful, with her tanned and exquisite body. Scattered all over was every prop and accessory to her many successful and multifaceted careers. She was a teacher, a doctor, an artist, a veterinarian, a business executive, even an astronaut. She was so smart that she could be any one of them, and she could change from one to another at any given moment. She was also a mom who did it all. She had babies, and amazingly, her body still looked the same—perfect. She was a "good mom," and she and Ken were the happy couple. Everyone loved her and wanted to be with her. She had the house, the cars, and the vacation home. It was all perfection!

Finally, the "voice" was in my hands. I knew instantly that Barbie represented my fears of not being good enough. Her perfect, plastic life was much like my own quest for perfection to prove the "voice" wrong. Like too many girls, I was raised to believe that girls can do it all. We were told that the world had changed and now there were equal rights. Girls believed they could be anything they wanted and, of course, the best at whatever they chose. This meant marrying "Ken" and having the perfect family with bunches of kids. They could be "super moms" that would cook, clean, do homework, chauffeur, play with the kids, and bake cookies (all with a smile), while simultaneously maintaining successful careers.

My anxiety mounted as visions of my former life ran through my head. My heart raced and my stomach turned as the "voice" taunted me. I supposedly had it all: the career, title, salary, husband, house, and babies. Perfect? Not really. Thoughts flooded me: the parade of au pairs and nannies, two-hour commutes, dreadful hours, guilt and shame from disapproving family members, middle-of-the-night drives home, arriving home to an ambulance or a fire started by the nanny. All this was commonplace; the stress and worry that resulted consumed me, and despite every success, I never felt worthy. In every facet I felt like a failure. This only chiseled away at who I truly was and why I was here. It was no surprise when eventually, this inner struggle manifested in an illness that no doctor knew how to treat. Ultimately, I was unable to get out of bed *or* care for my children. The "voice" had won, and this was what brought me to the basement floor where I now sat surrounded by this mess.

For all of us looking to improve our lives in some way we must take a hard look at this inner dialogue. The "voice" represents our conflicts and fears and is always deeply emotional. It is the biggest obstacle in creating any type of change in our lives. Therefore successful change will only result when we eliminate this negative banter. Doing so will reap huge rewards. It will not only impact your day-to-day living, but also your ability to cope with the larger challenges that lie ahead. In the end it will allow you to be kinder to yourself and, as in my case, even laugh at yourself.

Who is your "voice"? Maybe it's time for you to meet it. Just like Barbie, you can expose it by putting a face on it, a body, clothes, and, if you'd like, a name. What does your "voice" tell you? Many of us allow it to define who we are. It taunts us with what we can, ought, should, must, need, and deserve to do. Its words are so powerful that they can control our every action. Recognizing this self-heckling will uncover its purpose and bring us closer to eliminating it.

Once its purpose is revealed, we can examine how our actions are being affected. For example, some of us waste time and energy with procrastination. Others become trapped in the past or paralyzed with worry about the future. Many of us continually analyze ourselves and others. Some of us pretend to believe that the "voice" is protecting us from failure or hurt. As a result, we concede to its dominance and stifle our true desires. We walk gingerly through life, afraid to follow our dreams. We pretend that we are hoping for a different outcome, but inside, we know that will never come. The truth is that the "voice" is still at work, undermining our thoughts.

Consider now all the wasted time and energy that has resulted from listening to the "voice." Finally, let it go. Make the choice that Barbie and your own "voice" are no longer inside you. As for me, Barbie doesn't live inside my head anymore. In fact, she is more of an acquaintance who lives all around me as a constant reminder of where I don't want to go. Like me, you may never look at Barbie the same way again. Although I admit I like her much better now, most importantly, I like myself even more.

ABOUT THE AUTHOR

This article is an excerpt from Mary Jo Kurtz's first book, *Barbie Doesn't Live Here Anymore!*, due out later this year. Kurtz is a certified empowerment coach, writer, speaker, workshop facilitator, and President of Wellnecessity, a coaching and consulting company. Her specialties include holistic nutritional and health coaching and women's empowerment. She develops and delivers coaching programs for teens and young adults and is the creator of the award-winning Girls "U"niversity program. She resides with her husband and four children in New Jersey. To contact Kurtz or subscribe to her newsletter, visit http://www.wellnecessity.com.

48

The 9 Insights of the Wealthy Soul

Michael R. Norwood

When my father was slowly progressing through the phases of a terminal illness, as a final legacy, he revealed to me a sequence of 9 extraordinary "wealth-building" steps he nicknamed *The 9 Insights of the Wealthy Soul.*

On the surface his lessons appeared to be about building material wealth.

On a much deeper level these Insights held the secret for overcoming our greatest challenges and achieving the highest wealth of the soul.

My father himself had used these same Insights as an army pilot-trainee to turn several near-crashes into soaring flights. Later, these Insights were the means through which he would raise himself up from the devastating death of his beloved daughter—my sister.

Four years after my father's last great lesson to me, while actually writing a book on the subject, I awakened one morning perceiving a profoundly deeper significance of his 9 Insights.

I suddenly understood that they are the actual stages of *Transformation.*

Whether you desire to transform a dream into reality, failure into triumph, grief into grace, or a relationship breakdown into a bridge of love and higher understanding, these universal principles are the means through which you can naturally accomplish your goals.

Here is a summary of my father's *9 Insights of the Wealthy Soul.*

Insight 1: Insight

Just as a tree begins with a seed, so, too, is Insight the *seed* that begins your transformation. One of the greatest insights is simply the knowledge that *You Can*. You *can* overcome your greatest challenges. You *can* transform your dreams into your own living, breathing reality. You *can* create a new life for yourself and your loved ones.

Insight 2: Timing

The saying *timing is everything* is not just a nice expression. Without developing excellent timing you will always be fighting the natural ebb and flow of the universe. Just as most seeds sprout on a particular day in springtime, *you* can develop the ability to recognize the precise day of spring for all you do.

Whether asking for a raise, launching a business venture, or bringing up a difficult subject to a friend, loved one, or business partner, your ability to recognize the often brief moments of maximum opportunity will determine how much success and balance you achieve.

Insight 3: Patience

Only humans are impatient. Seeds do not attempt to turn into trees in winter. Eagles don't try to soar during lightening storms. And Mayflowers do not blossom in August. Developing patience—your ability to wait for the right moment in your life cycle to accomplish a particular task or goal—is all important to developing excellent timing and great success.

Insight 4: Surrender

What must you do to let go of your need to control things? How can you let go of your past mistakes and history that may be preventing you from moving forward? How do you spiritually surrender to *the process*?

Without spiritual surrender you will never be content, you will never have patience and excellent timing. You will never experience the joy and *flow* of having the greatest business and life partner you could ever possibly have: namely, *The Universe* and *God*.

Insight 5: Grounding

With strong roots a tree will survive any storm. When *you* create a strong foundation, your greatest efforts will withstand the many storms and challenges you inevitably face in achieving your goals.

Grounding is what you use to nourish and nurture your goals. Grounding is the books, tapes, schooling, seminars, and people you surround yourself with to support yourself in whatever you want to achieve.

Want to have a great relationship? Learn from those who already have one. Want to earn a million dollars? Read books, listen to tapes, and receive coaching by those who show you how. When you have ample grounding to support your dreams, the challenges that come along are merely temporary storms that ultimately make you stronger and more highly energized.

Insight 6: Balance

This is a tough one, especially for the most successful people. Even when a tree is well developed, without regular water, sunshine, and nourishment, it will not be healthy. What must you do to balance yourself?

How much sunshine do you get? How much exercise do you regularly do? How nourishing is your diet? How much quiet time do you take on a daily basis with yourself and your loved ones?

Life is a balancing act. Isn't the minute, hour, day, or month you save by working through your natural point of balance just another minute, hour, day, or month you subtract from your lifetime?

Take breaks to smell the roses along the way, and in fact, you'll naturally discover the universe rises up to become your partner rather than it being you against the world.

Insights 7, 8, and 9

Growth automatically occurs in direct proportion to your ability to empower yourself with the first six Insights.

Evolution blossoms when your growth takes you to a new and higher stage of life, unfolding a powerful Vision of your life you probably never foresaw.

Transformation occurs when you become something very different than that which you started off as. Your initial seeds of Insight become a tree of knowledge and accomplishment. You are ready for something greater than achieving for your own personal gain.

You, the student, become the teacher, the mentor, the leader. You are the vessel of seeds to birth a new generation. You enjoy the glow of knowing you have followed your highest path, which ultimately leads you to helping others follow theirs.

All along, you have been transforming into a balanced, wealthy, and fulfilled human being.

All along, you have been transforming yourself into a *Wealthy Soul*.

About the Author

Dr. Michael Norwood is the best-selling author of *The 9 Insights of the Wealthy Soul,* which has been featured in *The Wall Street Journal* and *The Atlanta Journal & Constitution*. Interviews of him have been broadcast on more than 300 radio and television stations worldwide. To subscribe to his "Wealthy Soul Newsletter" and to read his book for 21 days for free, go to http://www.wealthysoul.com.

49

INSPIRATION

Inspirational Tennis

Dave Kurlan

I was lucky to get some serious inspiration from sports. I played baseball, but tennis was the sport at which I excelled. There was an annual Labor Day Tournament where, heading into the event, I was the second seed, and my doubles partner—now a tennis pro and the former coach to Andre Agassi—was the top seed.

Before the tournament I had it all figured out: I would dominate the rounds leading up to the finals, and then my doubles partner would probably beat me in the finals.

However, when the tournament began, I played so poorly that I barely beat my first three opponents and ended up losing in the quarterfinals. That wasn't the outcome I'd imagined!

I was upset, humiliated, and felt I had let myself down. Sitting in the clubhouse and acting perfectly miserable, I caught the attention of John, the new club pro. "Is something wrong?" he asked. I whined my way through the day's events, and he sprang into action. I was about to get the lesson of my life!

John was a professional tennis player, recently off the pro tour after several knee surgeries. He said that I had great form, great talent, and great expectations but that I was mentally lazy. I protested, but he offered to prove it.

"You've seen me walk. I can't bend my right leg," he said, rolling up his pant leg to show scars like zipper marks that went in two different directions. "Here's what I'm going to do: I'll play against your two good legs with my one good leg and this racket," he said after reaching for a ridiculously warped wooden racket.

(This was 1973, when wooden rackets were the preferred choice over clunky metal ones.) "How much are you willing to wager that you can beat me?"

Well, I thought this was free money. Here I was, a very good player and with a good racket. He was crippled and holding a racket with which you couldn't possibly hit a tennis ball. If I was mentally lazy, surely he was mentally crazy. I had $50 to play with, and he accepted my wager immediately.

He limped and I jogged onto the freshly groomed, green clay court on which I'd spent my youth playing. I served first, a hard serve inside the service court. Imagine my surprise when John set up like a human tripod, bracing himself with the warped wooden racket positioned so that the ball would just bounce back. He didn't even swing that ridiculous racket, instead allowing the ball to bounce back to me. I approached the net and pounded the ball to the other corner of the court, but John anticipated the move and was already there in tripod position, ready to let the ball bounce back to me.

So the play went. I would pound the ball, and he'd be there already set up, as if he had some Star Trek "beam me up, Scotty" technology. Each time, the ball would bounce back to my side, until I'd get frustrated, make a mistake, and lose the point.

As the set progressed, about the only thing that changed was how long each point lasted. The volleys became fewer, my patience shorter, my frustration greater. By now, you can gather that this tour-hardened professional with one good leg and a warped racket beat me 6–0. I didn't even win a single point.

We returned to the clubhouse lounge, and after my embarrassment and anger subsided, he replayed the entire set—point-for-point and almost ball-for-ball—to explain everything I did mentally to get in my own way, raise my level of frustration, and eventually beat myself.

He went on to share some of the best lessons on goal setting, motivation, inspiration, and controlling my emotions that I would ever hear, and I've been teaching them ever since. "Your tournament goal was to get into the finals— nothing wrong with that," he said. "But you didn't have a more specific goal or a plan that you could execute. You have the skills, desire, and good intentions, and you're a better player than the other players you met today. Without setting specific goals and making a plan to achieve them you are unprepared for what is to come, haven't rehearsed for the various possible outcomes, and won't be able to control your reactions. You're being mentally lazy."

He said that before I could win a tournament I had to win a match. Before I could win a match I had to win a set. Before I could win a set I had to win a game. Before I could win a game I had to win a point. Before I could win a point I had to return the ball one more time than my opponent did. And, most importantly, before I could return the ball one more time than my opponent could I had to get to where the ball would be, set myself up, and be in a position to hit it before the ball arrived. He said, "And if you perfect that one thing—taking care of positioning, setting up, and executing, returning the ball where you want it to go—and do it consistently, you will beat everyone you ever play against!"

It was so simple—and it took time to get it right—but that lesson propelled my tennis game to the next level and formed the foundation of my future career in sales development consulting.

How does that lesson apply to you? Suppose your goal is to land a great new job. You can't land that job until you interview with a decision maker. You can't interview with a decision maker until you have a phone conversation with someone in Human Resources. You can't have a conversation with HR until you call them. You can't call them until you've responded to a newspaper ad or Internet posting by submitting your résumé. You can't submit your résumé until you identify a position for which you are qualified.

If you perfect one thing—dialing the phone and having effective conversations with prospective employers—and do it consistently, you will get that great new job you are looking to land.

Sometimes we feel overwhelmed by what we have to do. Other times, we aren't properly prepared to accomplish our goals. The next time you find yourself in either of these situations, ask yourself the following questions.

- What are the components or steps that would lead to a successful outcome?
- In what order must these steps be accomplished?
- What must be done in order to complete each step successfully?
- When can you start?
- How much time do you need?
- What resources do you require?
- Is your plan realistic?

When you're feeling overwhelmed or you need to make sure that you are properly prepared, break the goal down into the smallest manageable parts by following the simple steps outlined above.

ABOUT THE AUTHOR

Dave Kurlan is the founder of Objective Management Group, Inc. (http://www.objectivemanagement.com).

He is a top-rated speaker, internationally known for his ground-breaking work in evaluating salespeople, and the developer of the Dave Kurlan Sales Force Profile and other sales development tools. He is the author of *Mindless Selling* and *Baseline Selling—How to Become a Sales Superstar by Using What You Already Know about the Game of Baseball* (http://BaselineSelling.com). He writes *Understanding the Sales Force* (http://OMGEvaluation.Blogspot.com) and *The World of Sales and Selling* (http://www.squidoo.com/davekurlan). He is featured in *Inc.* magazine's video, *How to Increase Sales and Profits by 1000%.*

50

INSPIRATIONAL QUOTES

For Inspiration,
Look toward the Bookshelf

Michael E. Ruge

> I often quote myself, it adds spice to my
> conversations.
>
> – George Bernard Shaw

Graduation ceremonies usually include them; so do weddings and, of course, funerals. What are this mysterious things? Quotations, of course. Quotes are a quick dose of inspiration for any open-minded person. Many quotes get overused and stated to the point of saturation, while some are underutilized. Either way, quotes play an intricate role in our daily lives that can benefit everyone involved. For anyone that needs a pick-me-up, quotes are a great way to get the boost you need. People often look at quotes as long-lasting words from dead people, however, quotes are far livelier than one might think. Quotes can be flirtatious, engaging, motivational, and even healing.

Flirt with life by using quotes to make it through each day. Years ago, as a young student in a small school outside New York City, I had a friend that was constantly quoting what seemed to be every saying known to man. She lived her life vicariously through the words of others. It was what made her unique and interesting. Also, it seemed to be a way for her to interact with others. She'd share a famous saying or a quote from last night's late night comedy show. Whatever the mood was at school, she had a quote to fit it, and everyone seemed to enjoy her genuine passion for famous words. Just as her quotes made her unique, others can use quotes in a similar way to chitchat, make friends, or even fall in love. As the saying goes, crazier things have happened.

Engaging others through quotes can bring relevance to your message, whatever that message is. It's not that everyone doesn't already want to listen to you talk, but just in case we've got a few space cadets in the audience, try to use quotes to engage others in conversation. Quotes are be appropriate for speaking engagements as well as for more casual encounters. Approach others with some interesting quotes ready to sparkle off your lips at any given time, and I promise you'll be astonished at the reaction of those listening to you. People, for the most part, love to learn, and quotes can help put even the most confusing situations into perspective. To make others notice you, pack up your mental backpack with some quotations, and prepare to get noticed.

Get yourself motivated by reading the words of others. Some quotes should be kept to yourself and used for your own benefit. Before a big game one year our football coach came to talk to the team about an opponent that had beaten us the last three years straight. Coach noted that for the past three years we'd been knocking on their door, and now it was time to kick it down. I can still feel my heart rate rise as I think of those magical words. "Knock it down," he said, "knock it down." What a perfect way of putting our losing streak into perspective. It wasn't about us losing three years in a row; rather, we'd been making progress by knocking on the door, and now our progress was to come to fruition with a win. This quote, in particular, got our whole team so fired up that we won the game. Afterward, to be sure I wouldn't forget it, I wrote it down, and to this day, when I feel challenged, I read it again and again. To me, that one sentence is symbolic of strength, perseverance, and triumph. Not ready to kick down the door yet? Try reading up on some more subtle inspirational quotes; if you can't find any quotes you like lying around the house, look at quote books, or better yet, try religious texts. Those are always packed with famous guidance.

Most importantly, quotes offer an historical perspective that is unrivaled in many cases. Quotes can sum up generational feelings or, conversely, can intricately show one person's emotional core better then any other means. Quotes allow people to hear it from the source. Quotes offer an ocean of historical information for us to swim through, soaking up all the great words of our past in the process.

Not everyone will be passionate about quotes, and I can accept such a fact. There is beauty in diversity of opinions in this world, and we all know there is no shortage of opinions out there. However, if quotes aren't important to you personally, remember that in the end you may want something you've said to be remembered. As the old saying goes, "give, and you shall receive": give your time to understand the great words of others, and you will receive knowledge from those words . . . and maybe one day, we'll be quoting you.

> A pessimist sees the difficulty in every opportunity and an optimist sees the opportunity in every difficulty.
>
> – Sir Winston Churchill

ABOUT THE AUTHOR

Michael E. Ruge is a successful entrepreneur, expert negotiator, and dynamic community leader. As founder of several enterprises, his strong, interpersonal leadership style has positively influenced the bottom line of many companies. From the inspiring beauty of his wife's bed-and-breakfast retreat on Vancouver Island (http://www.LakeBB.com), Michael facilitates the development and growth of junior corporations worldwide through his vision, support, and mentor management. An inveterate traveler, Michael jaunts around the world to benefit various charity causes (http://www.aroundtheworldsafari.com). Michael has been collecting quotes for several lifetimes (well, at least one!) and has finally decided to share his collection with the world in his best-selling book, *Quote-A-Quote* (http://www.QuoteAQuote.com).

51

True Intimacy

Neill Neill

Time and time again, people tell me they are not experiencing real intimacy in their relationships. Sex? Yes. True intimacy? No. They long for a soul connection, a deep, tender love, a satisfying and fulfilling sexual love. They long for a deeper level of communication, not just the chatter of everyday life.

Seeking Communion

Human beings are hardwired to seek a deep love connection with another human being. I call this deep level of connection we all seek "communion." And communication is the key to keeping us moving in an upward direction toward communion.

When you meet someone, you begin to form a connection by talking with each other. That's communication. As you talk and listen, you get to know each other. As you get to know each other, you find you like each other. And since you like each other, you want to communicate even more. That is how the upward spiral toward communion begins.

Communication is the key because it is the only part of the process you have any control over. You can't just decide you're going to know someone better. You can't just decide you're going to like someone. The only decision under control is whether or not you communicate with them.

Accepting Your Partner, Warts and All

While it is true that good communication is the key to moving toward communion, we need to look more deeply into the roots of intimacy. True love is not that all-too-familiar but temporary state called infatuation. Infatuation fades over time. True, intimate love deepens over time.

The foundation of true love is acceptance. Can you accept your partner for who he or she is, warts and all? Acceptance of each other is and always has been the basis for love. Intimate love can't flourish without it.

When a couple is in trouble in their relationship, at least one of them is probably having difficulty in accepting something in the other. Nonacceptance leads to criticism, judgment, and damaged communication. Nonacceptance provides the road map to alienation.

Accepting the reality of your partner's shortcomings doesn't mean you have to like all aspects of that reality. But accepting reality, whatever it is, is the bedrock of good mental, emotional, physical, and spiritual well-being. And accepting the reality of your partner is the bedrock of a good relationship.

Your partner's behavior and its effects on you are both parts of reality. So if your reality is that your partner's behavior is hurting you, it would be unhealthy to pretend otherwise. You need to communicate this reality with your partner. Do it without judgment, but do it.

Accepting Yourself As You Are

Before leaving a relationship, or for that matter, before entering one, answer this: How completely do you accept yourself? Your inability to accept as reality something in another usually stems from difficulty you have in accepting the reality of who you are and what you are like.

Do you consciously give yourself permission to experience and be responsible for your actions, feelings, and emotions? Do you do this without putting yourself down? Can you be conscious of and be okay with your thoughts, feelings, and behavior, even when you don't particularly like the reality of some shortcomings you see in yourself?

True self-acceptance is based in consciousness of reality, whatever it is. If you tend to be a bit judgmental, for example, your easiest course would be to deny it and remain unconscious of it. Being conscious might be uncomfortable because as you come to accept who you are, you might decide you have to change and be less judgmental. That might be difficult and uncomfortable. It would be much easier to remain unconsciously judgmental.

Your road map to personal change is self-acceptance because it is based in consciousness of reality. Self-acceptance pays huge dividends in self-esteem and freedom. If you can fully accept yourself, it is easy to accept others. Then your entering or leaving a relationship is guided by the reality of the relationship itself, not by your need to avoid consciousness of things you might not like in yourself.

When both you and your partner can consciously accept yourselves and accept each other, it is possible for love with true intimacy to flourish and grow over the years.

ABOUT THE AUTHOR

Neill Neill, PhD, RPsych, D-CEP, maintains an active psychology practice on Vancouver Island, British Columbia, Canada. In addition to serving the needs of his clients in their psychological and spiritual healing and growth, he is Consulting Psychologist to the Sunshine Coast Health Centre, a residential alcohol and drug treatment facility for men (http://www.SunshineCoastHealthCentre.com). Dr. Neill is a columnist, speaker, and author of a new self-help work, *Living with an Alcoholic: Dr. Neill's Survival Guide for Women* (http://www.living-with-an-alcoholic.com). For a free copy of his e-book, *Codependency and Addiction*, visit http://www.neillneill.com.

52

Discover Three Simple and Easy Ways to Enhance Your Intuition

Elizabeth Manuel

I didn't really believe in intuition until four years ago. It really hit home for me the day my car was stolen. I woke up in the morning with the recollection of a dream about my car being stolen. I drove to work and kept "hearing" the message.

So what did I do? I ignored it, of course! I was receiving a very loud and clear message to move my car and not to park it in the parking lot. As I parked and locked my car, I was urged very strongly to move my car to a different spot. I said to myself, "They won't take my car—it's old. They'll take this nice Jimmy next to mine, and besides, it's raining, and I'm running late." So, I went into work and forgot all about the car.

After work I came out, and surprise . . . no car! I was stunned into disbelief. I walked back to my office, turned around, and came back to the parking lot, hoping for a different result. My car was definitely gone. What happened then? Police reports, phone calls, insurance, car rentals, paper work . . . hours of time and money spent on making arrangements to get a vehicle.

Then reality hit me hard. Initially, I went into victim mode. What did I do wrong? Why me? Why now? The answer is that I had failed to listen. I had ignored my intuition. I could have saved enormous amounts of stress, time, and money by listening to it. So why didn't I listen? Because it would have been silly—I had no rational reason to move my car to a different spot. If there had been a security officer at the parking lot verbally asking me to move my car to a safer location, I would have moved my car. But because it was internal guidance, my "gut," my intuition, I ignored it!

This was a turning point for me. I now rely on my intuition to provide me with the *truth* about situations, events, people, and places. I encourage you to recognize times when you wished you would have listened. How much heartache and struggle would you have avoided?

Unfortunately, we have been taught in the modern Western world that intuition is invalid, unusual, or perhaps even freaky. We have come to rely extensively on our five senses, although we are all gifted with a sixth sense. Since that fateful day, I have studied and learned a tremendous amount about intuition and God. After all, where does our intuition come from? The source of all there is supplies us with all we need if we would just heed our inner voices. We are all connected to this energy force, the creator, God, the Source, whatever you call it. The same force that beats our hearts rotates planets and turns a seed into a plant. We are all part of this energy. No one is exempt.

Intuition is a natural, normal, wonderful *daily* occurrence. I have mastered three joyful ways to enhance my intuition, and I am delighted to share them with you.

Decide

Decision is very powerful and sets into motion a wide range of energy. Absolutely everything in your life results from decision. Think about it—you make a myriad of decisions every day, and everything in your life is the result of making a decision. When you decide to "listen" to your inner voice, you will hear this voice every single day. Decide, and it is done unto you.

Deciding to really listen will increase your awareness of the times when you are following or ignoring your soul's guidance. Think about "gut decisions." The "gut" speaks from your soul. The mind gets caught up in stinky garbage. The "gut" knows before your mind can work it out. The gut does not reason, it simply knows, and herein lies the magic of it. Deciding to listen is the first step. Today, make it a habit to be conscious of your decisions.

Journal

Journaling is amazing. You get the opportunity to record the synchronicity, serendipity, and wonder of life. Journaling allows you to remember the greatest things that happen in your day. The more you acknowledge and appreciate the synchronicities, the more they happen. Every time you think something is a coincidence, think again. Write it down; read it over. You will be astounded at what is happening in your life. The answers are everywhere. The proof is *write* in front of you. Write it down, and you will see it! You are receiving messages—journaling is like putting them in a decoder to reveal the meaning. It's really easy! There are no hard and fast rules. You can type, you can write, or you can use a tape recorder and talk. This way, you can capture what you are saying (or thinking) to yourself and with it the voice of your intuition.

Laugh

Laughter will tap into your inner guidance faster than any other technique. Laughter performs miracles every day. Physically, psychologically, and emotionally, laughter is fun. Laughter releases mighty endorphins in our bodies, which feel great. Laughter changes our body chemistry in a wonderful way. When we feel great, we are not resisting the flow of life. When we feel great, we are literally in the flow. When you are in the flow, everything goes smoothly, *and* you are on top of the world. Why? Because you *become* open and receptive to receiving your guidance. You listen and act with confidence, without second-guessing yourself. Life really isn't so serious. Look around you and see what could possibly be funny. Choose to laugh today! Life really is funny when you stop to look at it. God really does have sense of humor. Laugh out loud—it's a real crowd pleaser.

Decide to *laugh* every day, and remember to *journal* your experiences. Then prepare to live an incredible life filled with abundance and joy. The river of life is designed by your choices. You can begin this minute to improve your life, no matter where you are right now. It all begins with your next decision.

Joy now fills my life. I rely on my intuition every day to make my life more joyful and easy. I now listen with full faith for my messages, and you can, too! Join me in sharing a magnificent, beautiful life.

Blessings to you!

ABOUT THE AUTHOR

Elizabeth Manuel, BEd, CACE, is dedicated to providing others with the tools to live richly, fully, and happily. Elizabeth has studied the Science of Universal Principles for well over 15 years; her motto is "happiness is a journey we embark on every day." Elizabeth is a certified Angel Therapy Practitioner, a yoga instructor, and a clinical hypnotherapist. She uses her skills to assist others in living with passion and joy. Elizabeth owns Metamind Consulting, through which she offers unique and thought-provoking workshops and seminars. Elizabeth is a member of the Canadian Association of Professional Speakers. Visit her Web sites at http://www.ElizabethManuel.com and http://www.metamind.ca.

Copyright © 2006, Elizabeth Manuel.

53

JOB PREPARATION

Things You Thought You Knew but Really Didn't: The Reality of New Jobs

Arlene T. Dyer

Getting ready to start work can be very exciting—there are so many things to do. First, put yourself on a budget before you receive your first paycheck because if you do not, you will find yourself deep in debt before you even get paid. Very few people realize going to work every day is very expensive.

What Do I Wear?

If their workplaces does not have assigned uniforms, many people are late to work because they cannot figure out what to wear. The Salvation Army and other thrift stores have plenty of attractive clothes to get you started.

What Should I Eat for Lunch?

Try to get into the habit of fixing your lunch instead of buying each day. Peanut butter and jelly, tuna, spam, or anything that is filling can make a nice, healthy sandwich that will hold you until you get home from work. Many successful men and women bring their lunches every day inside their briefcases.

What Time Should I Leave for Work, and How Do I Get There?

The bus, metro, and subway offer discounts for frequent travelers, and usually, they are dependable and less stressful. Make it your routine to take an earlier bus or train. That way, even if you are running late, you will still get to work on time. Remember that you are on probation, and being on time is extremely important.

The First Day

Before you leave home, be sure to eat a good breakfast. It is important to feed your body and brain. You cannot concentrate when you are hungry, and today is going to be a very long day. Your body needs fuel for energy.

You are given a brief orientation, and then you are taken around to meet more people. Your first break has come. Do you have any questions you wish you had asked? Are you taking notes and writing down the questions so you can ask them later? Remember that your break of 15 minutes starts as soon as you leave your desk and is over 15 minutes from that time. Figure out the distance from your desk to the rest room or the lunchroom so you will have complete control of your time.

Lunchtime has finally arrived. Now you can enjoy your lunch, the one you made at home. While you are sitting in the lunchroom, look to see if the company has a microwave so that you can bring some of the soup mixes that require only water. Also, notice if they have a refrigerator available to employees. Never take someone's lunch, no matter how tempting it looks. Once again, notice the time. You do not want to be late returning from lunch.

It appears as though the clock is moving so fast that your second break is now here. Now you have a better idea about what is going on and how you are keeping up with your assignments. If there is anything you do not understand, remember that you are in training, so ask questions. The only dumb question is the one that is not asked. Make sure the questions you wrote down earlier have answers beside them now. Be sure to do your followup.

The clock is now ticking toward the time you will be able to go home. Make sure you know the exact time you are off from work. You may notice people stopping work five and sometimes 10 minutes earlier, but you stop at the time assigned to you unless otherwise told by your supervisor.

While on probation, do not go to the neighborhood bar with your new coworkers. Everything that happens in the bar is discussed at work the next day at the water fountain or on the first coffee break. Keep your social friends and your work friends separate. The only time they should meet is at your funeral.

Most companies give Christmas parties. Many employees have lost promotions and sometimes even their jobs because of their behavior at the Christmas party. If you attend, be sure to leave while everyone is still on the first drink.

Office Policies

1. Be pleasant and courteous to everyone.
2. Do not participate in office gossip.
3. Keep a neat work area.
4. Clean up behind yourself when you finish eating lunch or while on break.
5. Don't put your feet on the office furniture.
6. Help keep the rest room clean.
7. Don't eat at your workstation.
8. Come to work on time every day.
9. Leave work when your shift is officially over.
10. Don't bring your personal problems to work.
11. Don't make personal calls or receive personal calls during your work time.
12. Give out your office number for emergency calls only.
13. Don't invite your friends to come by and visit.
14. As soon as you are eligible to join the credit union, do so.
15. Do not begin a personal relationship with a coworker. No matter how attractive you think that person is, it rarely works out.
16. Do not remove any office supplies from the office, for example, pens, pencils, rubber bands, staplers, push pins, or anything you know is the property of the company. You can be terminated for having stolen property on your person outside the building.
17. If you are having problems, talk to someone because your work will show signs that something is wrong.
18. Remember to respect all your company's rules and policies. Never share or give out confidential information regarding your company.

Your probation may be as short as 90 days or as long as six months. During this time, you will be making the decision whether this is something you can handle as a new career. You may need or want to be in another department, but this can only happen after you have completed probation. Always set your goals high. Make sure you are on time every day, are dressed appropriately, and have your mind set on the company's business. If your supervisor asks to see you, don't panic—he or she usually wants to get to know you better. Consider leaving the perfume or cologne off or put on very little as some people are sensitive to smells. When the employer and employee both want to be together, it is a marriage made in heaven. Most people spend more time with their coworkers than they do with their families.

Time management is one of the most important functions for anyone in any profession and, in fact, in life. How you handle your time, I believe, is one of the keys to success. Everyone has 24 hours each day. You have the power to determine how to get the most out of them. Some people will say the day goes by too fast for them to get anything done; others do not say anything, and they just keep on getting things accomplished. Planning your day the night before gives you extra time in the morning. Planning when you wake up takes precious time from that day. The sooner you wake up and get started, the more things you can accomplish. No matter how hard it seems in the beginning, you will soon be able to see the light at the end of the tunnel.

Congratulations and much success on your new job!

ABOUT THE AUTHOR

Arlene T. Dyer is an internationally known motivational speaker, author, group facilitator, radio personality, and publisher. She is the Founder and President of M.Y.S.E.L.F., Inc. (Making Youths Successful Employing Lifetime Formulas) and M.A.M.A. (Making A Major Adjustment). Her areas of expertise include careers, women's issues, abuse, at risk youth, achievement and peak performance, activists, authors, children, education, and the workplace. To contact Arlene, call (323) 754–6749 or visit http://www.arlenetdyer.com.

54

JOY

Joy Replacement Therapy:
Your Prescription for a Joy-Filled Life!

Anne Nelson

From your soul to your senses, joy is accepted, rejected, noticed, ignored, savored, severed, shared, withheld, increased, denied, or multiplied. You choose when and how to have joy in life. Your choice is influenced by the beliefs that are deep in your soul, planted in childhood and affirmed through the use of your senses and emotions as you became an adult.

What you believe is what you see—until you learn differently.

Think about how you grew up. Think about your home life, schooling, religious beliefs, and friendships. In all areas, well-intentioned people told you what they believed to be true. They all did what they could as parents and mentors to influence you, protect you, and teach you what they thought was best for you.

Did you hear statements such as the following?

- Money doesn't grow on trees.
- Being rich doesn't make you happy.
- We each have a cross to bear.
- Beware the hand of God.
- Children should be seen and not heard.
- Stop daydreaming—you're wasting time.
- With grades like that you'll never amount to much.
- It's better to give than to receive.
- You can't do that.
- It can't be done.

- It's a hard-knock life.
- Don't rock the boat.
- Don't go against the grain.
- Only in your dreams.
- Only the good die young.
- Life isn't a fairy tale.
- Boys like him are nothing but trouble.
- We all have to pay our dues.
- It's always darkest before the dawn.
- It's a weight you'll have to bear.
- There's a price to pay for happiness.

What other statements did you grow up with in your home, church, and school?

Joy Replacement Therapy

You can decide to change the negative beliefs you knowingly or unknowingly carry with you. You can unload those ideas that hold you back from accepting joy and abundance in your life. Joy Replacement TherapyTM is the way you jump-start your joy from a clean slate. This technique helps you change worn out thoughts or beliefs, one at a time. Move past an old belief by replacing it with a new one. Consider the new mantras below, or create your own, to replace ones that are not working for you anymore.

- Money doesn't grow on trees. → Money grows in my IRA.
- Beware the hand of God. → God's gifts of mercy and grace await us.
- Children should be seen and not heard. → Children should be seen and heard.
- Stop daydreaming—you're wasting time. → Daydreaming is a good use of time.
- You can't do that. → You can do anything.
- Don't go against the grain. → Be your own person.
- It can't be done. → Anything is possible.
- It's always darkest before the dawn. → This too shall pass.
- There's a price to pay for happiness. → Abundance is your birthright.

Put Joy Replacement Therapy to work for you right now. What other thoughts or beliefs would you change? Write down the worn out belief and then a fresh, new version. When your beliefs are what you want to believe, then you'll begin to create your own thoughts, feelings, and behaviors to generate more joy in your life.

To take it a step further, what you focus on in life, you get back in multiples, and what you focus on directly affects the flow of joy into your life each day. When you focus on some thought or feeling that negatively affects you in some way, you need to replace that thought or feeling. If you are looking straight ahead, you see one thing; if you turn around, you see something different. The picture changes. In the same way you need to pivot in your mind from thoughts or feelings that close off joy to those thoughts or feelings that bring joy into focus for you. Joy Replacement Therapy will help you turn a joyless perspective or situation into one of joyful abundance.

You generate joy in your life by seeing the joy in life. It then naturally multiplies over and over again. Joy Replacement Therapy is one quick way to shift your focus to joy. It's like a bubble bath for your soul. It simply feels good.

Deliberate Joy

If you live with deliberate joy, you reach the point where your life is full, but full of what you want. Living with deliberate joy gives you the ability to experience life around you on your terms. It is having good things in life flow to you. It is living guilt-free and feeling satisfied and confident about the choices you make. It is letting go of obligation and acting from an innate point of desire. It is a new level of self-discovery that brings you back to the point of being able to dream again, to recognize the miracles around you. Living with deliberate joy fills your soul with the warmth and love of all that is intended for you by your Creator.

Your life is what it is because of the choices you have made so far. As you already know, these choices will take you to either the pits or the possibilities in life. You have the power to make choices and changes that will give you the life you are intended to live—a life filled with joy. Everyone deserves joy in life. You deserve joy in life. Start today.

About the Author

Anne Nelson, author of Find Your Joy Zone: How to See What Makes You Happy and Love What Makes You Real, is an expert in the joy of daily living. Anne has studied her own and other people's lives, both to tackle what's missing and to openly celebrate what makes us thrive. Like night vision goggles for those dark corners of life, Anne's practical solutions bring out the Aha! in all of us. She is a speaker, direct sales entrepreneur, and the founder of http://www.YourJoyZone.com, designed to help you bring out the best in yourself—personally and professionally.

55

LANGUAGE

Live Your Life in Language

David Flack

How do you relate to yourself and others? What do you have in common with the voice in your head and the messages you speak?

It's language. Some say that ultimately, words are everything. Call it communication, conversation, or articulation—your expression of life lives in language. I say you *are* your words, and the vocabulary of your life is up to you. You get to choose your view of the world with the internal words you select— you are what you think about most of the time as even your thoughts are expressed in language. When you understand that adversity is inevitable but fear is optional (as is the drama of unnecessary and self-induced suffering), you see freedom of choice as your own personal power...expressed in language. Do you mainly think about what you don't have and can't do? More importantly, do you continually tell others what's going wrong and not working out?

If this is so, you may experience life as unfair and even cruel. You bounce from saintliness to martyrdom to what I call "victimhood." When real challenges come up, you're already beaten down because of your internal language. Some form of anger, denial, or sadness flows out of you, hangs over you, and haunts those around you.

The language in your life is not serving you. In some ways, this language is self-induced, and it can be strangely comfortable to complain and rail against the universe. Everybody does it, don't they?

Yes, they do—and this is an area of your life in which it is best *not* to fit in, to go along, and to blend in so that you can be miserable along with everyone else. I'm pleading for your awareness. See that you are too precious to throw away your own unique qualities with unexamined self-talk and chitchat. Consider the challenge of the world trying to "change" you when being yourself is the real gift, the real achievement in life. Accomplishing what others see as impossible, if only in your language, can give real satisfaction.

You could say (and therefore think or believe) that a glass is half empty, or that it is half full. I'm suggesting that it is both. For example, one person might declare, "it's a beautiful day," when another, with the same day in front of her, says, "yeah, but it might rain." Choose your words carefully—this is your life we're talking about.

When you expect a mess, you get one. However, putting possibility into your language *gives* you possibility. It's like starting the day with "good morning, Lord" instead of "Oh, Lord, it's morning." By declaring your life as rich, it becomes so…and you declare it with language.

Certainly, you will have challenges and obstacles ahead. Your intentions may be thoughtful, yet thwarted. Use the power of language to create what you *can* do and *may* have. The quality of your life arises from your language, so make language serve you. External problems are resolved with your internal emotions—be passionately productive for your profitability. Pablo Picasso was reported to have said, "I'm always doing things I can't do; that's how I get to do them."

Let's apply this by declaring the following out loud. Yes, read these statements aloud—use language!

- "I choose my words to create what I want in life."
- "I am accountable for what I tell myself and others."
- "I am capable of shaping my environment to serve others, which serves me."
- "I am committed to the language of positive possibility."

Start now to examine your choices, freely made, in the context of the language you use…and don't use. By being aware of what you say, you will deepen your understanding of the power that is yours for the taking.

It's a great way to improve your life, because language *is* life.

ABOUT THE AUTHOR

David Flack has been altering lives without apology for decades. He *accelerates* individual and company productivity, profitability, and possibility toward being extraordinary with exceptional skills as a professional coach, management consultant, and group facilitator. Also a published composer and songwriter, Mr. Flack has won numerous accolades as an inspirational speaker, teacher, and corporate trainer. His #1 best-selling book, coauthored with Dr. Wayne Dyer, Deepak Chopra, Mark Victor Hansen, and others, is *WAKE UP ... LIVE THE LIFE YOU LOVE: Finding Personal Freedom*, and he also wrote and published *Adopting Awesome Attitudes* (a book on cards). See http://www.TheAcceleratorCoach.com or call (210) 872–5490.

56

LEGACIES

Passing the Generational Torch

Leah Light

There are labels for mom's condition: senility, Alzheimer's, dementia. There are other labels, too, more often whispered in days past: she's off her rocker, a few bricks shy, lights on but nobody home. They all describe one whose physical existence has outlasted mental faculties.

Mom's frailty came on gradually over the past decade or more. Five of those years, she lived with me and functioned quite well, considering her advanced age. With a Medic-Alert button around her neck, I could leave her alone during the day, though not too many days in a row. She had a habit of "forgetting" to eat, her lifelong practice to counteract weight gain. At 80-something, her fragile frame carried no extra pounds. However, old habits die hard—habits like self-control, thriftiness, and staying busy.

During her prime Mom was such a busy bee. A homemaker, she did all the things that went with raising four kids and dozens of foster kids. She cleaned, gardened, baked, canned, knitted, and sewed. She wrote a community column for the local paper and taught art classes to the neighborhood kids. She crafted pottery and even composed music. She was full of energy and always on the go. Most times, she was cheerful, though she had her angry times, too. Whatever she was feeling, it was out there in the open and over quickly. No time for suffering in silence; that wasted energy when there were things to be done.

I wish I could tap into some of that energy now. It's been over two months since moving Mom to the home, and it's a big, thankless chore clearing out her old room. A Depression-era survivor, Mom certainly knew how to hang on to things. She gripped her possessions just as tightly as her fear of lack gripped her. Some things, like her beautiful pottery and artwork, are clearly treasures. Intermingled is a jumble of worthless items that I doubt even she cared about, kept by default, probably to avoid this kind of painstaking sorting. I begin organizing the mountain of stuff into three parts: discard, give away, and keep.

Of all the hats Mom wore, "writer" was primary. From her hundreds of pages of research notes she banged out numerous articles on her ancient manual typewriter. Some were published in newspapers. Some she "published" (photocopied) herself, and others are still in their original, handwritten form. Most are assembled into notebooks organized by subject matter. All are covered in dust.

Somewhat guiltily, I read through her writings, feeling as if I'm invading her privacy. My guilty feelings mount along with the discard pile, which contains her prized creations of a lifetime. As I spend hours sorting and breathing the dust from days gone by, however, my chore has an unexpected payoff—I'm gaining a new perspective of my mom as a woman, not just my mother, but as a person in her own right.

I'm entertained by Mom's stories of cute things kids and grandkids did. I find her angry notes of venting after arguments with Dad. Having cared for her own aged mother for seven years, Mom wrote about the challenges of caring for the elderly. I can certainly relate to that. As I read on, I'm hit squarely between the eyes by déjà vu. Mom had just put her own mother into a nursing home—the same facility, in fact, where I've just moved her. Mom's entry is dated more than 20 years ago:

> It's been a month now since putting Mother in the
> nursing home. All her clothes still hang in the closet.
> I'd really like to use her room, but I feel guilty about
> getting rid of her things, which she valued so much.
> What if I give them all to the Goodwill and then her
> mind returns, will she be mad at me?

As further déjà vu, I note that I was pregnant with my daughter when Mom wrote that entry, and as I write this, my daughter is pregnant with my granddaughter. The generational torch is being passed.

I've told Mom that she will be a great grandmother twice over, as my brother is also expecting a grandchild soon. Mom grasps this, and soon forgets; I have to repeat the news the next time I see her. She lives in the Alzheimer's/Dementia

220

unit at the home. Like other residents there, Mom has slipped into second childhood. She recounts events from 80 years ago as if they are going on this minute. Her eyes take on a misty, faraway gaze, and her voice becomes girlish. Sometimes she wanders the halls at night, like a toddler in search of her parents' bed.

Some of residents at the home are stuck on an emotion or retell a story repeatedly. On the other hand, Mom appears to be in the process of becoming "unstuck." She always had a mental grasp on everything, including uncomfortable feelings. This echoed her generation's mind-set: buck up and do your duty; no time for whining or self-pity. Staying in one's head avoids descent into risky emotional territory. Mom is likely way behind in feeling her feelings. The backlog has caught up to her now, and there are times when she laughs and weeps hysterically. She's no longer in control. And yet she is being freed from the stiff corset of willpower and self-discipline in which she lived most of her life. She's returning to a pure, childlike state that is real and in the moment. A child yells when angry, cries when sad, and laughs uncontrollably, without apology or restraint. Mom may appear to be a confused or crazy old lady. But if you look just beyond her softly lined face and into her enigmatic eyes, you will see a soul who is processing a lifetime of experiences.

In watching Mom's process I've been asking myself some questions that I pass on to those seeking to evaluate and improve their lives:

- What is my life's purpose, and am I fulfilling it?
- What do I value most? Am I making sure that's where I invest my time and energies?
- Do I hold in my life the possessions, people, and qualities that really matter to me?
- What do I need to let go of? Am I keeping things (or attitudes, beliefs, old methods, etc.) by default—not having questioned whether they still serve me?
- Am I growing? What can I learn? What do I need to unlearn?
- What am I contributing? Do I give because I want to, or out of duty?
- How do I feel about who I am and what I've done over the course of my life?

All these things, tangible and intangible, collectively make up the meaning of one's life and how well it is lived.

I treasure the gifts my mother passed to me, including honesty, a strong work ethic, and the joy of achievement. I have gained from her deficits as well; I see the value in taking the time to feel and just be. I'm also doing my best to let go of fears and other needless things that clutter my house and soul. I wonder what my daughter will learn when, one day, she sifts through the treasures and ponderings of my lifetime.

ABOUT THE AUTHOR

Leah Light is a published author, wedding minister, and intuitive counselor. She has entertained by giving readings since childhood. Over the years she has further developed her gifts to help people understand and heal themselves. Those abilities were tested personally following the sudden death of her husband of 19 years in 1998. Recovery came, in part, through writing of her experiences and spawning two inspirational books, *We Are Becoming: Insights & Impressions of a Psychic* and *Picking Up the Pieces: Becoming a Greater Whole*. For more information about Leah Light, please visit her on the Web at http://www.leahlight.com.

57

LIBERATION

Nine Keys to Spiritual and Physical Liberation

Sandy Paris

The physical universe is a maze of smoke and mirrors, complicated diversions that try to capture our attention and place it on the path of illusions instead of on the path of spiritual truth, love, and happiness. We are living in a swirling mass of positive and negative energies, vibrating to the frequency of the state of consciousness of the world's inhabitants.

This is clearly being reflected in the chaos earth has been experiencing lately, with hurricanes, tornados, earthquakes, and floods killing hundreds of thousands of people, animals, birds, fish, plants, and trees. This is contaminating the planet. The effect of these disasters is like a pebble being tossed into a pond and the ripples reaching out to all the banks on earth. Our water, air, and food sources are showing signs of this contamination.

It is apparent, at this time, from the reflection of all the chaos in the universe, that peoples' lives are not spiritually and physically in harmony. These imbalances are bleeding over into our personal lives. Many of us are experiencing problems with health, finances, and a lack of peace of mind. Spiritual starvation is rampant because attention has shifted to material distractions.

How can we survive and achieve spiritual and physical liberation during these difficult times? By taking responsibility and becoming active participants in manifesting balance and harmony between our own spiritual and physical lives. We can't change the world. However, we can change our state of consciousness, which, when enough people engage in the practice of self-discipline, would have an uplifting effect on the universal consciousness.

How and where do we begin? We begin by recognizing that there are two parts to each of us: our inner, spiritual selves as Soul, and our outer, physical bodies as ego.

Key 1: Our inner, spiritual self is "Soul." Soul is immortal, never dies, and lives in an *unchanging, timeless state of Pure Energy*. Soul is the observer and driver of our physical bodies, witnessing all events in this and past lifetimes.

Soul contains a collection of all the thought pictures of this lifetime as well as those from our past lives. Some of the pictures reflect our virtues, and others, our vices. When we come back each lifetime, we are given the opportunity to work off our weaknesses and vices for the supreme purpose of accepting and giving God's Divine Love, *Pure Energy*, back to life. Once we begin to wake up to ourselves as Soul, we evolve to a higher state of consciousness.

In other words, when timeless, spiritual *Pure Energy* enters the physical universe, it splits into two parts (positive and negative) and becomes *secondary energy*. This sets up the training ground for all our experiences and opportunities for learning. Our challenge, as Soul, is to blend the positive and negative energies back into the spiritual state of *Pure Energy*, neutral Divine Love, in our lives here on earth.

Key 2: We are Soul with a body, not a body with a soul.

Key 3: Our outer, physical body—ego—is mortal and is born and dies in a *changing world of secondary energy* made up of the dual aspects of positive and negative energy. Our bodies are like a car. The car can't drive itself. Soul is the driver and observer of our physical bodies.

Soul takes on a new body each lifetime so it can learn the lessons that only daily experiences can teach it.

Who is the life-force? God is the Creator and Life-Force. Holy Spirit is the guide. Soul is the driver. And the body with excessive ego is trapped in time and a changing world.

Key 4: How do we experience the unchanging world of *Pure Energy*? We have to suspend our old belief systems, bad habits, and unhealthy attitudes and elevate our consciousness above the concept that time and space control us. Then we master the freedom to see the whole picture—*Pure Energy*—instead of the parts—positive and negative energies. Finally, we achieve Spiritual Liberation. This takes many lifetimes, with a wide variety of experiences.

It takes discipline and practice to slow down and step through the illusions of time and space. It takes surrender of old habits, attitudes, and attachments, through the process of letting go. We begin to blend the positive and negative energies within ourselves into a neutral state of Divine Love—*Pure Energy*.

It is impossible to step through the eye of the needle to the spiritual state with karma.

Key 5: Master the art of spiritual liberation through contemplation. Find a quiet place where you won't be disturbed. Make yourself comfortable. Close your eyes. Empty yourself of any concerns or limitations you may be holding. Take three deep breaths, feel those concerns flowing out from you into a river of Divine Love, and watch them disappear. Bask in the lightness, and begin to sing HU, an ancient love song to God, for a few minutes. Then notice a bright beam of light and a gentle sound that melts your heart embracing and filling you with Divine Love. Open yourself to the guidance of Holy Spirit and the full acceptance of Divine Love. Within this state, let an image or feeling form within your heart with an attitude of gratitude. Explore this uplifting, divine state each morning. Throughout your day, step into your sacred state of accepting God's love—*Pure Energy*.

Key 6: After about 15 to 20 minutes, bring an image or feeling back, and write it down, as clearly as you possibly can, in words that match your experience. Be gentle with yourself and trust what comes to you, as long as it is uplifting.

Key 7: Make an action plan. Every gift has to become a physical action. Use it or lose it! A gift unused is a gift unaccepted and unappreciated.

Key 8: This is where we begin to make changes in our lives from the unchanging world. Create a physical container for your creative, spiritual seeds to sprout into your life.

Key 9: Practice the art of weeding your garden of life in the moment of *now* so the qualities of purity, grace, gratitude, and Divine Love begin to blossom in your daily actions and manifest in your experiences. This is a major step in blending the positive and negative energies in your life into neutral *Pure Energy*—Divine Love.

Become present in the *now*, paying attention to your choices. A simple technique to use is to ask yourself, "Will it be purity or pollution"? This goes for every aspect of life: food, movies, television, music, books, habits, words, deeds, and attitudes, which become thought pictures.

The world we live in is the world we have created with our thought pictures. Everything we see happening around us is actually a reflection of our own state of consciousness. We can't blame the actors on the stage of life for our manifestations. Life is really only a reflection of ourselves. This reflection is a gift showing us the lessons we have come back to earth to learn.

It is ultimately our responsibility to realize that we are already the finished dream. All we have to do is wake up, *now*, as the dream completed.

ABOUT THE AUTHOR

Sandy Paris is the author of *Loving Your Age at Every Age in the Good Times and Hard Times*, an international speaker, and a publisher. She is a modern-day expert on antiaging. Sandy has presented 33 years of inspirational and self-help speaking engagements to tens of thousands of people at locations around the world. Sandy's love for life is contagious, and her writing and speaking engagements reflect the infinite potential in all of us as ageless, timeless, and unlimited Beings. Visit her Web site at http://www.sandyparis.com, or e-mail her at sandyparis@mac.com.

58

Sit Humbly Before Your Buddhas

Laura Young

"They say you should write what you know," she offers as we sit sorting one more in an endless stream of boxes filled with papers. "Right now, this is what you know. They say no man stands so tall as when he stoops to help a child. This is kind of like that." My mother leans from her wheelchair to toss one more handful into the "burn" pile.

I had intended to write this chapter from the comfort of my home office, on my computer, with my cat on my lap, but while I was making those plans, life was happening, just like John Lennon said it would. So, instead I am writing on an old pad of paper, looking out over country fields two states away after a night disturbed by the frightened meows of a cat half feral after five months alone here. I am at my mother's house five months after her stroke. She is just 64 years old.

While I have been thinking high thoughts, trying to select what wisdom I would offer to help you improve your life, I have been immersed in helping my mother dismantle hers. The last six months have seen a series of hospital visits and days away from home as I have been plunged into my divorced parents' lives, as they each face life-altering health crises. Many times, I have felt anything but tall.

Considering her words, I haul another box to the fire and plunge my stick into the deepening pile of ash, fanning apart a McCall's magazine from 1973, encouraging the flames to gain purchase. Forty-three years ago, my mother began to collect these magazines. An innocent subscription to *Parents* grew to include *McCall's*, *Ladies' Home Journal*, and *Better Homes and Gardens*, each brimming with tips to transform her from an overwhelmed, unhappily married mother of four to a gracious, cellulite-free hostess with the right dress for every occasion, welcoming guests into a serene home adorned with timeless décor.

These magazines are as familiar to me as siblings, but the promised transformation never took place. I cast another stack into the fire. The irony is not lost on me.

My mother never stopped thinking about improving her life. In fact, 101 suggestions about how to do that would have appealed to her, and she would have intended to try every one. I watch a charred page dance in the heat, wondering if one day some other daughter in some other field will cast my own suggestions into her flames.

What can I offer you that will endure? What will last after these pages have long since yellowed? What has the deconstruction of two lives taught me? Certainly there are the time-honored truths:

- It is best to think twice before throwing toilet paper out the girls' room window when there are nuns around.
- Some styles should never come back, including anything from the 1980s and sky-blue sans-a-belt pants.
- In a small house, keep a handy supply of room fresheners and a sense of humor.
- If you all live long enough, someday, you will have to see your parents naked. Don't panic, everyone will survive it.

These guidelines will undoubtedly help you avoid a few jams and enhance your quality of life, but they aren't the most important principles.

Closer to the truth are words so overused as to have become cliché.

- You can't take it with you.
- Tomorrow is promised to no one.
- Love is all that matters.

These maxims hit closer to home the deeper one gets into middle age, but they don't tell you *how* to survive the changes that inevitably come.

But let's not talk mere survival. If you are reading this book, you want to go beyond the basics. You want to thrive. Like the authors, you intend to extract every drop of nectar from your journey, showing up fearlessly, passionately, and unflinchingly to all that life offers.

To you, I offer the most important skill I have learned: approach that which you fear.

Nothing clarifies life like death, and no one teaches more about living well than those who are dying well.

I live by the tenet that everyone in my life is a Buddha, here to teach me something essential to my path. This does not mean I enjoy every lesson, and I certainly have questioned the methods of a few instructors, but I pay attention nonetheless.

This is a difficult philosophy to adopt if one fancies oneself as "strong" and "independent." However, if you can learn the difference between humiliation and humility, putting the ordinary needs of the ego aside, you will gain the Buddhas' respect, and their aid will be invaluable.

I was a woman who loved people by doing things for them, finding this far easier than actually *being* with them. There is vulnerability in true intimacy that is too uncomfortable for many people to bear for long. *Eyes lock for a moment. Moment feels too naked. Here, let me get you more coffee.* Further, being with people I knew would die meant I might cry. I could appear weak if I revealed my fears. Perhaps my grief over being destined to die, surrounded by others just as mortal, would be too much for me to face head on, emotionally and spiritually, even if I could do so intellectually. Yet my commitment to living consciously never wavered. I knew showing up would mean moving into my pain.

Victoria Williams wrote, "That which you fear the most will meet you half way." My Buddhas began to show up in droves, both the dying and the bereaved. Impending death was my daily companion. In desperation I picked the one I most feared losing, sat at his feet, and wept. "This is so much bigger than me, right now. Will you help me?"

"Will you help me?" Four words that once signified the ultimate in humiliation for me became the bravest words I ever spoke.

My Buddha said yes. In fact, they all did, and my instruction began in earnest.

The lessons I have learned so far:

- When you say "this isn't my life," you are in denial. You are always in your life.
- It is possible to embrace someone as both living and dying as soon as you give up the need to label the present moment. All you have is the present moment.
- Inner beauty, grace, and dignity trump unwanted facial hair, saggy butts, and catheter bags every time.
- Self-care is not something to resume once the crisis is over. Crises have a way of stacking up. A centering practice such as meditation, prayer, walking, or any mindful activity is essential.
- Collapsing from exhaustion does not count as relaxation.
- Time alone to reflect is critical. No one can do your processing for you.
- No one will ever truly know what life and death look like through your eyes. They don't have to. Draw your own conclusions about the journey.

Enjoy the knowledge and wisdom contained within this book. Take bite-sized pieces, and chew them well. Incorporate. Integrate. Welcome every Buddha. Your lesson plan awaits.

ABOUT THE AUTHOR

Laura Young, MA, is the founder of Wellspring Coaching. An innovator in the field of wellness coaching, Laura draws on 25 years of experience, including extensive background in psychology, personal development coaching, pain management, martial arts, meditation, and yoga. She is a dedicated student of both Eastern and Western philosophy. She has a special interest in the transformative power of story and the uses of creative expression to promote wellness. Her Web site, http://www.wellspringcoaching.com, links to extensive writings on a number of personal development topics, including those highly relevant to mid-lifers. Private consultations and a full range of coaching services are available.

59

How to Simplify Your Life and Be Happier

Suhail G. Algosaibi

I've often found that people make their lives more complicated than they really are. To be sure, life is not easy in today's nonstop-action world. However, it doesn't have to be that complicated. We often put imaginary obstacles in our way. Decisions that can be made quickly are made more complicated than necessary.

Here are some things you can do to simplify your life.

Develop Clarity

Sit down for a few minutes and decide what you really want out of life. Imagine your ideal life. Make it as vivid and as detailed as possible. What kind of house do you want? What income and net worth would you like to have? What about family? If you don't have a partner, imagine what your ideal partner would be like. Ask yourself as many questions as you can think of. Use your imagination to its maximum potential.

Next, develop some goals to help you achieve your ideal life, and *write them down*. Studies show that writing down your goals and reviewing them on a regular basis dramatically improves your chances of achieving them. Be specific. If you have a target income in mind, write down exactly how much you what to earn and by when. Do this with all your goals. Make them SMART: specific, measurable, achievable, realistic, and timed.

Manage Your Time Better

Focus on the things that give you the highest ROTI (return on time invested). Do only the things that matter and give you a good return on your time. Delegate smaller-value things to others, or don't do them at all. Focus on doing the important things first.

Also, use time-chunking. This is a method where you dedicate a chunk of your time to one task only. Don't work on several projects at the same time (the old multitasking model)—this will only frustrate you. You can work on several projects at once, but dedicate time to only one task during a specific period of time.

If necessary, wake up an hour earlier, or go to bed an hour later each night. I often start my day at 7 A.M. and begin writing, long before my staff comes in and the phone starts ringing. I focus on one thing only for several hours.

Drop the Losers

Did you know that a lot of your success and progression in life has to do with the people you hang out with? We humans are like sponges: we constantly absorb information. Whether we like it or not, we get influenced by the people we spend time with. Make sure you stop hanging out with negative people that waste your time and energy. Find positive, successful people, and spend more time with them.

Don't be embarrassed to ask a successful person if he can spare a few minutes for you. Ask him out to lunch. You'll find that successful people are willing to teach others who are eager to learn. However, be respectful of his time, and make sure you don't overdo it. Work around his schedule. Record or write down his recommendations and habits, and implement them in your own life.

Motivate Yourself

Read and listen to motivational material. The fact that you are holding this book in your hands is a good sign. It's a great starting point. Seek out the authors that motivated you the most, and read their other materials. Go to their Web sites and register for their newsletters, if they have some.

Avoid Bad News

I always skim the newspaper in the morning, but I never read the bad news. When I read about human tragedy, it just depresses me. Of course, you should always remain well informed, but skip the gory details of the bad news items. Listening to bad news all the time has the same effect as hanging out with negative people. You have to be selective about what you let your subconscious absorb.

Make Decisions

It is better to make a quick decision than to make no decision at all. Making decisions will set things in motion, and it is much harder to stop once you get going. You can always correct your mistakes and learn from them as you go along. Here's a great quote on decisions: "Good decisions come from wisdom. Wisdom comes from experience. Experience comes from bad decisions." Also, make sure you don't suffer from "paralysis by analysis." As the esteemed sporting shoe manufacturer tells us, "just do it!"

Release Your Stress

You have to find ways to release all the tension that builds up over the days and weeks. You can do various activities like martial arts, going to the gym, meditation, yoga, or even simple things like taking a hot bath. A massage from time to time might not be a bad idea. Find something that relaxes you, and do it on a regular basis.

Don't Stop!

Implementing these simple steps will help you simplify your life and overcome any complexities—real or imagined. Beware, there will be setbacks! However, if you keep your goals firmly in mind and keep taking action, you will be able to overcome them and start living your ideal life.

ABOUT THE AUTHOR

Suhail Algosaibi, MBA, MCMI, AP, is a successful entrepreneur, consultant, author, and seminar leader based in the kingdom of Bahrain. He is the owner of Radical Marketing Consultancy, specializing in increasing the sales and profits of small- and medium-sized businesses. You can subscribe to his *free* marketing e-course at www.RadicalMarketing.com.

60

LOVE AND RELATIONSHIPS

Finding True, Blessed Love

Trish Regan & Doug Hackett

Have you always wished to attract your life partner, a love that is blessed and sacred, but have been having difficulty making your dream come true?

We have been married in what we call Sacred Partnership since 1992 and would like to share the process that we used to find each other. This process, we found, was partly intuitively given to us and partly learned from the wisdom of others. We experienced it in different ways and found that, in our determination to find true love, when we focused our attention on these steps, our meeting was inevitable and in perfect timing for each of our lives.

We both wished to find our beloved after years of heartache and experience in relationship, divorce, and other types of dysfunctional partnership. All our lives, we yearned to be whole and complete and to travel the pathways of life with our Spiritual Partner by our sides. We desired to be bonded in love, a love so powerful and deep it could take two souls and create a brilliant spirit of blended and unified light.

Spiritual Partnership takes the normal relationship to a higher degree of experience. It means that each person first is whole unto himself—one does not need another in order to be fulfilled, happy, and in joy. We do whatever it takes to find the essence of our inner selves so that we can love ourselves unconditionally, be it counseling, spiritual healing, or personal growth workshops. Then we can participate in relationships without having expectations that our partner will meet our needs, which frees the relationship to soar to heights of joy and freedom that can be an exquisite dance of oneness and separateness altogether within the sacred union.

The other aspect of Spiritual Partnership is that we honor the other's spiritual growth and exploration of his purpose on the planet and support his journey in whatever way that we can. We observe those aspects of the other's personality that aggravate or upset us as a mirror for that which needs healing within ourselves. We also take responsibility for our own feelings, refraining from blaming our partners for our problems and troubles. This shift from the old way of relationship frees the union to support each person's individuality at the same time that our lives are intertwined in unconditional love.

Five tried and true steps to attract your true, blessed love follow.

Heal and Complete Past Relationships

We know that it is difficult to find one's true love if one is tied to the past, to former relationships which bind one in dysfunctional connections or unfinished emotional baggage. When we are tied to the past or have anger or resentment tugging at our hearts, even though buried deep within our consciousness, our psyches are not prepared to receive the clear signal when a possible love comes into our lives. In fact, it is nearly impossible for our energy to connect with our possible partner because of the blockage of the flow of energy from our hearts.

What can be done is to sit in quiet, ask your heart who you need to make completion with, and allow that person to become apparent to you. When that person becomes clear to you, write a letter to him with the intention that you will come to compassion and forgiveness. If that intention is clear, it will happen if you write out all your feelings and spend at least a half hour doing so. This letter is not to be given to that person but is used to allow your feelings to emerge from your subconscious. By the end of the letter you will find that you feel very differently about this person and will be able to truly forgive and let go in the following process.

When the letter is complete, you can imagine that you are expressing the highest of yourself—you are in your highest radiance. In your imagination, allow that person to stand before you, and send love to him from your heart (you can see this as a pink light of love). Then send compassion into his heart. You can tell him that you thank him for being your teacher and that you love him and forgive him. And then see with your mind's eye if there are any unconscious cords or streams of energy attaching your body to his. Symbolically cut the cords, and let the person go to their highest destiny. This is very powerful and will free you to be open to the right and perfect partner for you.

Make a List of What You Want in a Relationship

Find a quiet space, and spend some time getting very clear about what you wish to bring into your life in a relationship. Make a list of all of the qualities you wish in a partner. Be specific, and write these qualities in present tense as if you already have them (for example, "I have a partner who loves me as much, if not more, than I love him").

Change Your Negative Beliefs

After you have made your list of qualities you want to manifest in your partner, read each one separately, and ask your inner self if you really believe that they are possible. Write down any negative beliefs that come up (such as "I will never find a woman who will love me as much as I love her"). Then imagine that belief written on a chalkboard in front of your mind. Erase that belief, and write the one you wish to manifest; feel what it will feel like to have that. Do this for each of the negative beliefs.

Feel Yourself Having the Relationship You Want

It is a common belief that if we can feel the emotion, the bodily sensation, and the sense of something for a few minutes with all our senses, we can bring that into our existence. Imagine that you are being held by your future beloved. You are feeling the immense joy and fulfillment that will come when you are in the arms of the one you love. Really be there, and "see" this scene from many perspectives (in front of the scene, behind it, and from different spaces). Exaggerate the feelings for 17 seconds, and then let them go.

Ask for This, and Then Let Go of Your Attachment

The next step is to ask the universe for this gift of love. Unless we ask, the universe does not know what we truly want. Be very clear.

The very last step is to let your desire and dreams go for the highest good and to the will of the universe and the higher plan for you. It is when we are attached to our desires that the energy keeps us from opening to receiving what we want and even, perhaps, something better. Our attachments prevent the other person from receiving our unconscious signals, and we may simply miss the opportunity of meeting our truest love by our unwillingness to be open to the highest and best that our souls have in store for us.

ABOUT THE AUTHORS

Trish Regan and Doug Hackett, a married couple in spiritual partnership since 1992, experienced a dramatic spiritual calling in 1994. They "jumped off the cliff," left their professional lives behind in California, and founded Dolphin\Spirit of Hawaii, offering spiritual dolphin swim retreats in Kona, Hawaii. Trish and Doug also travel internationally, bringing their Sacred Partnership, Dolphin Essence Experience, Be the Vision, Messages from the Masters, Empowering Magnificence, and Essential Joy workshops globally to assist seekers of Truth in their spiritual expansions and transformations. Trish is author of the book series *Essential Joy: Finding It, Keeping It, Sharing It.* Visit http://www.dolphinspiritofhawaii.com, call (800) 874–8555, or e-mail dolphins@dolphinspiritofhawaii.com.

61

LOVE PLAY TECHNOLOGY

Transform Your Relationship with Love Play Technology

Kara Oh

With the divorce rate looming over our society, there's a lot of pressure and fear about how to keep a relationship vibrant and filled with love. Here's a way to keep that sparkle of love alive or to reignite a sparkle that might currently be at a low fizzle.

It's often said that it takes work to make a relationship last. Through many years of studying, writing, and speaking about relationship issues I have learned that most couples don't quite know what that "work" is supposed to be. Mostly, they assume it isn't fun. So instead of thinking of it as work, I prefer to think of it as *Love Play*. Love Play is all about staying consciously aware of and focused on the *quality* of your relationship. The work part is keeping it at the top of the list of what's important to you.

When you're first falling in love, you're hyper-aware of the object of your affections, and you're so focused that you can't think of anything else, even when you try. It's fireworks, roller coasters, and can't-keep-your-hands-off-each-other pretty much all the time. You're feeling more alive than you ever thought possible. Inspired, you become a couple and settle in. Then, all too often, the fireworks become an occasional sparkler, the roller coaster becomes "It's A Small World," and the hands are more often holding up a newspaper. Ugh! Now that's what I call work.

So what can you do to turn things around, or, if you haven't gotten to that stage yet and things are still bright and shiny, how can you avoid the inevitable sinking of the ship? That's where *Love Play Technology* comes in. This technology will

239

help you shift your focus and awareness back to each other, back to being playful, back to how it was when you were falling in love. Love Play Technology is really simple because I've found that if advice isn't simple, people won't do what's required to make real changes in their lives.

Step 1: Recommit

To turn your love into something that really keeps you sparkling, you must first recommit to each other that your relationship is of supreme importance, just as you did at your wedding ceremony. Not married? It doesn't matter. Either way, you must let each other know that you are willing to do whatever it takes to keep your relationship alive, vibrant, and growing in love.

Recommit as Often as Necessary

Part of this technology is that you recommit however often the two of you agree is necessary for you to put things back on track and to keep your relationship the most important thing in your lives. If you have really let things slide, maybe you need to recommit once a week. Whether it's at dinner, on a walk, or in bed on a Friday night, you need to tell each other in clear and specific words that you are recommitting to each other and the love that brought you together.

As you develop the habit of expressing your love and commitment to each other, you can make the time span between recommitments greater. Maybe once a month, you light some candles, look each other in the eyes, and recommit. I would not recommend you go any longer than once a month. It's way too easy to get out of the habit. With the fast-paced lives we lead it's too easy to forget, and in no time you've let the relationship slide down several notches on the list.

Step 2: Prioritize

In step two you must make your relationship with each other your number one priority. One of the primary reasons couples fall out of love is that they just get too busy. They don't spend enough time together, they don't think about each other "in that way," they don't do all those things that they did when they were first falling in love, and they don't have fun together. Heck, they don't even have sex very often.

For this technology to work you must both make a pact that you will put your love at the top of the list. To turn this into a habit, you must actually make it item number one on your list of stuff to do each day. Otherwise, your relationship will turn into one of those faded old movies: it might be pretty good, but it lacks the sparkle, vitality, verve, and bright rainbow colors of life that caused you to fall in love way back when.

Each day, each week, or each month (depending on what you have agreed on together), you're going to have some ritual of recommitment to each other, and each day, you're going to put your love at the top of your to-do list. These two steps create the foundation of Love Play.

Step 3: Love

Step three is where the fun comes into the picture. You're poised to have your first recommitment ritual, and you're willing to put each other at the top of your to-do list as your number one priority. Now for the fun stuff: putting all this into action with real, tangible, and immediate results. The third step in Love Play Technology is to express your love to each other at least once a day, but in some fun, new, creative way.

You can share your love by appreciating each other, by giving notes, cards, or gifts, by doing a favor, running a bath, or creating some kind of surprise. Be thoughtful and attentive, and your Love Play will become an easy, enjoyable, daily habit. If your reaction is that this seems silly, think back. Was it silly when you were falling in love? No—it was fun, wasn't it?

Recommit-Prioritize-Love

The recommitment is a reminder that this is really important to you, prioritizing is so you will make it a daily event, and giving each other a little lovin' every day is the fun part, the part that will put the rainbow colors, the sparkle, and the play back into your daily lives.

You probably have some "I love you" habits that you share, like the quick "I love you" as you part in the morning. Keep doing them because they're part of the private rituals you've developed to make your relationship uniquely yours. But now add at least one fresh, new way to express your love each day. Make it a game, get creative, be playful, and have fun. You'll begin to focus on each other like when you fell in love way back when.

If you incorporate Love Play Technology into your daily lives, your relationship will be more fun, filled with bright rainbow colors, and definitely number one on your list of priorities.

ABOUT THE AUTHOR

Kara Oh is a speaker, workshop leader, and author of *Everlasting Love* (in which she introduces her Love Play Technology and offers lots of "I love you" ideas), *Men Made Easy*, *Women Made Easy*, and hundreds of articles on love, relationships, spirituality, and how to be happier and more fulfilled. You can find out more about Ms. Oh, her books, and her articles on her Web sites, HaveALifetimeOfLove.com, MenMadeEasy.com, HowToMakeAWomanHappy.com, and AliveWithLove.com. You can write to her at P.O. Box 21803, Santa Barbara, CA 93121, USA or at OhKara@AliveWithLove.com.

62

MEDITATION

Meditation—Cure of All Cures: The Magic Potion of the Soul

Crystal Dwyer

When I take on a new client in my practice as a life coach, I usually begin with a strategy of exploring what this individual's beliefs are about himself and his life. I then find out what the underlying daily thoughts are that support those beliefs. I always discover that whatever is showing up in this person's life, whether good or bad, is supported and perpetuated by these beliefs, the person's emotional responses, and the resulting actions they take or do not take each day based on these beliefs.

I have a number of exercises to help clients reveal to themselves some of the beliefs and values they hold that they may not even be aware of. I also utilize some wonderful therapies, such as hypnotherapy and Emotional Freedom Technique, to assist in clearing unproductive or destructive emotional beliefs and thought patterns from the body and mind.

Even with these wonderful techniques available for me to utilize, I must confess that the most important, lasting, and transformational support I can give to my clients is to teach them and encourage them to learn meditation and to practice it daily. Meditation is a beautiful and peaceful journey to the stillness within. When you quiet the mind and enter the silence of your own soul through meditation, you experience a restful vacation from the things that don't necessarily serve you much of the time.

The constant barrage of worrying, planning, rushing, and fretting that most of us deal with in heavy doses on a daily basis is the very thing that raises our stress levels to a point of compromising our immune function and overwhelming us mentally and emotionally. The societal expectations we have to produce and perform and to be successful at all things can, at times, take us to the breaking point physically, mentally, and emotionally.

Being in a state of meditation allows you to transcend the distractions of thoughts, emotions, and physical pain. Meditation allows you to go beyond into a state of just being. It is in this state of pure being that you access your higher self and connect to a universal flow of knowing and intellect. In this meditative state you begin to experience the infinite possibilities of all that you are. By setting simple intentions before your meditation, you truly can begin to activate those possibilities. As you practice meditation more, the results in your life begin to seem truly miraculous.

It is said that Leonardo da Vinci, William Shakespeare, and Albert Einstein all practiced a type of meditation. These brilliant people and many others discovered, through their practice of quieting the mind, the vehicle to the greatest self and the highest wisdom. This vehicle was not just available to them; it is available to all of us. Following are five simple steps that will get you started in your practice of meditation.

1. Choose a quiet space in which you can regularly meditate. It doesn't have to be an entire room. You can play soft music or light a candle—whatever gets you in a relaxed mood.
2. Sit comfortably. If you aren't comfortable sitting on the floor with your legs crossed, sitting in a chair with your feet on the floor is perfectly fine. Sit with a straight spine, your head even and your eyes closed.
3. Begin with three deep, cleansing breaths, breathing all the way down to the base of the spine, breathing in through the nose and out through the mouth. Then begin to breathe normally.
4. Start to let go of all thoughts by focusing on the inflow and outflow of the breath or by repeating, silently, a simple mantra over and over. The mantra could be something like "I am healed," "I am whole," or "peace." When a thought pops into your head, put your attention back on your breath or the mantra. Make sure you don't focus on the meaning of the mantra because that becomes a thought.
5. Try to practice your meditation regularly. Twice a day is very beneficial— once in the morning and once in the late afternoon or evening. One half hour per session is ideal, but even if you can only work fifteen minutes, each time, into your day, you will still enjoy wonderful benefits.

Meditation is done in a deeply relaxed state, allowing the entire body, and all of its functions, a vacation from stress. When you meditate, it is like taking a cleansing, refreshing plunge into a peaceful, boundless pool of awareness. You emerge cleansed of chaos and invigorated with a clear, pure perspective. The benefits of meditation range from better health, happiness, and awareness to experiencing pure bliss. Let meditation put you in touch with the unlimited potential that is already within you.

May you have great success in your transformation through meditation.

ABOUT THE AUTHOR

Crystal Dwyer is a highly skilled practitioner of transformational life coaching and a board-certified hypnotherapist. She has her own unique program utilizing the powerful tools of hypnotherapy, Emotional Freedom Technique, and meditation. By using these amazing techniques, she is able to assist her clients in overcoming the obstacles that keep them from being their best. With grace and humor she helps people move forward to create more of what they desire out of life. For more information about transforming any area of your life, visit her Web site at http://www.crystaldwyer.com, or contact her at crystalinphx@cox.net or (602) 343–1402.

63

Memory and Learning

Brian E. Walsh

Remembering is the storing and recalling of memories. It's a biological process that involves dedicated brain structures. When a memory is encoded, it is dismembered and handed off to different parts of the brain for storage. Getting all these pieces back together is an inaccurate process. Hence *re*-membering is not perfect. Knowing that memories are formed in different categories, and that they move between categories, can help in developing strategies for improving memory and learning.

Utilize Memory Organization

There are two broad categories of memory—nonconscious and conscious—and each has subcategories.

- **Nonconscious implicit memory** automatically stores experience and concepts and plays a role unconsciously in affecting perception and behavior. These memories are the basis for forming an individual's view of society and his or her place in it.
- **Nonconscious muscle memory** plays a role in the mechanical execution of a series of motions, as in riding a bike or playing a musical instrument, learned through repetition over time.
- **Conscious short-term memory** is the working memory. It's a place for stuff that you need to hang on to for only a short time. Maintaining information for only a few seconds, it enables us to remember a current thought, and so, for instance, take part in a conversation, keep a lecture in context as it progresses, or maintain the thread of a story or movie.

- **Conscious long-term memory,** although stored in our unconscious mind, is memory of the events and facts that we can consciously recall and verbally describe. It includes that of words, symbols, and general knowledge about our perception of the workings of the world.

The brain links information unconsciously, and you can intentionally help to maximize this effect. As you perceive new input, match it as best as possible to material already in your memory by using images, sounds, key words, and concept maps. A vital ingredient for memory is reviewing, and it is effective only when done at specific times after absorbing the information, say, for instance, after one hour, one day, one week, and six months.

Manage Stress for Enhanced Learning

It is the management of emotions that gives learners greater command over their learning. Overwhelming stress has a detrimental effect. Researchers have evidence that high stress experienced by a pregnant woman can distress the fetus, resulting in learning difficulties for the child later in life. Among infants and toddlers, high and chronic levels of stress can make learning more difficult, perhaps even shrinking the part of the brain associated with memory.

Traumatic events and enduring stress can take a toll on a person's physical and psychological health. The memory and accompanying negative emotions of a stressful incident or condition, at any point in life, can lay dormant for many years. When triggered by some later stressful event, they can evoke negative beliefs, desires, fantasies, compulsions, obsessions, addictions, or dissociations. This toxic brew can inhibit learning and memory and generally fracture human wholeness. Unless the person feels emotionally secure, it is almost impossible for the "thinking" parts of the brain (neocortex and frontal lobes) to function effectively. The metaphor I like to use is that of a clear pool of water with silt resting on the bottom. Imagine a bunch of kids getting into the pool and disturbing the silt. The pool will no longer be clear.

How can we overcome this condition? Here are a couple of suggestions. Take three slow, deep belly breaths. This has an immediate effect of slowing down the physiology and putting you back in balance. Another way to bring calm and balance to a stressful circumstance is to disassociate by imagining yourself in a helicopter, looking down at "you" in your situation. This perspective tends to remove emotion from the mix, and the perspective provides clarity.

Maximize Primacy and Recency Events

Imagine that I recite to you a list of 30 items. I then ask you to write them down after I finish. You would remember things that are:

- at the beginning of the list
- unusual
- repeated
- at the end of the list.

The remembering of the first and last items is helped by what is known, respectively, as their *primacy* and *recency*. Every study session has primacy and recency opportunities. If you study for one hour, then take a break, you get one of each. If you study for 25 minutes, take a short break, then study another 25 minutes, you get double the primacy and recency events. How great is that?

Stay Hydrated

If you are dehydrated by only five percent, your cognitive abilities are reduced by 30 percent. Of course, you may not notice this since it happens so gradually. Dehydration not only causes fuzzy thinking, but it is also a major cause of fatigue. When I begin a workshop, I ask everyone to drink some water and then take three deep belly breaths. The moisture coats the air sacs and enables more oxygen to enter the blood. The three breaths take this fresh, oxygenated blood directly to the brain.

ABOUT THE AUTHOR

Brian E. Walsh, PhD, author of the best seller *Unleashing Your Brilliance*, is an international speaker based on Canada's west coast. He completed a 30-year corporate career by heading up his company's China operation in Beijing. He has also lived in Canada's Arctic, where he served as a Justice of the Peace. He holds a commerce degree and a PhD in clinical hypnotherapy. His training includes detoxification acupuncture, Emotional Freedom Technique (EFT), and neuro-linguistic programming (NLP). Visit Brian's Web site at http://www.UnleashingBrilliance.com.

64

MISCONCEPTIONS

Things Are Not Always as They Seem

Barbara McRae

I'd like to share with you a story that my spiritual teacher and dearest friend told me. Once upon a time, there were two seekers of enlightenment climbing in the Himalayas. One seemed more surefooted and climbed at a faster speed. He was conflicted about whether to wait for his friend to catch up or to keep going at his own pace. Finally, he decided to continue without his friend, journeying in a way that felt natural for him and allowing his friend to do the same.

It was a long and arduous trip to the top of the mountain, the home of the Enlightened One. When the faster climber finally arrived, he was granted a meeting with the wise master. He was very pleased with himself and hoped that his friend would have the same opportunity one day. Soon he was in the master's presence. He bowed respectfully, and when he looked up at the Enlightened One, he was amazed to see the face of the friend who had been left behind! Things are not always as they seem.

Everything That Occurs Is Perfect, Even If It Doesn't Appear to be Perfect

The story clearly illustrates how we make assumptions about the paths that others take and how we really don't have all the information—we just think we do. Every step we take is just perfect as it is. Each of us has our own path and expression. We have our own timing. We are each responsible for ourselves and no other.

By shifting our focus to what others are doing, we inhibit our growth. It's important to listen to inner guidance and honor the path within each of us so that we don't get in our own way. Refrain from being concerned about the progress or lack of progress that others seem to be making. If we had the Big Picture, we would see how each person is contributing to the whole (even someone who acts like Attila the Hun!).

I'm reminded of an incident that enraged one of my clients. Erin is a conservationist and values all life. She loves the outdoors and tends her garden faithfully. One morning, at 5:30, her sleep was cut short by loud noises coming from a neighbor's backyard. She looked out the bedroom window and couldn't believe her eyes. A row of 30-year-old elm trees was being chopped down, leaving unsightly stumps near her property line. Many of the cut limbs dropped on her side of the fence.

Erin couldn't understand how anyone could butcher those beautiful trees. Her neighbor never gave any indication of his intent and had made no arrangements to clear the limbs from Erin's property. My client's first reaction was to rant at her neighbor. But she resisted. On a deeper level she knew this action would just fuel the fire and could turn into a nasty feud. (She has learned that what goes around, comes around.) Yet she was struggling with her emotions. Every time she stepped into her garden, she was reminded of this brutal act. She felt that her peaceful haven had been violated.

Erin realized that she is not a vengeful person and that the trees were gone and nothing she said or did would change that fact. She took the high road, allowing herself time to privately vent and grieve, and finally she came to the state of acceptance.

Accepting the Actions of Others Restores Balance

Getting to acceptance of an incomprehensible, hurtful situation requires wisdom and strength. It is when we accept the behavior of the other—without judging or condemning it—that we contribute to balancing these harmful energies. So, rather than focusing on what the other has done, we need to handle our own violent thoughts. As we do, others will adopt this new behavior for themselves.

Research has determined that once critical mass is reached, others can easily tap into it and make a similar choice. In our example, when sufficient individuals match Erin's behavior pattern of transforming thoughts of violence and destruction, others benefit. We are all part of a process, spreading "idea seeds" affecting each other throughout our culture. Whether we realize it or not, our thoughts, emotions, and behaviors can pervade an entire group.

Everything that happens is perfect, although it may not appear so at first glance. We don't have all the answers, but a grander purpose of the tree-cutting incident may have been to allow Erin an opportunity to recognize her violent reaction, learn to balance the volcanic eruption within herself, and thereby contribute a peaceful resolution to the world. This illustrates how each of us can take responsibility and make a difference.

About a month later, the same neighbor placed his home up for sale. Erin believes that she may have contributed to this event. By making the choice to let go of her anguish and substituting peaceful behavior, she was no longer emotionally stuck to this person. Maybe an opening was created for a new, more like-minded neighbor to move in. Stranger things have happened. Be open to the concept that things are rarely as they seem.

Consider the notion that there may be hidden meaning in all events and that these events cause you to evolve. When conventional thinking prevents your understanding of a situation, elevate your point of view. See with the eyes of your soul, not your ego.

This material is excerpted from *More Drama, Less Fun—Your Roadmap to Personal Freedom.*

<u>ABOUT THE AUTHOR</u>

Barbara McRae, MCC, is a nationally known Master Certified Coach, a best-selling author, and an internationally syndicated columnist. Barbara is a recognized expert in professional coaching, as profiled in *BusinessWeek* magazine, *USA Today*, and *The New York Times*. She coaches remotely via telephone, facilitates workshops, and has been featured in various media outlets, including radio, TV, national magazines, and newspapers. She is the author of *Less Drama, More Fun*. For free assessments and resources, visit http://www.enhancedlife.com.

65

MISTAKES

Mistake Salad

Alan Cohen

A mother seeking to inspire her young son to progress with his piano lessons took him to a concert by the famed virtuoso Ignacy Paderewski. After the two took their seats, mom noticed a friend a few aisles away and went to chat with her.

When mother returned, she discovered her son was missing from his seat. She began to search for him, but he was nowhere to be found. Suddenly the house lights dimmed, the curtains parted, and a spotlight shined on the gleaming Steinway piano on stage.

There, to the woman's horror, she saw her little boy sitting at the keyboard, innocently picking out the notes to "Twinkle, Twinkle Little Star."

Embarrassed beyond words, she began to rush to the stage to retrieve her mischievous little musician. Before she could get there, however, the great piano master emerged from a stage wing and approached the child. Paderewski leaned over and whispered in the boy's ear, "Keep playing." Then he reached his arms around the boy's and added a bass part with his left hand. With his right hand Paderewski improvised a running obbligato. Together, the seasoned master and the young novice turned a potential disaster into a triumph that inspired everyone.

Are you so sure your mistakes are just mistakes? Or could they be building blocks to a success beyond any you imagined?

When my friend Dorothy goes home to visit her family each Thanksgiving, her mother serves the traditional "mistake salad." The dish was born many years ago, Dorothy explains, when mother was using a cookbook to make a salad. In the process, mother accidentally included half the salad ingredients from a recipe on the left side of the open cookbook and half the ingredients from a different salad recipe on the opposite page. Everyone enjoyed the salad so much that she continued to serve it every year. So it was really no mistake at all.

Then there was the fellow named Alfred, who invented dynamite. When Alfred's brother died, the city newspaper confused the two and printed an obituary noting that the deceased's most notable act was the creation of the explosive, subsequently adapted to manufacture bombs. Stunned to consider that his name would forever be associated with destruction, Alfred sought to leave a more positive legacy to humanity. So he instituted a prize for people who contributed to world peace. Now the Nobel Prize, established by Alfred Nobel, is the most coveted and respected award in the world.

Everything is part of something bigger, and mistakes are no exception. Every minus is half of a plus, waiting for a stroke of vertical awareness. In his brilliant book *Illusions*, Richard Bach explains that every problem comes to you with a gift in its hands. If you focus only on what went wrong, you miss the gift. If you are willing to look deeper and ask for the insight, the problem dissipates, you are left only with the learning, and you advance on your path.

Gallup conducted a poll asking people what was the worst thing that ever happened to them. Then the pollsters asked the same people what was the best thing that ever happened to them. The surveyors found an 80% correlation between the worst and best experiences. Four out of five people reported that the worst thing that ever happened to them turned out to be the best.

A Course in Miracles tells us, "It takes great learning to understand that all things, events, encounters and circumstances are helpful." The Course also notes that trust is the bedrock of a true master's belief system. Trust implies faith that there is a wiser plan afoot than the one that meets the eye. Only the inner eye, the insight of higher wisdom, can make sense out of apparent human error.

We all make mistakes, and plenty of them. Enlightenment does not ask you to be perfect; it simply asks you to be open to a bigger picture that embraces your humanity while rising above it. True perfection has space for imperfection. Think of your life as a grand mosaic. When you examine your acts with a magnifying glass, you see many flaws. Step back, and you discover that every little piece has an important place in a grander design. It is our belief in mistakes, and dwelling upon them, that makes them seem more real than eternal love.

Within you is a child who wriggles off into unacceptable places. Also within you is a Paderewski, a master who knows how to transform child's play into a masterpiece. You can regret your errors, and those of others, or you can honor them. At the very least, mistakes are opportunities to practice forgiveness. At the most, they are invitations to acknowledge perfection. Ultimately, real forgiveness means seeing good where others find fault. A friend is someone who sees through you and still enjoys the view. You become your own best friend when you do the same.

Salad, anyone?

ABOUT THE AUTHOR

Alan Cohen, MA, is the author of 20 best-selling inspirational books and tapes, including *The Dragon Doesn't Live Here Anymore* and the award-winning *A Deep Breath of Life*. He is a contributing writer for the *New York Times* best-selling series Chicken Soup for the Soul. Alan's syndicated column, "From the Heart," appears in new thought magazines internationally.

66

Understanding Your Relationship with Money

Anne Hartley

Whenever we say that we want more money, less debt, or more possessions, what we are really saying is that we want a feeling. Money and possessions have no power. Power comes from the feeling we get from having money and possessions. In order to determine your money values, you need to determine what feelings are most important to you. If you want to have a lot of money so that you can do what you like, when you like, you're seeking a feeling of *freedom*—this is your value. If you want to live in a beautiful home and live an affluent lifestyle, then you want to feel *prosperous*. If you want to know that there will always be enough money to pay the bills, retire in peace, and know you'll never have to worry about money again, you want to feel *secure*.

Recently, I moved into an old home, which I intend to renovate. My house has a very old but functional kitchen, which I don't like much but which I know I can live with for a while. This old kitchen has turned out to be one of life's blessings in disguise as I've learned quite a lot about money values from it.

When my eldest daughter, Lisa, first saw the kitchen, she said, "The first thing you have to get rid of is that kitchen." Lisa likes nice things and doesn't like to wait for them. My youngest daughter, Laura, is more security conscious, hates spending money, and likes to save, and she said, "There is nothing wrong with that kitchen. Why would you want to change it?"

The kitchen evoked three different responses in three different people, and that's the way it is with money. We are all different, and how we earn, manage, spend, save, and invest our money depends on our money values. The key to achieving your financial goals and living a life you love is to know your money values, then find a way to manage your money that respects these values.

Once I realized that my kitchen was a gauge for assessing money values, I decided to make the most of it. I started listening to what people were really telling me about their money values when they made any comments. A carpenter commented, "Nice kitchen." When I asked him if he was being sarcastic, he looked genuinely surprised, and I learned from subsequent conversations that he is very security conscious. When my former secretary, Lisa, came to visit and said, "Good size kitchen," I recognized this statement for what it was—a nice, neutral comment that was more about politeness than real feelings. So when I said that I disliked it and intended replacing it, she said, "Well, I didn't want to be rude by commenting on it." Another friend said, "Don't worry about the inside, what's important is to get the outside of the house looking good first."

What all these people told me is how they feel about money and what is most important to them. The most common money values are freedom, prosperity, and security. Although it is important to honor your money values, it is equally important how you do this. When you pursue a feeling to the exclusion of all else, you may find yourself in financial difficulties.

It would be easy to assume that everybody with the same money values has the same need, but they don't. One person's desire for freedom may mean that he simply cannot work for an employer, while another person may be quite happy working for an employer provided he is not tied down by financial responsibilities. One person may want more money so he can do what he likes, while another may not care about money but wants the freedom to be creative.

To discover your own money values, ask yourself these questions: If I was really happy and money was no object, what type of home would I live in? Who would I live with? Where would I live? What work would I do? What would I do with my leisure time? Who would I share my leisure time with? What would I look like? When making your choices, write down everything you think, and don't discount an idea because it seems too grand or too small. Once you've completed this exercise, look to see if one value is more dominant than any other. This is the value that you need to honor in a responsible way. Usually, one value will stand out, but this isn't always the case—some people can have two values that are equally important to them, and in this case you need to honor both values.

All money values have a positive side and a negative side, and learning to balance the two is the key to success. There's a lot we can learn from security conscious people because they are good with money. On the negative side, though, they can be overly cautious and as a result miss out on opportunities. In contrast, if you value prosperity, you know what's important to you, and quite simply, beauty is something that makes you happy. However, this needs to be balanced with being responsible and making choices that are going to help you over the longer term.

Whatever your money values, there is always a way to earn, manage, and achieve goals in a way that honors what's most important to you. If you are in a relationship with a partner who has different money values than you, you have an opportunity to learn, grow, and prosper. Couples with differing money values who work together are often the most financially successful because they balance each other. Sometimes, in a relationship, one person gives his power away to his partner, giving up his own desires for the sake of harmony. In an equal relationship, both parties have an equal say. If your partner refuses to respect your needs or to take responsibility for himself, then you need to look at what opportunity your relationship is presenting you with. You may need to love and respect yourself more. You do this by setting standards and letting other people know what you will and will not do.

You also need to be aware that if you are not prepared to change your behavior in any way, and that applies to the really extravagant as well as to the extremely security conscious, what is behind your behavior is fear. In this case, money problems are just a symptom of a deeper issue that needs to be dealt with.

Your money values hold the key to financial freedom, so rather than cursing money, start loving it, and look for the gift in your current situation.

ABOUT THE AUTHOR

Anne Hartley is the author of four books: *Love the Life You Live, Life Lessons, Love Your Money, Love Your Life*, and *The Psychology of Money*. Anne works as a life coach and trains others to be life coaches using her values-based approach. She lives and works on the northern beaches of Sydney, Australia, and coaches and trains students by phone anywhere in the world. If you would like to receive her free newsletter, you can visit Anne's Web site at http://www.hartlifecoaching.com.au, or write to Anne at P.O. Box 769, Mona Vale, NSW 2103, Australia.

67

The Bowl of Light

Sally K. O'Brien

I am going to be a first-time grandmother in August. I'm ecstatic about having my first grandchild. One of the first things I will share with my grandson or granddaughter is the "Bowl of Light" story that I learned when I was an *alakai*, advanced student, of Ho'o pono Pono in Hawaii. My *kumu*, teacher, said Pali Jae Lee and Koko Willis's book *Tales from the Night Rainbow* is an excellent, authentic source for this story and so many others.

In ancient times, in Hawaii and throughout the world, each child born was said to have a Bowl of Perfect Light. If the child was taught to respect and love his or her light, the child would grow in strength and health and could swim with the sharks, fly with the birds, and know and understand all things.

If, however, the child got into *pilikia*, trouble, with thoughts of fear, worry, doubt, judgment, anger, resentment, envy, or jealousy, he or she would drop a stone into the Bowl of Light, and then some of the light would go out because light and stone cannot occupy the same space.

If the child continued to get stones in the bowl, the light would eventually go out, and the child would become a stone. Just like a stone, the child would no longer grow, nor was he or she capable of movement. However, as soon as the child tired of being a stone, all that was needed was to do *kalana*, forgive this aspect of himself or herself, and turn the bowl upside down to let the stones fall out. All the light could then shine again and grow even brighter than before.

This was the way the ancient Hawaiian *kupuna*, grandparents and elders, took care of their *mo'opuna*, grandchildren. They would give them a bowl each morning, and at the end of the day they would call their grandchildren to their sides and look at how many stones were in their bowls. If it had been a good day, just one or two stones in a bowl, the child was told to simply turn the bowl over. Yet if the bowl was filled with stones, then in addition to turning the bowl over, the child would be told to go into the ocean and wash away all thoughts from the day.

You can apply some strategies from the Bowl of Light concept in order to improve your own life. First, select a bowl—wooden, ceramic, or any vessel that is pleasing to your eye and that will represent your Perfect Light. Next, choose some stones from a store or the beach, or perhaps some rocks from nature. These will represent the thoughts, feelings, and behaviors you know are negative. Then experiment for one day: live in the moment, and become conscious of your thoughts, feelings, and communication with your friends, family, coworkers, customers, and so forth.

For example, if you encounter an aggressive driver on your daily commute, do you take a deep breath and relax, or do you become angry and resentful? If you experience less than satisfactory customer service in a busy store, do you find yourself silently judging or criticizing, or do you remain calm and not become upset?

If you're not physically able to place a stone or rock in the bowl, you can imagine yourself placing a stone into your bowl as you observe yourself during the day. Finally, at the end of the day, you might arrange to give yourself a quiet, private time to go over each of the stones or rocks you have physically or mentally placed in your bowl.

As you caress or touch each stone, reflect on the significance of each of the stones and physically wash them in water to symbolically cleanse them. Ask yourself the following questions: Did that thought deserve a stone? Am I worried, doubtful, jealous, judgmental, fearful, envious, resentful, or angry about that situation? How might I see it differently and choose a better response the next time I'm experiencing something similar?

Now you can forgive the individuals who hurt your feelings and then forgive yourself for your reaction. Last, dump the bowl over, and let the stones pour out. If you find that one-day experience was beneficial, notice and observe how your reactions and behaviors change after using the bowl and stones for 30 days. You might even choose to log or journal each day and celebrate your little victories as you master and let go and surrender to seeing or hearing differently a situation that in the past would have given you a stone in your bowl.

Another suggestion is to create a chart that records how many stones you had each day. Celebrate when you find five stones or less to empty from your bowl at the end of the day. You might even find yourself singing the African American spiritual "This Little Light of Mine," as I do when I want to feel empowered. I'm looking forward to teaching my grandchildren that song, in the same way the ancient Hawaiians left spoken legacies for their descendents.

I will tell my beloved grandchild this: many days I find I need to change, to make a better choice in the moment, so I pick up my bowl, turn it upside down, and let the stones roll out. I start over again so the Perfect Light I am can shine even brighter.

ABOUT THE AUTHOR

Sally K. O'Brien has a master's degree in speech and for 19 years has been a professional teacher, author, speaker, trainer, and life coach. She's been a Reiki Master for 10 years and offers tele-seminars for life coaching, memoir writing, and Reiki distant energy healing at http://www.sallykobrien.com. Since moving to Grays Harbor in 2003, Sally has focused on Reiki level trainings, individual-client Reiki sessions, and special memoir writing workshops for women at her location on the beautiful Pacific Ocean. Her spiritual memoir, *Love Offerings to the Universe*, is available on her Web site and on Amazon.com.

68

The Question Is Not How Smart You Are; Rather, It's How You Are Smart

David Lazear

Scientific research has shown we all have within us multiple ways of knowing, learning, and processing information. Yes, we are all smart in a lot of different ways nobody ever told us about, especially when we were in school!

Here's the real issue, and it deeply concerns me: *we've been lied to about our intelligence!* We've been given some very inaccurate and frankly dangerous information about our intelligence and what makes us smart. And most of us bought all or part of these lies!

So What is the *Truth*?

New research is in that calls into question almost everything we used to think about human intelligence.

1. **Intelligence is not fixed at birth!** In the past we thought our intelligence was a matter of heredity and that it could be measured through different tests that would tell us our intelligence quotient (IQ). However, these tests do not take into account the many different environmental and cultural factors that affect the development of our intellectual capabilities. *We are all much more than our IQ ever gives us credit for!*
2. **Intelligence can be taught, learned, and improved!** Because our intelligence capabilities are part of our biology and neurology at birth, *they can be strengthened and enhanced at any age and almost any ability level!*

3. **We are smart in many ways, not just one!** There are at least eight ways we're intelligent, eight ways we know what we know, understand, gain knowledge, and learn. *The eight intelligences are already in us!*

What Are the Eight Kinds of Smart?

- **ImageSmart** (*visual-spatial intelligence*)—uses the sense of sight and being able to imagine and visualize an object, including making mental images inside the head.
- **LogicSmart** (*logical-mathematical intelligence*)—uses numbers, logic, scientific reasoning, and calculating to help solve problems and meet challenges.
- **WordSmart** (*verbal-linguistic intelligence*)—occurs through written and spoken words, such as in essays, speeches, books, informal conversation, debates, and jokes.
- **BodySmart** (*bodily-kinesthetic intelligence*)—uses physical movement and performance (aka learning by doing) to understand.
- **SoundSmart** (*musical-rhythmic intelligence*)—learns through sounds, rhythms, tones, beats, music produced by other people or present in the environment.
- **NatureSmart** (*naturalist intelligence*)—the knowing that occurs in encounters with animals, plants, physical features, and weather conditions of the natural world.
- **PeopleSmart** (*interpersonal intelligence*)—uses person-to-person relating, communication, teamwork, and collaboration with others.
- **SelfSmart** (*intrapersonal intelligence*)—the knowing which comes from introspection, self-reflection, and raising questions about life's meaning and purpose.

How do you awaken, stimulate, or otherwise activate an intelligence? Following is a set of miniexercises, puzzles, and games you can use to "trigger" your intelligences and make them part of your daily experience.

Tips to awaken your ImageSmart

1. Work with "artistic media" (such as clay, paints, colored markers, and pens) to express an idea or opinion, for example, what you think the year 2050 will be like.
2. Do intentional daydreaming; for example, dream about the ideal vacation spot with as much visual detail as you can muster.

3. Practice internal imagination exercises—visualize yourself in a different period of history, or have an imaginary conversation with a character from literature or history.

Tips to awaken your LogicSmart

1. Practice analytical thinking by comparing and contrasting two objects.
2. Create a convincing, rational explanation for something that is totally absurd, for example, the benefits of the square basketball.
3. Participate in a project requiring the use of the "scientific method." If you are not a cook, try making brownies from scratch following a recipe.

Tips to awaken your WordSmart

1. Read a story you enjoy, and write your own sequel.
2. Learn the meaning of one interesting, new word each day, and practice using it during the day in conversation.
3. Make a speech on a topic about which you have a great deal of interest and excitement.

Tips to awaken your BodySmart

1. Perform a dramatic enactment. Play charades using current events or modern inventions.
2. Practice activities that require physical activity such as folk dancing, jogging, swimming, and walking. Try walking in different ways to match or change your mood.
3. Carefully observe yourself involved in everyday physical tasks such as shoveling snow, mowing grass, washing dishes, or fixing your car to become more aware of what your body knows and how it functions.

Tips to awaken your SoundSmart

1. Listen to different kinds of music to shift your mood; for example, play relaxing, instrumental music before or during a potentially stressful or anxiety-producing activity.
2. Use singing to express an idea.
3. Hum to create different kinds of vibrations inside of your head; for example, try the vowels one at a time, using different volumes and pitches.

Tips to awaken your NatureSmart

1. Get involved in a planting project either in your own home or somewhere in your community.
2. Spend some time with an animal. Allow yourself to really "get to know" this fellow creature. Imagine it has human qualities—what is it thinking? feeling? wanting?
3. Go for a walk, and consciously focus on the impact of the environment on your five senses, on your emotions, and on your spiritual awareness. See how fully you can experience the walk!

Tips to awaken your PeopleSmart

1. Get into different structured situations in which reliance on other people is required for the successful completion of a project.
2. Practice listening deeply and fully to another person. Cut off the "mind chatter" that often occurs when you are listening to someone else talk, and stay focused only on what he or she is saying.
3. Try to guess what someone else is thinking or feeling based on various nonverbal clues, then check your accuracy with that person.

Tips to awaken your SelfSmart

1. In the midst of a routine activity, practice acute mindfulness, that is, an intense awareness of everything going on, your thoughts, feelings, physical movements, and inner states of being.
2. Practice watching your thoughts, feelings, and moods as if you were a detached, outside observer. Notice patterns that kick into gear in certain situations, for example, the "anger pattern," the "playfulness pattern," or the "anxiety pattern."
3. In 25 words or fewer, write your answer today for the question "who am I?" Keep working on it until you are satisfied. Look at it again each day for a week, making revisions that you feel are needed.

I promise you that the more you call on your innate intelligence potentials, the more they will become a regular part of how you live your daily life. After a while, almost without thinking, you'll find you are automatically "cooking on more burners" simultaneously. To keep all *Eight Kinds of Smart* fully awake and ready to help you think, learn, and work smarter, exercise them every day!

ABOUT THE AUTHOR

David Lazear inspires and empowers people to awaken their full intelligence. He translated Howard Gardner's research on multiple intelligences into life-changing practice! David is the best-selling author of 10 books on applications of multiple intelligences and has over 30 years of international experience in the development of human capacities in both the public and private sectors. Each year, he conducts hundreds of workshops for business and educational organizations. He is the founder of the David Lazear Group, which specializes in programs, printed resources, and media that demonstrate the how-tos of applied multiple intelligences. Visit his Web site at http://www.DavidLazear.com.

69

NEEDINESS

Is Neediness Ruining Your Relationships?

John Gray

In a recent survey conducted at MarsVenus.com, "neediness"—clingy, controlling, possessive, and/or demanding behavior—was one of the most commonly cited reasons for ending a relationship. Dating couples are calling it quits because they feel they either cannot or do not want to please their partner! It's simply *too much work*! If you're a member of the dating world, and you are confused about why it isn't working for you, the answer lies in a better understanding of how the opposite sex thinks.

First, what qualifies as "needy"? In some cases a person may be considered needy if others are repeatedly unable to *make him or her happy*. In everyday conversations this person may be referred to as "high maintenance" or "difficult." Other attributes of a "needy" person are that he or she can be demanding, sometimes to the point of being rude or inconsiderate of others. He or she may also have a difficult time thinking of others or placing them first. Truly needy people desire to be the center of attention. Unfortunately, these qualities are not very appealing or attractive to someone searching for a mate.

Unfortunately, there are often times in a relationship when you may not get your needs met, and this can inspire "needy" behavior. Discussion board members at MarsVenus.com frequently mention feeling at the end of their ropes to get their needs met by their partner and the lengths they go to in order to be heard—everything from repeated calling and e-mailing, to conversations demanding to know where their partner was, and why he or she didn't call. *It really does not inspire a man or woman to hear your concerns when he or she feels he or she is being yelled at or stalked!*

While the behaviors just discussed sound a bit irrational, they are created when a seemingly healthy man or woman is unable to get what he or she wants from the relationship. We're here to tell you that there is another way. Men and women are not doomed to late night "drive bys" or stalker phone calls to find happiness in their relationships. The first and most important thing to understand is that men and women have different needs and therefore give to each other differently. Think of it this way: if your favorite meal is sushi, on some level, don't you think everyone must love sushi because you do? We expect on some level that if we want to be treated one way, our partners must want the same thing. But that assumption is a big mistake!

Both men and women have basic, primary needs. Women need to feel cared for, understood, and respected, and men need to feel trusted, accepted, and appreciated. One example of what happens in the real dating world is that women want to be called on a regular basis. When a man does this, it tells her that he *cares* about her. When he doesn't, it makes women feel *disrespected*. On the other hand, when a man doesn't call, he wants to be *accepted* for who he is and not made to be a "bad guy" for not calling. When a woman becomes angry or disappointed in him for not calling, he begins to feel like she doesn't *trust* that he's good enough for her, and his motivation to call diminishes even further.

Neediness is created when perfectly sane and normal people do not get their needs met, especially if they are genuinely interested in the person they're dating. Feeling powerless to change your partner's behavior and get what you want out of a relationship inspires the feelings and actions of a needy person. Someone who seemed like he or she was "relationship material" is suddenly unattractive and demanding.

If you have felt the ugly needy monster creeping into your dating life or current relationship, there are two possible obstacles in your way. One, you're dating or in a relationship with someone who is not aware of what you need and how to give it to you. There are specific ways to ask the opposite sex for what you need that *motivates* them to want to give it to you. You may simply not be asking for what you want in a way that your partner can clearly understand. Remember, men and women are different!

The other possibility is that your partner may not be motivated to meet your needs, and that may be a sign that the end is near. Relationships can be challenging at times, and we all have to find the energy to give to our partners, sometimes when we least feel like it. You would be surprised how easy it is to save a relationship as long as you act before it's too late.

If you're not sure which of these two issues is the real problem, it may help to get objective feedback. At MarsVenus.com, we have a Relationship Coaching Program that can help you identify your issues and show you exactly what to do to find a solution. For more info about this program, visit http://www.askmarsvenus.com/SG.

MarsVenus.com—remember, we're always here for you.

ABOUT THE AUTHOR

John Gray is the author of 15 best-selling books, including *Men Are from Mars, Women Are from Venus*, the number one best-selling relationship book of the last decade. In the past 10 years, over 30 million Mars and Venus books have been sold in over 40 languages throughout the world.

An expert in the field of communication, John Gray's focus is to help men and women understand, respect, and appreciate their differences in both personal and professional relationships. In his many books, CDs, DVDs, tapes, workshops, and seminars, he provides practical tools and insights to effectively manage stress and improve relationships at all stages and ages by creating the brain chemistry of health, happiness, and lasting romance.

Dr. John Gray has appeared on *Oprah*, *The Today Show*, *CBS Morning Show*, *Good Morning America*, *The View*, *Politically Incorrect*, *Larry King*, and others. He has been profiled in *Newsweek*, *Time*, *Forbes*, *USA Today*, *TV Guide*, *People*, and *New Age Journal*, among others.

Dr. Gray, a certified family therapist, is the premier Better Life relationship coach on AOL. In 2001, he received the Smart Marriages Impact Award.

John Gray lives with his wife and three children in northern California.

70

Harness the Power of Your Natural Negotiating Style

Dee McCrorey

Harness: To bring under control and direct the force
of something.

The first step people often take when honing their negotiating skills is to read an assortment of how-to books and attend a class or workshop. Mastering negotiations, however, requires a three-prong approach: learning the fundamentals of negotiating, understanding the tactics associated with successful outcomes, and developing a negotiating style that feels natural to you.

Your negotiating style is your calling card. When you develop a style from the inside out, your negotiating persona becomes more than a compilation of strategies, tips, and tactics.

Your negotiating style comprises four key areas.

Philosophy

A negotiating philosophy encompasses your belief system—your principles and social and personal values—the core of who you are as a person. It's what makes you tick.

What *type* of negotiator do you want to become? Are you interested in learning about the art of negotiating and effectively persuading others to take action by following your lead? Or, perhaps, you enjoy the spontaneous, creative process of negotiations as they unfold before your eyes. Maybe you prefer to become the power negotiator, where your research and planning result in big financial wins. It might even be a combination of all three.

What underlying motivations would you need to satisfy before calling a negotiating outcome a win-win situation? During negotiations we aim to satisfy our tangible and intangible needs. Tangible, or *formal*, needs are those we can see, touch, or somehow measure. This is not always about money, but more often than not, it is financially related. Intangible, or *psychic*, needs are those driven by emotional appeal or emotionally based results. A negotiator's formal and tangible needs contribute to his negotiating philosophy.

For example, you might find yourself negotiating with someone whose formal needs require that he stays within his budget. He will likely use language to this effect, such as asking about the bottom line, how your product could save him money, or why dealing with you would offer a better value to dealing with one of your competitors.

Although all of the above might suggest a tangible need, the last could suggest a psychic need as well. The word *value* in this case might literally refer to money, or it could represent the person's value system. Other value-related words to listen for include *principle*, *quality*, *trust*, and *credibility*.

Boundaries

Understanding your core philosophy allows you to explore your personal and professional boundaries. What boundaries do you consider negotiable, and which ones are not negotiable?

Negotiable boundaries provide you, or your counterpart, with flexibility when making decisions. We use the term *boundary* not in the context of limits, but in that of choices and consequences. Without clearly understanding your personal and professional boundaries you may find yourself expending far too much energy and effort in attempting to define them *during* negotiations. Your objective is to reach a mutually beneficial agreement based on smart, prepared, and skillful negotiating that leverage your Natural Negotiating Style™.

Nonnegotiable boundaries are typically value-driven and thereby make it difficult or even impossible to reach a compromise during negotiations. Given that we may not be aware of our own boundaries and are even less clear about the steps needed to understand those of a counterpart, nonnegotiable boundaries may be the most challenging to maneuver during negotiations.

For example, a personal negotiable boundary might be your need not to work late evenings because you value dinnertime with your family, but this need is flexible if your team is working on meeting a critical deadline. Your nonnegotiable boundaries might mean, though, that you never work weekends.

What will your response be if someone challenges one of your core nonnegotiable boundaries during negotiations? If your counterpart suggests an idea or solution that clearly goes against your personal ethics, what action will you take? Will you walk away? Are you comfortable addressing the boundary issue on the spot? Or will you tactfully shift negotiations in a different direction?

Social Style

What is your natural communication preference when negotiating? Do you prefer to work alone or in groups? How do you interact with others in a team setting? Do you feel the need to *position* yourself as leader, or do people naturally gravitate toward you in a leadership role?

Where do you "discover" your energy? Do you feel energized when you're around people or when you can surround yourself with numbers and data? Perhaps you like working alone as an individual contributor. Are you more comfortable in the speaker's role, or do you prefer listening to speaking?

Think about the last time you participated in a group setting where you didn't know anyone else in the room.

- Did you speak out of nervousness?
- Did you speak in order to position yourself?
- Did you listen on the sidelines and allow others to take the lead?
- Did you process information internally, expecting to discuss it later?

Was this behavior typical of your communication style, or was it an exception? If it was an exception, what made it so, and what were you *feeling* during your silence?

·

Leadership Style

Leadership begins with the self. Before we can lead others we need to understand what leadership looks and feels like for us. Are you comfortable shifting outside your comfort zone when conditions call for it?

Your leadership style determines how you approach and position yourself during negotiations. You might be the type of person who seeks out new people, situations, and changing conditions. This could translate to a Natural Negotiating Style™ that is both comfortable in dealing with unknowns during negotiations and that provides the ability to think on your feet in order to take advantage of unexpected opportunities.

Perhaps your leadership style is self-directed and your social style is more along the lines of someone who prefers to listen to the nuances of a conversation. You could build on these strengths to develop a style that allows you to listen on multiple levels during a conversation—a powerful negotiating skill—to what someone is both saying and *not* saying, for example, allowing you to uncover hidden agendas.

Summary

Playing to your strengths in developing your natural style should not come at the exclusion of developing other skills you will need to become a solid negotiator. There is not *one right way* nor *one path* in mastering negotiations. Over time you will add or swap out items in your negotiations toolbox, but by following this process, you will hone and harness the power of your Natural Negotiating Style™.

ABOUT THE AUTHOR

Dee McCrorey, innovation coach, trainer, and speaker, is founder and CEO of Risktaking for Success, LLC, a venture that works with corporate teams and individuals to design nimble entrepreneurial workplaces. Dee's winning-formula workshops and seminars provide corporate leaders and managers with a competitive edge, a process she'll capture in her ultimate guide for corporate entrepreneurs, scheduled for a fall 2006 publication. Her passion for investing in the next generation of leaders includes alliances with Women Unlimited, Inc. and TiE (Talent, Ideas, Enterprise), a global not-for-profit organization. You can visit her Web site at http://www.RisktakingforSuccess.com and her weblog at http://www.TheCorporateEntrepreneur.com.

71

Networking

Five Steps to Creating a World-Class Social Network in Any City

Alex Benzer

One of the secrets to success in life is having a web of friends and associates. I've moved around a fair amount in my life, and one thing that my friends have noticed is that I quickly get to know a large number of people within a short time after moving to a new city. In fact, it seems that I know more people within days of my arrival in a new city than most of my friends who have lived there for years.

How does this work? And how can you can learn and use this yourself? It certainly helps to have an outgoing personality. However, if you implement the following steps, you stand to get results in leaps and bounds beyond what you have been getting so far. The following protocol works especially well if you've just landed in a brand-new city, knowing hardly anyone at all. If you've lived someplace for a little while, you just have to pretend like you're a newcomer and implement the same steps.

Step 1: Have an attitude of openness and interest

First, it's important to internalize the key determinant of your social success: *an attitude of openness and interest.* People tend to find interested people interesting. If you show genuine interest in the people you meet, they tend to reciprocate by showing genuine interest in you. Also, an attitude of openness generally works better than one of "I wonder what I can get out of this person." If spiritual law says that the world tends to reflect your attitude back to you, then if you approach a person thinking how you can enrich the person's life, you tend to get that back in return.

Step 2: Honor all invitations

An invitation is an act of humility. Someone has opened his door and heart to you and has requested your company. Honor that. An invitation is a gift in an intangible form and should be treated with the same amount of reverence and consideration that a tangible gift merits.

Let me elaborate a little bit on what I mean by accepting all invitations. The event could be anything: a birthday party, a dinner, a baby shower, a professional networking event, a gallery opening, a free event, or a pay event. Show up. There will be times when you don't know the host very well. Show up. There will be times when the event seems a little too far away. Show up—you just never know who else is going to be there and what could happen. Get the machinery of fate in motion. At other times you may feel that you won't know many people at the event. That means you should *show up*—if you avoided meeting strangers, you'd stay in your living room for the rest of your life. Remember that there are only two kinds of people: friends and future friends. And if you said you would show up, *show up*, even if you don't fully feel like it at the last minute. Be impeccable with your word because your word is your honor.

Of course, there will be times when you have conflicts and can't attend the event, and that's acceptable. Decline politely, express your regrets, and do your best to attend the next event.

Step 3: Honor all contacts

Now that you've shown up, you'll speak to a variety of people. Some may not initially catch your attention. That's okay—honor the contact anyway. If you speak to someone, no matter how briefly, exchange contact information with that person, making sure to get his or her e-mail address. Each friend you make increases your potential for meeting even more people, so be inclusive. Nobody has enough friends, and you're no exception.

Step 4: Follow up on all contacts

Now you have e-mail addresses from a bunch of people. Most people wait until there's something pertinent to contact that person about. And 99 percent of the time, that means they will never contact that person again. Not you. You will send a note to all the people that you meet within 48 hours of meeting them. I prefer to do it the day after, just because that way I know I'm not missing anyone, and I'll remember them well. If you wait a week, you will usually forget entirely, and after that they may not remember who you are. So do it the next day. It doesn't have to be anything fancy—just say it was nice meeting them, mention something about your conversation, and close by saying that you look forward to keeping in touch.

Step 5: Give back

Now that you have accepted all these fabulous invitations, it's time to issue some of your own. The absolutely best way to do that is to host an event. You have compiled all the contacts you have made over the past few months into an e-mail list, and now you will send them all a witty invitation. For a big party I like to have at least 120 invitees (about a quarter will show up). For a dinner party I invite about 40 to get 10 guests. I like to throw my parties on a Saturday night to maximize attendance since many professionals are too tired to party on a Friday night. I recommend four weeks' advanced notice for your event (and two weeks at the absolute minimum). That way, people can block out that Saturday evening beforehand, and you get priority over any other events that may be going on that night.

Your party will be a reflection of who you are, so have a compelling *theme*. The more you make people dress up and do things for the event, the more compelling your event will be, and the more likely it will be that they will show up. An interesting aspect of human psychology is that the more effort people have to put in to attend your event, the more committed they will be to attending, and the more they will enjoy it once they show up. *Two* concurrent themes are even better than one. One of my most successful events was when guests were asked to dress in pajamas *and* bring a funny poem.

So be open, show up, meet, follow up, and give back. Like everything else in life, the more you participate and give, the more you can expect to meet new people and expand your social circle.

ABOUT THE AUTHOR

Dr. Alex Benzer is the author of *The Tao of Dating: The Thinking Man's Guide to Success With Women* and the companion booklets *The Tao of Sexual Mastery* and *The Tao of Social Networking*. His works blend Eastern wisdom and Western science to create spiritually oriented, practical guides to greater fulfillment and success. Dr. Benzer has degrees from Harvard, Cambridge, and UC San Diego School of Medicine and is a clinical hypnotherapist in Los Angeles. The aforementioned works are available at http://www.thetaoofdating.com. *The Tao of Dating* for women is expected in summer 2006. Dr. Benzer can be reached at ab@thetaoofdating.com

72

NEURO-LINGUISTIC PROGRAMMING

The Map is Not the Territory

Christoph Schertler

In NLP (neuro-linguistic programming) we talk about people's "maps of the world."

This term describes a person's unique experience of reality. A map is not reality itself, only a representation of it, just as a map of Yellowstone Park is not the park itself, but a two-dimensional simplification on a piece of paper that has enough information to enable a visitor to navigate through the park. Likewise, we humans create maps of the world around us that help us to function in our daily lives. These maps include all the necessary information and ground rules we need to master a given situation. A pilot has various "maps" related to flying a plane, such as knowledge about aviation, engineering, and weather patterns. These maps allow the pilot to fly a plane and make the right judgment when facing a wide variety of situations in the air. In the same way, spouses have maps regarding marriage, singers have maps regarding music, and so on. Our maps—a mixture of a compass and a measuring gauge—enable us to make sense of a situation and therefore are at the very core of our success in life.

Imagine you flew to a different continent and visited an exotic civilization, where the citizens yelled at each other to express affection and turned their backs on each other while communicating. If you judged this style of communicating by your maps for social interaction, it would appear to be dysfunctional, to say the least. You would be confused by such behavior, until someone told you the reasoning behind it. Why? Because you don't have the right map to make sense of this exotic civilization's social etiquette. Your map for successful communication and kindness includes eye contact, smiling, and moderate volume and voice tones as ground rules; yelling and turning your back on another conveys hostility on your map.

Sounds like a funny scenario to imagine, doesn't it? However, you do not have to fly to a faraway culture to find this kind of misunderstanding and confusion. All you have to do is find another human being, be it your spouse, friend, colleague, or teenage kid. The truth about us human beings is that we all have our own unique maps of the world, and as a result, we misunderstand each other. The way you see and judge a situation is unlikely to be seen and judged that way by others. Yes, a shared cultural background and similar life experiences do lead to similar maps, but even then, significant differences remain.

Life is a system of systems in which countless maps are connected to each other; we share maps as groups (nationality, culture, religion, language, supporting the same sports team, etc.) and at the same time have our individual maps (values, behaviors, beliefs, and personal history). Of course, the mixture of maps being so complex means that every person is unique in his or her perception of the world.

This complexity is what makes life so colorful . . . and challenging. It is also the recipe for success for reality TV shows like *Big Brother*, *Wife Swap*, or *Survivor*. By selecting people with different or openly conflicting maps and forcing them to spend time with each other in close proximity, quote-raising drama is guaranteed. Your family or office life might sometimes feel that way, too.

What can you do to get by in a world that is set up in such a way for conflict? One way is to try accepting that other people's maps are real to them, even if they don't make sense to you. You do not have to share their opinions, but try to demonstrate that you understand how the situation looks, sounds, and feels when experienced through their maps. Place yourself in their shoes, and you will begin to see their maps' perspectives. Ask yourself, "If I were that person and had that kind of map, how would I make sense of this situation?"

If you have no idea what other people's maps look like, you can ask them questions that bring forth the criteria by which they judge a situation, such as "what about this [situation, person, place] is important to you?" or "what does this mean to you?" or "what would your best outcome look like?" The more you learn about how they arrive at their conclusions, the more clearly will you understand their maps.

The next step is to demonstrate that you have an understanding of where they are coming from. You can do this by making comments or asking questions that indicate that you understand them. An easy way to do this is to backtrack other people's words and repeat what they have just said in nonjudgmental, nonmimicking ways, e.g., "It sounds to me like you feel that. . . ." "XYZ seems to be important to you." "I hear you saying. . . ." Try not to overdo it; otherwise, the conversation will seem unnatural and might irritate the person you are talking to. Another thing you can do to improve the quality of your communication is to ask the other person to clarify what exactly he or she means when using general terms, e.g. "What do you mean by XYZ." "Who are 'they'?" "You said this happened a while ago; can you be more specific?" Again, use this technique with care and when appropriate. Using such communication skills will demonstrate your ability to listen and your willingness to understand, which will increase your chances for a harmonious and productive conversation with that person.

Some of our maps are impoverished. Actually, most of them are. What do you know about indigenous tribes living in the Amazonian rain forest? If you are like most of us, not much. How about Bavarian folk dancing? Equity trading? Scuba diving? Maintaining friendships? Raising children? If you feel that one or more of your maps needs to be enriched, use your common sense to do it. If you want to enrich your maps regarding being a parent, read good books about good parenting, attend parenting classes, share your experiences with other parents and with schoolteachers, and spend more time with your kids (or children you are close to, if you haven't any children at the moment). Remember, there is no copyright on maps, so if you have a role model who exemplifies everything you value, by all means, analyze his map and make it your own.

There are over six billion people on this planet, and each one of us has a unique identity, values, beliefs, capabilities, and behaviors, all of which influence the type of map we create in order to make sense of the world around us. By becoming more aware of the maps you use to navigate through life and by respecting other people's maps, you can move toward improving your communication skills and becoming your greater self.

ABOUT THE AUTHOR

Christoph Schertler is a certified NLP Trainer/NLP Coach and feels passionate about empowering others. He has trained with some of the forerunners in the field of neuro-linguistic programming and has experienced how NLP transforms and enriches people's lives firsthand. He is currently working on growing his own NLP business, PEC—Personal Empowerment Coaching, LLC, based in southern California. If you are interested in PEC services or want to learn more about NLP, visit http://www.pecoaching.com and sign up for the free biweekly e-zine "NLP—The Secret Science of Self-Empowerment." All contact details can be found on the Web site.

73

ORDER

Boss It or Toss It?:
That Is the Question for Your Life

Anita Jefferson

Do you know where you are going? Do you know where life is guiding you? Are you plagued by stress? Are you happy? You can have a balanced, fulfilled, and happy life. The question for your life that uplifts and restores balance and happiness as your perpetual state of mind is, Do I *boss* or *toss*?

Making this powerful but simple choice—to *boss* or *toss*—makes all the difference. Whenever you are dealing with stressful or unsettling situations, you can choose to improve the state of your life. The choices you make affect your state of mind, regardless of whatever is happening in your life at present or has happened in the past. Learning how to control your reactions is one of the most powerful, positive, and productive choices you can make. You can train your emotions. You can control your reactions. You can choose what is beneficial for you without feeling guilty or selfish or ignoring the stressful precipitator.

When you choose to *boss* a situation, you are really saying that you are in charge of your reaction to it. Because you are choosing self-success, you begin to realize that you are the boss of your state of mind, regardless of how emotionally draining or how challenging the situation may be.

Let's use a common professional example to illustrate the point. You are asked to add another work task to your already demanding workload that you cannot refuse to do. A *boss* state of mind makes the choice to plan how to integrate this new task by considering options. Some options could be to divide the responsibilities with a coworker, link it to a current function, plan implementation strategies, or devise a timeline to get the task finished. The personal success strategy here is factoring in the available options that enrich the state of your mind instead of complaining, stalling, elevating the stress serotonin, or inviting other work-related consequences that could spiral beyond your control. When you decide to *boss* a situation, you are big on self-success and recognize the mature state of mind that is required for responsible living. In essence, you are choosing your own success route.

A *toss* it person is adaptable, too. If your life is like those of most modern-day multitaskers, your to-do list is filled with at least 10 to 25 things to finalize in a day or week. In order to function best as a multitasker so that you are not always overwhelmed and frustrated, tone down your pace of activity. Scientific study and enough reports and articles about health confirm the damaging effect of stress—increased weight, insomnia, hypertension, diabetes, anger, snappiness, suicide, and strokes or other cardiac problems are known results of accelerated rates of stress. However, when you learn to *toss* in your life, you gain control over these ill effects by minimizing your stressors.

Plan better. Rather than stress about the frenzied pace of life, add balance to your list. Add things that create calm, rest, or relaxation. It is not necessary to plan just stress-inducing activities; plug into your list ways you can tap into your inner peace by rewarding your diligence in intervals. Take time to pause. Pace the frenzy. For instance, it may be that four of the things you need to do are in the same area—simply group them together so that you can get four things quickly checked off your list, then allow yourself to sit quietly for a few minutes right where you are and breathe in a relaxed rhythm rather than immediately rushing off to do the next thing on your list. Another way to turn off your stress sensors is to connect with something active that you love and that brings needed relief. Rather than putting off exercising, woodworking, gardening, or aerobic dance by adding them to the end of your task list, move these things up, and intersperse them into your habits or routine so that you add balance and give yourself a mental and physical break. Deliberately escape the rat race. This will in itself ease tension and recharge your energy. Then you can bounce back to the other things on your list with enthusiasm. With a mind that is not overengaged, you may even discover new loves or passions.

Make the choice. Dealing with choices is productive. At first you may battle with the effort, thinking it is a waste of time or that you aren't really getting anywhere. Do it anyway. Take the time, and be disciplined to stop and deliberate the choice—whether to *boss* or *toss*—that you make. Take the time to change from wishing your life was better or different to knowing you can choose to make it so. The wishbone can never replace the backbone. Have the backbone to push on while you are on your path of discovery, and go beyond wishful thinking to making a definitive change. Don't even think about stopping. It is always too soon to quit before you have made a choice. Get into your mind, look and see what pictures are inside, and then paint your pictures in vivid color, as an achiever would do.

Here are five simple ways to *boss* or *toss* vivid, vivacious colors of paint onto the canvas of your life.

1. **Say no.** Be mature enough to know what "enough" feels like. Don't overschedule your time with extra events, projects, or invitations. Busy-ness is not a status symbol. Make healthy choices that add to the state of your life and elevate your state of mind.
2. **Write down your plan.** Write a daily to-do list. Relieve anxiety by using pen and paper or a PDA to remind yourself of what you have to do. Don't forget to add in relaxation, reflection, or self-growth to your planned list. You will be excited and energetic during the day because you have determined your productivity and progress.
3. **Learn.** An active, engaged mind is a safe mind. Explore, and expand your knowledge base. You will be surprised at what you will uncover.
4. **Simplify.** Make your options simple. Go back to the basics. Even spend time making a pro or con chart, and list the benefits or negatives of your actions. Then distill your choice to simple, doable tasks.
5. **Red light.** Red light, or stop, and affirm yourself. Say to yourself, "I am happy" or "I am an achiever."

Minimize your stress before negative health effects take their toll. Start your discovery, get excited, and begin to build a new life for a new you. Make a personal commitment to change your life by controlling the choices you make, for the better. Answer your life question. Know where you are going. You can play a part in deciding where life is guiding you. Make informed, intentional choices, enjoy yourself, and paint on your canvas all the way to happiness, health, fulfillment, and balance. It is your life, and you are in charge of living it robustly and to the fullest. Tap into your inner power for strength. Make a conscious decision to *boss* or *toss*.

About the Author

Educator, speaker, trainer, author, and talk radio show host Anita Jefferson is the owner of WordSmith Revisions Communications. She has authored *Climb Every Obstacle: Eliminate Your Limits!* (http://www.climbeveryobstacle.com) and *For the BEST of You and Getting Things Done.* Download your free gift and subscribe to the "Obstacle Climber" newsletter. Her expertise is leadership, customer service, and life enrichment. She helps clients discover personal fulfillment, link profit to inner development, and restore a healthy balance. Listen to her radio show, "Anita Answers," on Monday nights at 8:00 (http://www.love860.com).

74

OVERCOMING RESISTANCE

What's Stopping You?

Linda Sapadin

Your Favorite Don'ts

What are your favorite don'ts that prevent you from doing what you need to do to be successful or happy?

Perhaps you believe you don't have the talent, the money, the confidence, the know-how, the energy, the time, the looks, the brains, the motivation, or the willpower. Ten big don'ts! And there are many more. Hence if I neglected to mention your dearest don't, add it on now.

What do these don'ts stop you from doing?

"I don't know," shrugged Jeff. "I have no idea what I want," whined Winona. If you, like Jeff or Winona, don't know what you want, how are you ever going to get it? Don't tell me you still believe in Santa Claus bringing you what you want. And by the way, how would he know what you want if *you* don't even know?

Marilyn Monroe once said, "I wasn't the prettiest. I wasn't the most talented. I simply wanted it more than anyone else." Obviously, there was a lot about Monroe's life that didn't work, but if you're open to learning, then know that anyone in life can be your guide.

If your mind easily zooms in on why you *can't* do something, here's some important advice for you.

- **Do what interests you, even when there's more pain than gain.** When I first began skiing, I loved the sport—despite falling on almost every turn. Black and blue bruises be damned, it was too much fun to give up!
- **Learn to tolerate feelings of inadequacy.** There are days when you will feel incredibly dumb or klutzy. These are "bad days," not a life position—unless you choose to make it so.
- **Quit comparing yourself to the best.** Sometimes people think they can't even *try* an activity (like writing or public speaking) because they won't be any good at it. They compare themselves to the best and fall short. Cut that out! No, you're not the best. You're not even average. You're just a beginner. Let yourself be one. Don't belittle what you're doing. Don't call yourself nasty names. And don't give credence to others' wisecracks.
- **Take an action.** Thinking, reading, talking, or wishing you could do something is often a good way to begin. But if you want to pursue an activity or reach a goal, you must take the plunge and do it. Thinking is no substitute for action.

If you still find yourself stuck and can't get moving to do what needs to be done, go back to your list of don'ts. Treat these don'ts as naughty children who are behaving badly. Give them time-outs. Now that they are stuck in their room, you are free! Take the opportunity to go and do what you've always wanted to do. No excuses. Do it now!

Discover Your *But*

If you know what it is that you want to do but you still haven't gotten around to doing it, it's time for you to discover your *but*.

Here's Jared's *but*: "I'd love to play the guitar, *but* I'm so busy I can never find the time."

Here's Zoe's *but*: "I'd love to quit my boring job, *but* I'm afraid I won't be able to find another one."

This word *but* is tricky. It's a tiny little word that yields great power in our lives. Our job is to make this power work *for* us rather than *against* us.

Let's see how this works. What feelings are generated for you as you read these two sentence stems?

"You're doing a good job, *but. . . .*"
"You're a nice guy, *but. . . .*"

Were you feeling angst about what would follow the *but*? Were you anticipating bad news? If so, you're right on the money. A *but* sentence has two parts: one positive, the other negative. The essential message of such a sentence is what follows the *but*. What precedes it is just there to soften the blow or provide the excuse.

Hence if you want to defeat the negative influence of a *but* sentence, here's what you must do.

Strategy 1: Place the *positive part* of your statement *after* the *but*. Doing so will help you become more action oriented. Notice the difference:

"I hate working on my resume, *but*
I want to revise it by the end of the day."

"I want to revise my resume by the end of the day, *but*
I hate working on it. *"*

Can you feel the optimism in the first sentence? Can you feel the resistance in the second sentence? Ending on a more positive note helps fight the resistance!

Strategy 2: Replace the word *but* (which connotes resistance) with *and* (which connotes connection). Compare these sentences to Jared and Zoe's *but* sentences.

"I never seem to find the time, *and*
still I'd love to play the guitar."

"I want to quit my boring job, *and*
I need to find a job before I can do so."

By making the shift from *but* to *and*, you prevent resistance from snuffing out desire. In addition, giving significance to both parts of the sentence practically implores you to do something to create a resolution.

"I never seem to find the time, *and* still I'd love to play the guitar; perhaps setting aside time on Sunday evenings would work."

"I want to quit my boring job, *and* I need to find a job before I can do so, so I'll contact a headhunter and investigate job opportunities."

People typically speak with little awareness of how their word choices affect their actions. Now that you know better, however, make it a point to use the word *but* to *contribute to*, rather than diminish, your power.

Change your language, change your life.

ABOUT THE AUTHOR

Linda Sapadin, PhD, psychologist, author, and motivational coach, is known for her sharp insights and exceptional ability to provide timely and timeless advice. Her self-help books, *It's About Time! and Master Your Fears*, earned her extensive media coverage, including appearances on *The Today Show*, speaking engagements at the Smithsonian, and featured articles in *The New York Times and USA Today.* Her new book, *"NOW I GET IT!" Totally Sensational Advice for Living and Loving,* provides inspiring and valuable advice for building competence, enriching relationships, and overcoming self-defeating patterns. Contact her at DrSapadin@aol.com, or visit her Web site at http://www.psychwisdom.com.

75

Improve Your Life by
Improving the Lives of Your Children

Kathleen Oqueli McGraw

> Children begin by loving their parents; as they grow
> older they judge them; sometimes they forgive them.
> – Oscar Wilde

When asked to author a chapter about improving one's life, I immediately thought of improving the lives of children. Most parents would agree that when their children are happy, they themselves are happy. Therefore when parents improve the lives of their children, their lives also improve. The following are stories of two families, amalgamations of families with whom I have worked, which illustrate my point.

There once were two families, the Bienvilles and the Ibervilles, from a small town named Vieux Carré. These families were very much alike. They were both two-parent households. The mothers and fathers of both families worked outside the home. They both had two children, a daughter and a son. They were both middle class and lived in the same neighborhood. Last, both families wanted the best for their children. Unfortunately, here is where the similarities ended and the differences began.

John and Marie Bienville's children were named Wendy and Tanner. The Bienvilles believed that they were a typical family, but anyone on the outside looking in would adamantly disagree. John and Marie fought over parenting decisions regularly. Wendy and Tanner disregarded their parents' rules habitually. John and Marie overindulged their children, and Wendy and Tanner manipulated their parents. They were not a happy family.

John and Marie did not understand that overindulgence and ineffective discipline were counterproductive to teaching their children respect. Therefore they continued to parent their children in the same way throughout their lives. Unfortunately, this story ends with Wendy and Tanner still living at home when they are in their forties.

John and Marie did not understand why they needed help with their parenting styles. They had been told many times that their children lacked discipline. Their family members and friends were willing to offer advice in response to John and Marie's numerous complaints about their lack of control over their children's behavior. However, John and Marie did not ask for help. They compared their children to others and were certain that their children were very special. Clearly, everyone else must be wrong!

Wendy and Tanner knew how to get what they wanted from their parents. Wendy would refuse to clean her room, preferring to talk on the phone. She knew that her father would not give her an allowance if her room was messy. Nevertheless, she also knew that her mother would increase her allowance as a bribe to do chores. Tanner would not do his homework, preferring to play video games. He knew that his father would take the video games away as soon as the report card came in the mail. However, he also knew that his mother would buy him two new games if he promised to raise his grades. John and Marie used ineffective methods of parenting, and their children did not take responsibility for their actions.

John and Marie did not attempt to work together in the best interest of their children, so they and their children continued to suffer!

Mitchell and Jane Iberville's children were named Trisha and William. Although the Ibervilles believed that they had a great family, they also believed that there was always room for improvement. When Mitchell and Jane saw their children behave in ways that were inappropriate, they evaluated their parenting styles and decided that since they had both been reared differently, they needed to coordinate their beliefs and actions. They sought advice from family members and friends, heeding suggestions that were in sync with their value system. And most importantly, they worked together as a team.

Trisha and William thought that they were the unluckiest children in the world. Trisha would sneak and watch television at night when she was supposed to be in bed. She did not think that it was right that she had to be in bed a whole hour before all her friends. However, Trisha had trouble waking up every morning for school and missed her school bus regularly. Mitchell and Jane agreed that Trisha could stay up later on weekends, but only if she went to bed on time every night during the week. They also agreed that if Trisha did not wake up early and was not ready for school on time, she would have to go to bed an hour earlier than usual.

As typical with older brothers, William would tease and pick on Trisha, making her cry. He did not think it was fair that he had to play with her when his best friends lived around the corner. However, when William went over to his friends' homes, he would repeat the curse words he heard them say. Mitchell and Jane agreed that William could invite friends over on the weekends, but only if he stopped taunting Trisha. They also agreed that if William said another curse word, he would not be allowed to play with anyone. Trisha and William followed the established rules, and Mitchell and Jane stuck to the agreed upon rewards and consequences.

Mitchell and Jane sought the assistance of a parenting coach. The coach supported them as they set parenting goals with attainable outcomes. The coach encouraged them as they assessed current parenting challenges and as they identified their priorities for future goals. Mitchell and Jane actively participated in coaching sessions and used the recommended resources. They read parenting books, watched documentaries featuring child specialists and childhood development experts, and attended parenting skills and education classes. Mitchell and Jane noticed huge improvements in their parenting styles and in their children's behavior. Amazingly, so did everyone else!

Children are happiest when they grow up in a home where their needs are met and where they are shown love and respect. Children prosper in homes where both parents are consistent and dependable. Children flourish in homes where age appropriate rules, rewards, and consequences are spelled out for them. Parents improve the lives of their children by demonstrating effective communication and conflict resolution skills and by implementing successful, positive discipline techniques. Parents also improve their children's lives by teaching them to accept responsibility for their actions or inactions.

Some parents may not know how to effectively parent their children, and they may not be aware that they are causing harm. Most parents learn how to parent from their own parents, repeating a lot of the same mistakes. With the assistance of a parenting coach, parents can set their goals, expected outcomes, and preferred behavior changes. Coaches support parents, guide them to stay on track, help them to work together, and provide them with resources to improve their skills. The parenting coach's qualifications should include education and training in coaching, childhood development, parenting styles, parenting plans, family dynamics, positive discipline techniques, and childhood health and mental health issues. The parenting coach should also have experience working with children, adolescents, and families.

Parenting coaches can help parents who are married, divorced, or never married to coparent their children in ways that are in the best interest of the children. Moreover, coaches can show parents how to be more involved in the different areas of their children's lives.

Parents improve their lives by being invested in improving the lives of their children!

About the Author

Kathleen McGraw is the founding partner of Kathleen McGraw, LCSW & Associates, LLC, a mental health, mediation, facilitation, and coaching firm. Kathleen is a Licensed Clinical Social Worker and has both a master of social work and public health from Tulane University. She is a psychotherapist and family mediator. She is a life, relationship, communication, and parenting coach. She is also a professional trainer, speaker, writer, and facilitator. Kathleen coauthored a book to be released soon, *A Guide to Getting It: Vibrant and Lasting Relationships*. Contact her at Kathleen McGraw, LCSW & Associates, LLC, 3350 Ridgelake Drive, Suite 287, Metairie, LA 70002, USA, (504) 836–3883, http://www.McGrawandAssociates.com, kathleen@McGrawandAssociates.com.

76

PASSION

Money Is No Object: Passion is Your Currency

Catherine B. Eagan

(Excerpts from *How to Discover Your Purpose in 10 Days*.)

Have you ever wondered what billionaires Bill Gates, Oprah Winfrey, and Warren Buffet have in common with you? It's an exciting possibility. You may say it's definitely not the fame or the fortune. So what is it? Each of us has been given a slice of divine brilliance that, when uncovered, developed, and applied, has enormous compensating rewards. It's called a ruling passion.

Your ruling passion comprises the ruling or governing desires and convictions in your heart. It is an intense, driving, and overwhelming sense. It is a deep-seated interest, which causes an energetic pursuit of an aim or devotion to a cause. It is the subject or cause for which you feel passionate. It causes your juices to flow. It excites you and commands your utmost attention. It might be a wrong you feel compelled to right. It can ignite your anger or stimulate your most important interest. You must learn your ruling passion and follow it.

Most people a live life null and void of the passion to fulfill their personal greatness. In a recent Gallup poll, research indicated that over 70 percent of working people are dissatisfied with their jobs or careers. It's no wonder that customer service is such a problem in society today. If people herald Blue Monday, Hump Wednesday, and Thank God It's Friday, then clearly their passion is misplaced.

Ruling Passion and Your Career Choice

What Oprah, Bill, and Warren understand is that career decisions should be governed by your ruling passion. Selecting an occupation that you are passionate about enables you to excel at unparalleled levels. This is why identifying and pursuing your passion is key. If obstacles are encountered, they can't sidetrack you or deter you from achieving your best.

What Awakens Your Ruling Passion?

Seeing others do what you love to do gives rise to the passion. You may even say "I can do that" or "I can do that better than they." While in graduate school at Harvard University, I met Del Meriwether, a world-class athlete and medical doctor. He said he was watching the Olympic track-and-field competition on TV and decided, at age 30, "I can do that." He decided to train and run the 100-yard dash. He not only beat impossible odds, but also qualified in the 1971 Pan American Games for the 100-yard dash, set a world record, and won a bronze medal! Featured on the cover of *Sports Illustrated* in 1972, he was dubbed "The Amazing Dr. Meriwether." Your ruling passion is often ignited when you see someone else doing what you are gifted and talented to do. What's amazing about you?

Have the Courage to Follow Your Passion

My husband often tells the story of his college roommate, who had always been musically inclined but attended the University of Michigan as a premed student. Because of his love of music, he decided to take his elective courses in the music school. He loved it and wanted to pursue the music curriculum, but his parents urged him to become a doctor. Therefore he continued taking courses in both areas and struggled with what to do with his life. He knew he had a burning passion to play music. He knew if he became a doctor that he would only be doing it to please his parents. Therefore after a period of time and serious contemplation he decided to change his major because music was his ruling passion. His parents wisely supported him in it. Eventually, he married, and he and his wife formed a duet. For many years they have performed all over the world and have been highly successful. They cannot imagine doing anything else. It takes courage and honesty to pursue your passion.

Identifying Your Ruling Passion

Each one of you has gifts, talents, and natural abilities. When they are developed and fueled by your passion, success is inevitable. A clue to determining your passion is the ease and confidence with which you pursue your lifework. Your ruling passion could be:

- the arts
- entrepreneurship
- meeting the needs of the poor and downtrodden
- music
- religion
- politics
- entertaining people
- teaching
- homemaking
- investing
- helping the sick to be healed (healthcare)
- improving the environment
- making people laugh
- saving lives
- inventing

In this short list, there are thousands of careers or life pursuits that can be undertaken with joy, excitement, and fulfillment. Ask yourself the following questions to unravel your ruling passion.

1. If all of your financial obligations were met and you had an unlimited supply of money, what would you do for work? What problem would you try to solve? Whom would you help? What contribution would you make to society? What type of legacy would you like to create?
2. What are your deepest, heartfelt dreams that you would like to fulfill in your lifetime?
3. What can you do today and every day to fulfill your destiny and receive the accolade "The Amazing . . . ?" You fill in the blank.

Money Is No Object: Passion is Your Currency

Hundreds of thousands of people have used their ruling passions as their currencies. Look at every rags-to-riches story: these people were are all fueled by courage and sheer ruling passion to make a difference with their gifts. All you have to do is read the Horatio Alger Association's list of Americans who have received the award for outstanding achievement in spite of adversity. The list includes such notables as Mary Kay, Ray Kroc, Joe Dudley, Thurgood Marshall, Boone Pickens, Oprah Winfrey, and a host of others. Read their life challenges to encourage yourself.

For example, the man who invented the lifeboat began at 12 years old. He had no money, learned on the job, was mocked for developing an iron boat, and spent years proving his invention to a doubting society. His name was Joseph Francis. Living in Boston, a coastal city, he learned of the unimaginable number of shipwrecks and life-threatening horror stories that occurred at sea. Even at his young age, he was deeply affected, which gave rise to his life passion. He birthed the idea to create a life-saving boat. From the ages of 12 to 18 he dedicated his spare time to building and developing a life-saving boat prototype, fully equipped and tested to save lives. Joseph Francis's name became great because of his commitment to pursuing his ruling passion, which gave rise to one of the greatest life preservers—the lifeboat.

Most people want to be successful. We have learned that if you do not pursue your ruling passion, then your greatness will be trapped on the inside. Langston Hughes said it best: What becomes of a dream deferred? Does it dry up or does it explode?

ABOUT THE AUTHOR

Catherine B. Eagan is a multimillionaire entrepreneur, speaker, teacher, and world-renowned financial coach. A Harvard University graduate, a former private banker, portfolios of over $250,000,000, and the best-selling author of *Dominating Money and How to Discover Your Purpose in 10 Days*, Catherine coaches and trains thousands worldwide on how to achieve financial independence, while discovering their passion and fulfilling their purpose. She established *The Wealthy Women* Seminars and Teleconferences to aid women in managing assets and building wealth. Visit her Web site at http://www.catherineeagan.com, and learn key tips to build wealth.

77

PERCEPTION

It's Not the Room, It's the View

Heather K. O'Hara

It has been said that the eyes are the windows to the soul. And, as much as I believe this is true, I also believe that every window has two vantage points—one for seeing in and one for seeing out.

What is most familiar to a soul is its own image, and it is constantly drawn to what it recognizes as itself. When our eyes stop to gaze on something magnificent, when the view is so magical that it takes our breath away, it is our soul reaching out to touch the miracle of its own reflection.

I have been asked many times why I have chosen to fill the pages of my Web site, Quantum-Grace.com, with nature photography. The answer is simple. Focusing on the beauty around us is a gentle reminder of what we are made of. From the smallest dewdrop to the largest mountain the beauty that surrounds us is who we really are, and it is our choice to see it or not to see it.

If it is majestic mountains our eyes are drawn to, we are being reminded of our own enduring strength. If it is the center of a rose, we are reminded of our tenderness and innocence. Oceans reflect the power, rhythm, and grace of our eternal selves, and a drop of rain, our simplicity.

We are often encouraged to close our eyes and look within. This is something I do myself, every day. But in a world sometimes overflowing with persuasive randomness and magnetic emotion, it is not always possible to maintain the peacefulness of inner vision. The Universe is very practical, however, and sometimes our greatest revelations come when we open our eyes and see all that we are made of right before us.

Free will is having the right to choose what to focus on and what not to focus on, and your choice of focus is your rite of passage. It's as if we are each holding a camera, and while looking out through a tiny "eye," we have the freedom to focus on whatever brings us joy.

You don't have to focus on what doesn't make you happy—just move the camera a little to the left or a little to the right until you find the awe-inspiring landscape of your soul. These are the pictures worth a thousand words because these are the pictures of your own integrity and beauty, and they're the only ones worth keeping.

On a daily basis we are surrounded with the energy of millions of people going millions of places doing millions of things. If we allow ourselves to get caught up in their pictures, we are allowing others to determine what we should be looking at and focusing on, and we miss the magical progress of our own natural evolution.

Nature is the mirror of humanity, and it reflects the affirmations of the soul. Within nature are found the same qualities that our own spiritual essence holds. The qualities of strength, courage, passion, patience, trust, and love are within us as well as outside us. And it is up to us to notice them.

We need not hurry as there is no urgency in evolution; and we need not scale Mt. Everest to claim a view of our own endless magnificence. It takes only a moment to look out a window and find the bluest edge of the sky. Honor yourself today, and immerse yourself in what you are made of—remembering that it's not the room you are in that determines who you are, but the exquisite view on which you focus that is you.

ABOUT THE AUTHOR

Heather O'Hara is an award-winning author who encourages us to look beyond the ordinary and find the extraordinary. A contributing editor for various publications and author of two books, *AXIS, The Song in the Center of the Soul* and *Living on Level 7 (Choosing a Life with a View)*, her passion for inspiring others has evolved into a wealth of empowering articles; many collections of original poetry; and a free, inspirational newsletter that is now received in more than a third of the world's countries. For more information on Heather O'Hara, please visit her Web site, http://www.Quantum-Grace.com.

78

PERSPECTIVES

Don't Take Your Inner Brat to Work!

Pauline Wallin

Is your inner brat taking over your job? Everyone has an inner brat. It's the part of us that's still a two-year-old. It lives on in the dark recesses of our minds, no matter how much we've accomplished.

The inner brat gets furious at the slightest inconvenience. It feels entitled to get what it wants, when it wants, and it complains when things don't go its way. Your inner brat not only makes you miserable; it makes work unpleasant for everyone else.

"Hmm," you might be saying to yourself right now. "That describes someone I work with." It's always easier to spot someone else's inner brat than your own. But take a moment now to reflect on yourself, and answer the following questions.

- Do you frequently complain that something isn't fair?
- Do you get angry at least once a day?
- Do you hate at least one person at work?
- Have you almost quit your job on the spot because you were upset?
- Are you a spreader of gossip?
- Do you frequently "forget" to do work or pass on messages that other people are waiting for?

If you answered yes to any of these questions, you probably don't enjoy your job very much. And when you're in a negative mood, your inner brat brings you down even more. Research has shown that while some jobs are more stressful than others, dissatisfaction has more to do with your attitude than with the job itself.

For example, consider two women, Abigail and Betty, who work as nurse's aides in a hospital. Abigail complains, "All I do is clean up other people's messes. Patients don't appreciate what I do for them. If I'm five minutes late or if I forget to wash out a bedpan, I get yelled at. When I first started here, they promised I'd get two breaks a day. Now I'm lucky if I even get one. I hate this job."

Now here's how Betty sees her job: "I like to know that I can make the patients more comfortable. They don't always show appreciation, but I guess I wouldn't either if I was in as much pain as they are. Sometimes I get so busy that I forget things, and my supervisor gets mad. She's got the administration breathing down her neck and can't afford any patient complaints. There are days when I don't even get a break, but the time sure flies by on those days. Even though it's a hard job, I like helping people."

The Key Is Changing Perspective

You can see from this example that your job is what you make it. It makes no difference whether you work inside or outside, at a desk or behind a counter, or whether you wear jeans or a suit to work. If you focus on the negative, you will never enjoy your job, no matter what you do or how much you get paid.

Abigail in the above example has a strong inner brat. She complains and finds fault. She perceives herself as a victim. Not only will her inner brat make her irritable and hard to get along with, but it will deprive her of the opportunity to feel good about herself.

Betty is more positive about her job, but at the same time she is also realistic. She's aware of the hard work and lack of appreciation. However, instead of dwelling on what's missing from her job, she focuses on why she chose to work there in the first place. She gets tired and stressed, but she also goes home with a sense of satisfaction and accomplishment.

No one is cheerful 100 percent of the time. Still, people who don't let their inner brats make mountains out of molehills suffer less stress, are less angry, and are more optimistic about the future.

There are many things you cannot control at work. For example, you have no control over your boss's moods. If your boss is in a bad mood, he or she might take it out on you. But you don't have to let your boss's inner brat push your buttons and unleash your own inner brat.

Some aspects of your job may be monotonous or unpleasant. But even then, you can view them in a different way, for example, by setting up a challenge, such as racing the clock, or by doing things in a different order or with different tools. By doing so, you gain a sense of control over your work, thereby reducing both physical and mental stress.

"How can I possibly like my job when I work with impossible people!?"

Who hasn't had to work with someone who was unpleasant, uncooperative, or a troublemaker? Such people not only bring their inner brats to work with them; they allow them to take over. It's even worse when the inner brat belongs to your boss.

The main problem with other people's inner brats is that they trigger your own inner brat. Thus when Mary fails to relay an important phone message to you because she's angry at you, this gets your own inner brat screaming inside your head, "How dare she do that! She's not going to get away with this!" Then your inner brat spends precious time brooding or plotting revenge.

Here are some things you can do when confronted with other people's inner brats.

- Ask yourself who "owns" the problem. Did you do something wrong, or is the other person overreacting? If it's the latter, don't feel that you have to fix things. Just minimize your interactions with the person, and don't complain or gossip to someone else.
- If your boss is overreacting, say something to acknowledge her feelings, such as, "I can see why you're upset." But don't try to explain or defend yourself at this point. Wait until your boss has calmed down.
- When a coworker's uncooperativeness affects your ability to do your job, ask yourself if this is the first time. If so, offer to help him expedite his end of the job. If the person is habitually uncooperative, it's time to start documenting your efforts and later bring it to the attention of a superior if things don't

improve. But do so in an objective way, documenting only facts, not your opinions or feelings.

- Keep in mind that focusing on other people's bad moods, sarcastic comments, and uncooperative behavior will drain you of energy. Wouldn't you rather save your energy for something more productive or enjoyable?
- Finally, remember that it's easier to spot an inner brat in someone else than in yourself. Are you sure it's the other guy's inner brat that's upsetting you . . . or is it your own?

ABOUT THE AUTHOR

Pauline Wallin, PhD, is a psychologist in Camp Hill, Pennsylvania, and the author of *Taming Your Inner Brat: A Guide for Transforming Self-Defeating Behavior* (Wildcat Canyon Press, 2004). Visit http://www.innerbrat.com for more information, and subscribe to her free, monthly "Inner Brat Newsletter." Dr. Wallin is also available for workshops and presentations. Call (717) 761–1814.

79

Nothing Happens in Life or Business Until Somebody Says Yes!

Lynn Pierce

Think about this: even when there is no one else involved in a decision, like whether you're going to exercise today, you still have to say yes to yourself to make it happen. And if you don't enjoy the activity, there's probably an internal conversation going on where you have to give yourself a very persuasive argument to get to that "yes"!

How do you get to the point of saying yes to yourself or having someone else say yes to you? You've been doing it naturally, without any conscious thought, since you were a toddler convincing another child to give you the toy he or she was playing with.

How do you think you got a date each time you've wanted to go out with someone new?

How did you convince your last employer they should hire you for the job instead of another, equally qualified person? How do you get your kids to do what you want them to do? Or do you?

Remember that time you really wanted to eat at your favorite restaurant, and everyone else in your group had different ideas? You convinced them by talking about how great it was, the atmosphere and the particular dishes you thought they would enjoy, didn't you? The way you talked to them was based on the rapport you had with each individual and the group. You took their personal preferences into consideration and gave them the benefits of your restaurant based on their needs and desires. You thought you were being nice, and you were right.

You know how to persuade people to see your point of view and how it benefits them, don't you? You got them to say yes. That's called sales.

Don't be afraid of the word sales. The truth is you're already much better at sales than you give yourself credit for. In fact, you spend quite a bit of your time every day in sales. Just look at the sales talents you just discovered. It's how you get a date, a job, a spouse, a client. It's the basis of every relationship you have because sales is nothing more than good communication skills used for a specific purpose.

Does that shock you? I can hear you reading this and saying to yourself, "She isn't talking to me—I don't like sales, and I would never trick people like that."

There are three myths about sales I'd like to dispel.

1. Most people don't consider themselves to be in sales if they aren't employed as a salesperson.
2. Sales is hard edged, manipulative, unpleasant, and confrontational—with a winner and a loser.
3. If you are nice and considerate to people, it will be taken as weakness.

Those statements couldn't possibly be true if you look at the way you use persuasive communication skills, otherwise known as sales, in your day-to-day life. Sales is persuading people to go along with what you want because it's to their benefit—as in the case of your children—or showing someone how you have the best solution to her problem in business. Just like you did with your restaurant choice.

No tricks.

Isn't true business development about building relationships with your clients? So, in reality, relationships are relationships, whether business or personal. It's really all the same at the most basic level. Learning the techniques and strategies of persuasion is of great benefit to you in all the relationships in your life because the success and well-being of all relationships is based on the ability to understand and be understood, which comes down to good communication skills.

Are you a parent? Do all your kids happily cooperate with you? They can if you learn how to appeal to them each in the way they best receive information. It may look like they enjoy being difficult, but to a large extent, it's more likely that you have different personality styles, and that's where your communication problems come in. What is a carrot to you, in terms of the carrot/stick theory, may look more like a stick to someone with a different style. Once you know how to reach them and speak to them in a way that works for them, things will be much more relaxed in your relationships.

Wouldn't it be great if your spouse always understood what you were trying to say, and wouldn't your life be easier if your kids or your employees actually took the action you wanted without having to say it more than once? What would it be like if you could get things accomplished in a way that seemed effortless?

This isn't a dream; it's a very attainable reality. The first step is to understand that there are four major personality styles, and a lot of communication conflicts can be resolved by acquiring a good working knowledge of how each personality best receives information and what criteria they use to make decisions.

If that's a piece of knowledge you don't yet possess, learning to communicate effectively with people who have different personalities from yours could literally change your life, not to mention lead to a huge increase in your income!

If you have your own business, I'd like to help you become so sought after that people come to you asking to do business. That requires two things.

1. You have to set yourself apart from everyone else.
2. Your potential clients need to recognize that you are different.

Chances are you aren't the only person doing what you do in your area. You probably have some competitors. Ask yourself these questions.

- Why is someone going to do business with me rather than someone else?
- What do I have to offer that my competitors don't?
- Why are people making a tremendous amount of money very quickly and easily, while I'm working really hard and not getting their results?
- What are they doing differently?

Let's say you're an accountant and you want to get 10 new clients.

- How are you going to approach these prospective clients?
- Do they already have an accountant and you want them to move over to your company? Are they people who aren't yet sure they need an accountant?
- Why should they do business with you rather than the brother-in-law of their best friend? What do you do to serve your clients that your competitors don't?

One thing we know is that people will do business with someone they like and trust over someone they feel no allegiance to, every time. So the question is, How do you develop that kind of rapport in a short amount of time? The same is true in your personal relationships. The more rapport you have and the closer someone feels to you, the more likely you are to get to "yes" with him.

Now that you know you really do have persuasive sales skills, ask yourself what level they've reached and where you could use some additional fine-tuning. Your financial independence and peace in your home could be the result.

ABOUT THE AUTHOR

With over 25 years in sales and marketing, along with 30 years studying human behavior, Lynn Pierce, "The Sales Therapist," mentors entrepreneurs and information marketers to reach the pinnacle of success. Tell Lynn what the life of your dreams looks like, and she'll create the blueprints to get you there, along with the sales system to fund it. Lynn Pierce's personal growth and business acceleration systems help her clients get three times the results in half the time with one tenth of the effort. Claim your free minicourse, "9 Steps to Getting to YES Without Selling," at http://www.LynnPierce.com.

80

Are You Running Your Life, or Is It Running You?

Jan Hornford

Sometimes our lives can feel like an endless to-do list, where we leap from one task to another. It can feel like our lives are running us rather than the other way around. If this is how you are feeling, it is time to consider how you are spending your time and energy.

The simple fact is that each of us has the same 24 hours a day. We cannot create more time. What we can do is manage our energy and our thoughts to change how we experience time and make considered choices on how we are spending our time.

It is all about spending your time and energy on what is most important to you. Honoring your priorities and focusing on one thing at a time will help you lead a less stressful life and will allow you to accomplish more with less effort. Making conscious choices about how you spend your time and energy will enable you to start running your life and to experience life as moments to enjoy rather than as a to-do list to complete.

Dangers of Multitasking and Multithinking

We often fill up our time with thoughts of the past (thinking about all the things we did not get done) or the future (thinking about all the things we have to do) instead of where we are right now. We often try to complete a number of different tasks at the same time. Splitting our thoughts and attention in this way contributes to the sense of feeling rushed and pulled in many different directions.

When we multitask, we often end up with a number of things half done, which leaves us feeling anxious. When we only listen to our child or colleague with half an ear while we think about tomorrow's meeting, we create an experience that is stressful and unfulfilling for both us and the other person.

Being Fully Present

What if you could focus all your energy and attention and place it on what you are doing in this moment? What would be possible for you then? When we give our full attention and presence to whomever we are speaking or to whatever we are doing, we step off that hamster wheel of frenetic activity and enrich our lives and the lives of others.

Choosing to focus your thoughts and energy in the present moment and doing one thing at a time, and doing it well, will not only help you to accomplish more, it will help you to create a more peaceful experience of time.

How Are You Using Your Time?

We are constantly confronted with multiple possibilities of how to spend our work and personal time. There is not enough time to do it all. We often must give up one thing in order to have time to do another. We often get caught up in doing all sorts of things that we think we should be doing but that are not very important to us. We end up spending our time and energy doing things that do not bring us joy or a sense of fulfillment because we never take the time to really think about what we are doing and why.

Many people spend up to 35 hours per week watching television. Is this a real priority for you? Perhaps you would rather choose a movie or one really good television show that you enjoy and let the others go. This would free up huge amounts of time for you to do many other things.

When you know what is most important to do and have clear priorities, then it is easier to make choices on how to use your time. When we focus on things that are important to us, we make more effective use of our time, and we feel better because we are spending our time doing what is important and meaningful to us—and we will likely accomplish more as a result.

Setting Priorities

Setting priorities will help you make conscious and informed choices on how you are using your time. It is all about living with purpose. Honoring your priorities and focusing on one thing at a time will help you to have a less stressful experience of time and will allow you to accomplish more with less effort.

When you are setting priorities, consider the following questions.

- Why am I doing this?
- Is this something I need to do or is it something I want to do?
- Or is it neither? Who else can do this?
- Is it important that I do this right now, or can it wait?
- Will doing this support my goals and my values?

It is important to recognize the priorities in all aspects of your life: work, relationships, self-care, home, and responsibilities. You can then make choices that enable you to fulfill your priorities and can choose to let the less important things go for now. Be honest with yourself about what you can do and what you want to do. Priorities will change day-to-day, week-to-week, and year-to-year. Different things will be more important to you at different times in your life.

Schedule Your Priorities

Schedule time to take care of your priorities, and set a completion date. Be sure to build "flex" time into each day: 30 to 60 minutes of time that you block off. This time can be used to deal with the unexpected or for things that are taking longer than you anticipated.

Spending your time focused on priorities will increase your peace of mind and bring greater meaning and purpose to your life because you are focused on what is really important to you in all aspects of your life.

Coaching Questions

Of the activities you are doing now, which ones energize you? Which ones drain you? What do you want to have more of in your life? What is most important for you to have in your life right now? (Consider all your roles and responsibilities.) What is stopping you from doing these things?

Take Action
How Are You Really Using Your Time?

Over the next week, carry a notebook and write down what you are doing for every minute of your day. Keep a record of how you spend your time and energy for the next seven days.

After one week, consider the following questions.

- How are you using your time?
- What are you missing out on because of your current lifestyle?
- Is there time in your life for the things that are most important to you?
- How can you make more time for what you value most?

Action Steps

List three ways you misuse your time, and then list three things you can do to minimize these activities. For example:

- **Misuses:** checking your e-mail every hour on the hour. **Action:** only check e-mail in the morning and after lunch.

Identify three areas where you might be able to delegate tasks or ask for more help, and then list three actions you can take to help you create more time in this area. For example:

- **Area:** Household chores. **Action:** have each family member take on an additional household task.

ABOUT THE AUTHOR

Jan Hornford is a life coach and certified retreat coach whose passion is to help individuals reconnect with their own wisdom and power and to support them in creating the lives they want. She offers a variety of courses and retreats that are designed to help you reclaim your self and experience the peace and sense of wholeness that comes from knowing your purpose and living authentically. Visit her Web site at http://www.futureperfect.ca for more information and for the free, four-week e-course "Living Authentically: Honouring Your Truth in Everyday Life." Contact Jan at (403) 313–4064 or at jan@futureperfect.ca.

81

QUESTIONS OF LOVE

Play 20 Questions and Revitalize Your Love Life

Ellyn Bader & Peter Pearson

Do you remember the game "20 Questions"? You could ask 20 questions to elicit and eliminate and finally discover what animal, vegetable, or mineral the other person was thinking about. We use a variation of this game to enrich your love life and build a stronger bond in your most intimate relationship.

In our work with couples we like to help them formulate a vision of the kind of life they would like to create together. A powerful vision involves recalling and revising the important dreams you had when you first got together and identifying new hopes as well. Sometimes this means exploring "little buds" that are unconscious, but waiting to blossom. A vision contains something you really want and evokes enough passion that you are willing to invest sustained effort to bring it about. Your vision contains strong desires that are aligned with your values and supported by a plan.

In order to think creatively about the type of relationship you desire, ask each other a few of the following 20 questions on a dinner date, or set up a special time to explore these together. They will help you connect on a deeper level than the usual topics of careers, kids, vacations, politics, and movies. They can illuminate areas of joy, passion, and connection. Most couples ask each other questions like these when they first meet, but as time hurtles by, these meaningful questions get neglected and then abandoned. They'll be the starting point for an interesting and stimulating conversation that will create the foundation for your vision.

Developing Your Partnership Vision

- What things in your life bring you the greatest pleasure?
- What things do you look forward to each day?
- What excites you about the future?
- In what settings are you the happiest and most comfortable?
- On your drive to work, what consumes your mind the majority of the time?
- In a regular day, what do you find yourself thinking about the most in addition to work?
- If you could change one or two things in your life, what would they be, and why?
- What accomplishments do you value most in your life so far?
- If you had three wishes that would come true, what would they be?
- When you reach the rocking chair stage of your life, what do you wish you had done that you didn't do?
- Is there a belief or attitude that seems to interfere with creating or pursuing a big dream?
- What activities do you most like to do by yourself?
- What are a couple things that you appreciate about our relationship, and why do these things seem significant?
- How strong is your desire to do something together?
- Describe a memory of a time when you felt like we collaborated well.
- What kinds of projects or activities would you consider doing together?
- What projects or activities do you think we do well together?
- What talents or strengths do you believe we each bring to a future project?
- What question would you ask that we have not included?
- **Bonus Question:** What would be the next step you suggest we take from here?

Here are some guidelines to help you get the most out of these conversations. Treat your partner's answers with respect. Please don't argue or negatively judge any of your partner's responses. Be like a compassionate reporter who is exploring an unknown subject. Ask your partner to do the same for you. Approach it like the game of 20 Questions. You will be delicately ferreting out the overlap in all the answers to arrive at what is most meaningful to each of you. Don't simply race through the questions. This process takes time and dedication, yet returning to these questions will pay huge dividends in your life together.

The More Detail Your Vision Has, the More Compelling It Will Be

Sarah and Jim used this exercise repetitively over time. From the beginning Sarah answered what excites her about the future by saying "leaving a legacy." Jim responded to the question of what kinds of projects or activities he would consider doing together by saying that he'd like to work on something together for the well-being of their children. As they asked each other these questions again and again, their responses evolved. Their answers would incubate and stimulate additional ideas. One session would prove to be a springboard for the next. Sara and Jim eventually decided they wanted to do something for their children, which also met Sarah's desire to leave a legacy.

Their answers kept returning to doing something that reflected their interest in teaching and also strengthening the family. They both believed the old saying that if you really want to learn something, then you should teach it. They decided to begin with teaching a Sunday school class together. After sitting through some tedious Sunday school classes when they were children, they decided they would make it enjoyable for themselves and the kids. They became increasingly passionate about creating a very different learning experience for kids in Sunday school.

Alert! Alert! In the beginning stage, do not discuss potential obstacles. The best way to kill a budding dream is to ask, "Well, how is *that* going to happen?" or "Are you really serious about wanting that?" Asking these questions will surely strangle emerging desires before you see the bigger picture.

Rather, Sarah and Jim jumped in and discovered they enjoyed teaching together. Through trial and error they learned a lot about collaborating and how to better negotiate when they had sharp differences of opinion. However, they also discovered they did not like the bureaucracy telling them what to teach. Over time they kept returning to their vision questions. Eventually, they started a small, interfaith Sunday school with other families who had a similar vision. The project was more work than they had anticipated. Much more. But the work they had put into building a collaborative vision and learning to negotiate sustained them through the tougher times.

You will know you have accurately described your vision when:

- the results are hard to achieve; success will require "stretching."
- you are excited when you think about it.
- the results of the vision are meaningful to you.
- the results make a difference in your life and your partner's life.
- the results are visible, can be written down, and, at least to some degree, can be measured.
- the results will reflect your strengths and core values.

Your vision will evolve as you move toward it. You will meet obstacles along the way. Ask yourself an important question: "What will I have to do that I don't want to do to realize this vision?" Every worthwhile vision carries with it some undesirable tasks. Don't let these make you believe your vision is wrong. Accept that your vision will involve some challenges that you won't enjoy.

Realizing your vision as a couple will require new skills in problem solving, negotiation, and decision making. They're not always intuitive. And remember: you can't create a flourishing relationship just by fixing what is wrong. You achieve your vision by building on the best in each of you.

ABOUT THE AUTHOR

Drs. Ellyn Bader and Peter Pearson are founders and directors of The Couples Institute in Menlo Park, California. As therapists, workshop leaders, authors, and speakers, they are dedicated to helping couples fulfill their dreams. Their presentations educate, enlighten, and entertain, while giving innovative, practical ways to help improve relationships. Peter's couples workshop, "Coming from Your Heart," comes with an unusual money-back guarantee and attracts couples from across the country. Peter and Ellyn have been quoted in multiple national publications as well as featured on over 50 radio and television programs, including "The Today Show" and "CBS Early Morning News." Visit http://www.couplesinstitute.com for free articles to help you develop the best possible relationship skills.

82

Learn to Choose: The Seven Types of People to Avoid on Your Way to a Happy and Fulfilling Relationship

June Marshall

If you are looking for a relationship, it takes patience to find someone you can respect, whose heart is open to you, and whom you can be with without driving you up a wall. Good mate material is out there, but while you are looking, don't waste your time and money on the Dirty Sevens. The underlying problem with the Dirty Sevens is a kind of selfishness that makes them incapable of giving your needs fair play. They lack empathy (the ability to put themselves in your shoes).

Who Are They?

Don't give up your freedom and happiness for these guys and gals. They will always put you and your needs last.

Ladies, read on to see who these men are and what you can do about them.

1. **ScarMan.** Talks continuously about his ex and the past, to the exclusion of everything else, including you. You feel like saying, "Hello! You are out with me!" If you want to feel first in a man's heart, throw ScarMan back on the dating beach.
2. **SideMan.** Married or living with someone, but looking for some excitement on the side, with no intention of creating a real relationship. Walk away, and don't look back. He wants to use you. If it takes a lie, he will lie to get what he wants, without a thought for the pain he causes.
3. **CrazyMan.** Has so many quirks, a hospital wing of psychotherapists couldn't figure him out. He'll drive you nuts if you give him a long-term try.

315

4. **GuyMan.** Likes guys better than girls, but pretends to be straight. The fact that he is lying to you about his sexuality is what makes him one of the Dirty Seven. Let him go on his journey of discovering his true identity without you.

5. **YAPpie (Young and Poor).** Has the benefit of youth on his side, but not much else: no money, and no job prospects. You pay for everything and drive him around, too. Do less for him. He is a species of parasite that survives by living off women and will eventually move on.

6. **OLMan (Old Loser Man).** The YAPpie, grown older but not wiser. He has not provided for his future. He is looking to you to do that for him. He was lazy, selfish, and clueless in his youth and has remained the same in his old age. Do not get involved with him until you find out where and how he lives. Go there with him. If he is penniless, especially beware of how he lives.

7. **BagMan.** Difficult children from different marriages, some of whom live with him, multiple alimony payments, and lots of bitterness over past woes are just some of the baggage this man brings to the relationship. Give up on him before you are left holding the bag.

And now, men, read on about the Dirty Seven ladies to avoid. Some women are no angels, either, when it comes to selfish behavior and placing their mates in unhappy situations. If you are looking for happiness, stay away.

1. **The PMS Queen.** Blames her constant mood swings and disruptive behavior on what part of the menstrual cycle she is in. She is either pre-, positively, or postmenstrual. But whatever part of the cycle she is in, you are getting on her last nerve, and she will let you know with tantrums, grumbling resentment, and self-pitying crying jags, all aimed at you and why you are to blame for not making her life perfect. Let her stew. It is not up to you to teach her coping skills.

2. **Needee Nellie.** An emotional black hole of never-ending need. She will call you hundreds of times a week to receive assurances that you love her, will follow you around, and will generally make you the center of her empty life. Though flattering, her incessant need becomes cloying and suffocates your love.

3. **Material Girl.** Only interested in your money and what you can buy for her. Never grateful, she always demands more. Her empty mind is filled with consumer goods and her empty life with self-grooming activities. Gold diggers have been around for centuries and remain destructive and incapable of love. Pass them on your way to someone who can really bring happiness into your life.

4. **Shopaholica.** Incessantly searches for someone she thinks is better than you but will let you spend time and money on her until she finds him. Have enough self-esteem to know that this woman's character, or lack of it, will never bring you a sense of being loved or appreciated.
5. **The Wedding Belle.** Spends all her thought and effort on the storybook wedding, but after it is over, lets herself go. She has accomplished her goal and feels that she need not make any further effort. Recognize her by her obsession with weddings, whether her own or her friends'. You will regret getting entangled with this dead end as a mate.
6. **The Mom.** Thinks that she always knows best and that you are one of the silly kids she needs to dominate and boss because you don't know any better. Do not consider being happy with this type of woman, who must prove you wrong at all costs.
7. **Psycho Babbler.** Dissects the relationship until it dies of terminal examination. Insists on pulling apart and scrutinizing every declaration of love, like tearing apart a flower to discover its mystery.

Love Yourself

Care enough about yourself to avoid these people as mates. They have a lot of work to do on themselves before they will be capable of being loving, empathic beings. Be loving enough to yourself to allow only loving people into your life, and don't think you will be able to fix any of the Dirty Sevens. It is hard enough to continually improve your own character and ability to love without being on a rampage of reform to change the Dirty Sevens. One of their characteristics is that they do not want to change their behaviors and expect you to change yours so that they can be parasites instead of truly equal partners in love.

About the Author

June Marshall is the author of two love and relationship books, *Booby Trapped: Men Beware of the Dirty Seven Sisters!* and *The Dirty Seven: Ladies Beware!* She has appeared on television and radio and has given talks and seminars on the topics of mateability, behavioral standards, and self-esteem in the dating arena. She has also written numerous articles for various publications. Visit her on the Web at http://www.loveshowbyjune.com, or write to her at Newmedia Publishing, 94 Hawthorne Avenue, Park Ridge, NJ 07656, USA. You can call her at (201) 505–1133 or (201) 421–7145, or e-mail her at june@newmediapublishing.com.

83

Creating Everyday Rituals for Magical Living

Deborah Roth

In the technically brilliant sterility of our modern age, I believe we're aching to find new ways to make meaning in our lives. Truly transformative ceremonies and rituals allow us to infuse a sense of the sacred into our ordinary lives, to recognize major life events in profoundly satisfying ways, and to remember our connection to our deepest selves and to each other.

While I was researching my master's thesis 10 years ago, I discovered that each discipline—anthropology, religious studies, psychology, drama—had their own definitions of "ritual." The one that most resonates with me is actually a blend and focuses on the notion of ritual as "transformance"—transformative performance. Ritual becomes transformative when we direct our intention and attention to create a particular outcome, when we activate all our senses, and when we participate in powerful, symbolic actions. Sharing bread becomes an act of community building; throwing a rock into a stream signifies the letting go of old wounds; lighting a candle sheds new light and hope in a time of uncertainty.

A ritual is more likely to move us deeply, to begin to propel us toward wholeness, if it contains several important elements.

1. **Clear intention.** What is the purpose of the ritual? What do you want to accomplish? The more focused you are, the more powerful and evocative the ritual.
2. **Creating sacred time and space.** How do we set this enactment apart from our everyday lives? We must physically create the time and place away from the bustle of our daily routines—in effect, constructing the "container"

within which we may encounter the quieter, deeper parts of ourselves.

3. **Use of symbols.** Symbols are the language of the unconscious. If our intention is to make a shift in some area of our lives, superficial Band-Aids won't work. We must begin at the source, somewhere deep in our psyches, and tickle the core issues to the surface. Symbols serve to focus our attention on the work of the ritual and to evoke powerful memories and emotions.

4. **Stimulating all five senses.** Some of us resonate strongly with visual symbols, while others respond more to auditory or kinesthetic stimuli, like music and dancing. Ingesting special "brews" or ritual food activates our sense of taste, while scented candles and incense tickle our olfactory senses and directly trigger our limbic systems, the emotional centers of our brains. By integrating all these modalities into our ritual, each of us can find meaning, regardless of our sensory strengths or weaknesses.

Once we understand the key ingredients of transformative ritual, how do we go about structuring it in a way that is both easy to enact and powerful in its experience? Clearly, there are as many ways to create meaningful rituals as there are people to produce them. The recipe I offer here is one I have worked with for many years, drawn from my early teachers and mentors and my own research into the power and magic of ritual.

1. **Purification: Cleansing the ritual space and ourselves.** This can be done using incense, water, or essential oils, to name a few options. For instance, "smudging" is a common practice in many Native American traditions which involves using a feather or your hands to surround yourself with the smoke and aroma of burning sage. However it is done, it is the first step in creating sacred space.

2. **Ritual invocation: Stating the purpose or intention.** Verbalizing with clear intention what we wish to accomplish provides a solid foundation on which to build all the ritual actions that follow. Whether our goal is to celebrate a rite of passage (birthdays, menarche, retirement), to heal an emotional wound, or to honor our unique gifts (just a few examples), we must express that intent in order to begin to manifest it.

3. **Creating sacred space.** This can be done in conjunction with the purification process, simply by walking the perimeter of our ritual space with burning incense. Or, in a group ritual, we can also define our space and our purpose by inviting everyone in the circle to share who they are and why they are there. Whatever method we use, the intention is to create an energetic container which holds ritual time and space apart from our ordinary

319

reality.

4. **Invoking the directions/elements: Honoring fire/water/air/earth energies.** When we face each direction and invite the energies of each of the four elements into the circle, we recognize and honor our connection to nature and the world around us. It reminds us also that we embody those same elemental archetypes within ourselves.

5. **Meditation: Concentrating awareness inwardly.** Guided visualizations, silent meditation, and focused breathing are just some of the ways we can move from outer space to inner space. It is a powerful way to deeply ground our intention on the internal plane.

6. **Work of the ritual: Creating something tangible or sharing stories.** Ritual "play" can be as whimsical as creating valentines for ourselves to promote self-love or creating a web of yarn within a circle to celebrate our connectedness. Or, it can be cathartic, like smashing an egg (outdoors, of course!) filled with our rage over the abuse we have experienced, or perhaps simply sharing our feelings about topics that are often taboo in the rest of our lives, like anger or death.

7. **Raising energy: Usually by sound and/or movement.** We bring life to our ritual work in many different ways: by dancing, drumming, chanting, or toning. This is truly the part of the ritual when we most fully and literally embody the energy we have created up to this point.

8. **Grounding energy: Renewing our connection with the earth.** Once we have raised energy, it is necessary to ground it; otherwise, we will leave the ritual feeling spacy and disoriented. We can do this simply by placing our hands on the ground and breathing deeply, visualizing our connection to the earth. Or, we could ingest some form of ritual food at this point, or clasp hands in a circle—any action to tactically, physically feel firmly "planted."

9. **Opening the circle.** Every ritual must have a clear beginning and ending. At this point we can thank the elemental energies for supporting us in our ritual work, acknowledge the shifts that have occurred, and begin to reflect on how we can use these ritual gifts to make a difference in our lives. In a group ritual, this is also the time to engage in some final, fun grounding, in the form of hugs and feasting!

Through all of these stages we see how the four key ritual elements—clear intention, safe and sacred space, symbols, and sensory stimulation—can be woven into the overall experience.

Enacting ritual with a clear structure in mind should not stifle creativity, but rather enhance the feeling of operating within a safe, sacred, energetic container. With those parameters in place the magic woven during its enactment becomes a spontaneous and unique cocreation of everyone present—even if it's only you!

ABOUT THE AUTHOR

Deborah Roth, MA, PCC, is a certified Life Transition Coach and Relationship Coach whose passion is to guide individuals and groups to the next level of success and fulfillment in their lives, work, and relationships. Her approach is holistic and incorporates helping each client fully realize and honor the connection between his or her mind, body, and spirit. She is also an interfaith minister licensed to perform weddings and loves designing creative, meaningful ceremonies to mark other important life passages as well. You can learn more about her programs and workshops and sign up for her free quarterly newsletter at http://www.SpiritedLiving.com.

84

Some Simple Rules for a Satisfying Life

Andreas Stark

Life has taught me that success, abundance, prosperity, peace, and happiness are all created through exercising a planned routine. To create a happy and prosperous life, we need some instructions, or rules, for living.

Rule 1: Spread love. In order to produce great achievements, we have to take great risks. The greater the required achievement, the greater the personal risk involved. The greater the love we show and give, the greater the vulnerability, but the greater the return.

Rule 2: Learn from life. We have to learn from the lessons in life. When we do lose, as we all will from time to time, we should lose gracefully and learn from the lesson that life has taught us through the experience, turning it into a positive to build on.

Rule 3: Show respect. We need to respect others as we respect ourselves. Above all we should respect ourselves and show that respect. In today's society, there seems to be a great lack of self-respect. Just look at the way people behave and dress.

Rule 4: Be responsible. We need to take full responsibility for all our actions. Always do things for the right reason and from a position of love for your fellow man. Remember that anything done for the greater good will always succeed.

Rule 5: Be ethical. Live a life that is honorable and ethical. Especially in today's world, there seem to be a lot of questions about ethics and deceit. It is very important to stay true and honest to the fundamental rules of ethics and fairness.

Rule 6: Admit fallibility. Remember to take immediate action when you realize you have made a mistake. It is very important that you admit when you have made a mistake and that you take immediate steps to correct the mistake. It is a sign of maturity and of courage to own up to your own fallibility.

Rule 7: Show forgiveness. Do not let little things interfere or destroy a great relationship. Whether in your personal life or in business, relationships are precious and should not be taken lightly, so when minor disagreements occur, do not let these destroy the relationship. Show forgiveness, and move on.

Rule 8: Allow change. Be open to change, but do not compromise on your values and ethics. Through change we grow and learn. Too often, however, people tend to change for opportunistic reasons and are willing to forego all that is good and valuable for immediate gratification or greed.

Rule 9: Learn to listen. There are times when it is better to be silent than to speak. Too often, we feel the need to say our piece, but there are many situations in life where it is better to be quiet and listen. It is through listening that we learn the other person's point of view and get a better understanding of the situation under consideration. This could be a hard rule to master for some of us.

Rule 10: Create abundance. Create a loving and harmonious atmosphere in the home. When we create an atmosphere of love, we create the foundation for happiness, abundance, and prosperity. Remember that it is through giving that we receive the greatest joy and rewards.

Rule 11: Practice quiet reflection. Spend some time alone at least once a day. This is the time you can spend to meditate and reflect on the happenings of the day. This is your opportunity to recharge and to connect with your inner self. Here you will create the foundation for your abundance and prosperity.

Rule 12: Give of yourself. Remember that in any relationship your love for each other exceeds your need for each other. In other words, it is in the giving of yourself without any attachments or expectations that you receive the greatest satisfaction and rewards.

These twelve simple rules, when followed in a consistent manner, will bring you lots of abundance, prosperity, and happiness. They will create a life experience that you will gladly look back on. They have certainly helped me in reaching my life and business goals. It will take time to learn and practice these rules faithfully, but the time spent will surely pay benefits in your life's journey. Always have unwavering faith in what you set out to do, as long as it is done for the right reasons and within the universal rules of ethics.

ABOUT THE AUTHOR

Andreas Stark, MSc, is a consultant, entrepreneur, and teacher. He and his wife, Regina, have an independent energy consulting business that specializes in earth sciences and in teaching and training. Andreas has written many educational course manuals for the energy industry as well as for postsecondary education. He is currently taking PhD studies at Rushmore University. Andreas has been a long-time student and practitioner of meditation techniques to help in the creation of abundance and prosperity. He is currently expanding the training side of the business into the field of general help and education for the poor and Third World, where a drastic need for hope and prosperity exists.

85

SELF-DOUBT

Awaken the Genie Within

Linda Salazar

Ancient lore tells us that there's a magical Genie who lives in a lamp and that the person who possesses that lamp has the power to invoke wishes and desires beyond our wildest dreams. If I told you that Genie lives in you, would you believe me? Maybe not.

But if I told you that there was another character who lives in you and complains, whines, and was negative about your day-to-day life as well as your dreams, would you believe me then? I'll bet you would because we are all far too familiar with this character, whom I call the Gremlin.

The Gremlin is that part of you who keeps your fears, anxieties, and doubts alive and well. His entire purpose is to maintain control over you, keeping things status quo, even if you're not happy with the status quo. He believes his purpose is to keep you safe by not allowing you to take risks, to speak up for yourself, or to create changes in your life that you know in your heart need changing. And he definitely wants to make sure the Genie doesn't make an appearance because once the Genie shows up, the Gremlin knows he's no longer in charge.

For way too many years I lived with the Gremlin as the one in charge, until I learned how to quiet him enough to awaken my Genie within, making him my full-time partner and only allowing my Gremlin to visit occasionally.

Now you may ask, "Why allow the Gremlin to visit even occasionally?" Because it's important to realize your Gremlin will always be there. You're human, and it's only natural to have both negative and positive thoughts show up throughout your life. But the trick is to be aware of your Gremlin when he's around so you can consciously quiet him enough to allow yourself to feel a little bit better about a situation. As you do this, you give the Genie within the chance to come to the surface and help you find better solutions, ask different questions, and attract into your life more of what you do want, instead of what you don't want, which, by the way, is what the Gremlin does—he attracts what you don't want.

To get you started in shifting from your Gremlin thinking to your Genie thinking, I'd like to share with you Five Tips to Quiet Your Gremlin and Five Questions to Awaken Your Genie.

Five Tips to Quiet Your Gremlin

1. Let your Gremlin be when he starts up with you. Focus more on your body, and see where he's showing up in your body. Does your head hurt? Is your neck stiff? Is your stomach in a knot? Breathe into those areas until you feel some relief.
2. Give your Gremlin permission to rant and rave for a bit. Don't judge him; don't panic over what's being said or resist anything. Just let him be. Allow all the Gremlin's ranting to pour out. Sit back and enjoy it for a change. Put a smile on your face as you listen calmly. Separate yourself from that Gremlin who's doing all the whining and complaining.
3. Ask him questions. Get as intimate as you can with him. Find out what sets him off. Then give him answers as if you were talking to a four-year-old, trying to calm him of the dark before falling asleep.
4. Pick a name for your Gremlin and talk to him out loud. Using his name, tell him that everything is going to be fine and that he can take a rest for now. Keep talking to him until he's less noisy. Talking out loud will create a shift inside you that won't happen when you just think about the conversation. By the way, my Gremlin's name is Gertrude.
5. Be gentle with your Gremlin. Visualize your arm around him, soothing him, comforting him, allowing him to rest his head on your shoulder. Remember, he's scared—he doesn't want you to fall down, and he believes he's doing what's best for you.

Once your Gremlin is under your control, this is when you want to connect with the Genie within. Your Genie is that part of you that creates comments, ideas, and questions that allow you to feel like you're moving forward instead of being stuck. He'll have you feeling better about yourself overall.

Five Questions to Awaken Your Genie

1. What's working in my life for me?
2. What's my intention in this moment?
3. What wants to be born from this?
4. What would be my best choice at this time?
5. What can I do for myself right now to feel a little bit better?

Learning to move from your Gremlin thinking into your Genie thinking takes time and patience. The Gremlin's been in charge a whole lot longer than the Genie, so be loving and gentle with yourself as you develop this skill. As you are, it'll occur to you one day that your Genie's been showing up more than your Gremlin!

ABOUT THE AUTHOR

Featured on radio, on TV, and in the *LA Times*, Linda Salazar is the founder of Awaken the Genie Within® Coaching. Clients ranging from CEOs to actors say that her unique coaching method harmonizes their work and souls. With a degree in communications Salazar received her coaching certification from Coach U and is a member of the International Coaching Federation. Her unique method works for people of all careers and cultural beliefs. Salazar is the author of *Parents In Love; Reclaiming Intimacy After Your Child Is Born* and the creator of the *Awaken the Genie Within®; Manifesting Your Heart's Desire* CD series. Visit http://www.awakenthegeniewithin.com.

86

The Vital Element: Self-Esteem

Lois Marie Gacher

You've decided to improve your life. Where do you start? Do you begin with a new relationship, with a new career, or move to a new city? The answer is no, none of these, for there is one constant: *you*. The same *you* will be there, wherever you choose to go, whoever you're with, whatever you choose to do. That's why the place to start improving your life is at the beginning, with your own self-esteem.

When you feel good about yourself, you have good self-esteem. You realize that anything outside yourself is exactly that—*outside* your self. You know that your self is fine. It's the outside that needs fixing. When you recognize your own worth and know that you have value, nothing anyone can say or do will have any effect on your self-esteem. Your feelings can always be hurt. Your self-esteem can be hurt only if *how* you see yourself is determined by someone other than yourself. You know the truth of your worth, and if someone else's opinion of you tries to diminish you in any way, it doesn't matter.

We can be our own worst enemies. We can go from feeling good to feeling bad because of our own thoughts—those little voices in our heads that are ready at a second's notice to criticize us. The moment we perceive that something we have done is not up to some standard we have set for ourselves, we immediately put ourselves down.

Sound self-esteem is maintained by not listening to that little voice, by remembering that no matter how badly you think you did, you did the absolute best that you could have done at that time. Low self-esteem is caused by criticizing or condemning yourself for not living up to *your own* standards. We have a tendency to set our standards high, often too high to succeed. Then when we fail to meet our own expectations, we criticize ourselves for failing. There is never any reason for putting yourself down or for any loss of self-esteem. Change how you perceive life, and your life will change accordingly.

Most of us find it easier to overlook the mistakes of others, yet continue to be hard on ourselves. As if there wasn't enough in the present to attend to, we often insist on dredging up the past to torment ourselves. When you cannot change the outcome of conditions that you wish were otherwise, all you can change is your attitude toward it. With sound self-esteem you no longer find it necessary to place value judgments. You would no sooner judge another than you would judge yourself.

If you pick up a fork to eat dinner and then discover you're having soup, you don't insist on eating with a fork. No one would. You would change your utensil for a spoon. Yet often we stick with a poor decision we've made, even though we know there is a better choice available. Change is how we make progress. To resist change is to miss opportunities. What's the most prevalent fear that keeps us from making a change? Fear of failure. Fear of mistakes. Yet to not even try is failure already, and mistakes are only lessons.

The most important thing is to be aware of and awake to what is going on in your life. Once you are aware that some choice you have made is not working for you or has had a negative impact on your life, you gain the option of changing it. If you choose to continue doing it, at least you are aware of what you are doing, and you can take responsibility for your actions and whatever continuing reality they create. Or, once aware of what reality you have created, you can opt to change it for a better, positive reality, one that makes you happy. But you can do nothing without being aware of what is going on and how it affects you.

Whether it is a physical fender bender or an emotional heartbreak, the situation exists for us to *get* the lesson. Once we extricate the lesson from the turmoil, the experience is free to leave us. As long as we choose to judge it by hating, resenting, or ignoring it, it will remain. When it becomes neutral, being neither good nor bad, the emotion binding it to us is loosened, and it is free to go. In any difficult situation, ask yourself what the experience is trying to teach you. Underlying it is a fear. Discover what that fear is, reason out why it is in your life, and it will lose its power and cease to exist.

You create more of whatever you give your attention to. What you focus on, you will experience. Focusing on negatives will generate more negative situations. The more you focus on the positive things, the more you will create positive situations in your life. You always have that choice to change your thinking and to change the conditions of your life. Every moment, with every choice, you create your life every day. There are no wrong choices. You can be just as happy as you make up your mind to be.

Recipe for Success: Start with high self-esteem. Mix in equal measures of respect and responsibility. Respect yourself and others, their rights, privacy, and property. Take responsibility for your actions and words, spoken or not. Add logic and imagination to realize your full potential: logic to decide what you want to do and imagination for the most original ideas. Reason it out. Make sure it makes sense. With logic and imagination, success is yours.

Compared to the universe, we are an infinitesimal part, yet we are of significance because each of us is unique. No one else is exactly the same as you. Therefore no one else can have the same impact on the world as you. Every action has meaning and purpose and results in a reaction. The point is to learn and grow from our experiences, both pleasant and not so pleasant. Love yourself for you have value, and treat others with the same respect. The joy of living is reflected in high self-esteem. The more secure our self-esteem, the better we can treat ourselves and others. Improving your self-esteem will improve your life and our world.

ABOUT THE AUTHOR

Lois Marie Gacher has been an intuitive self-improvement counselor for over 13 years and in customer service for over 20 years. As a professional writer, she is author of a workbook for improving self-esteem, *Rise and Shine*. Her company, High Esteem Seminars, LLC, uses this workbook in their self-improvement workshops, "Realize Your Potential" and "Inner Personal Actualization," as well as in their customer service training seminars. High Esteem Seminars feels self-esteem is so vital for success that they base their Customer Service Representative training in self-esteem. They are the only company to offer this dynamic combination. Visit http://www.highesteemseminars.com.

87

Is Your Calculator Broken?:
Being on Your Case versus Being on Your Side

Relly Nadler

Many individuals have "faulty evaluation systems." They are rarely satisfied when successful and are overly critical of their performance, even if they win, and win big. This can become a rigid pattern. In the past it may have driven them to great successes, but over time it can become a burden and an anchor from being more successful.

These individuals tend to continually try harder and often fall short in their own eyes. They will readily admit that they are hard on themselves, but they believe it is the *only* way to push themselves to their best performance. It is as if they have a calculator that is defective, but they do not realize it is always off one digit. When evaluating themselves, the calculator should read 1,000, but instead, it reads 100, or it should read 100 but instead reads 10. They get upset about the reading but don't realize their evaluation system is faulty or broken. Instead of "being on their side," they are always "on their case."

There are three major, unintended consequences of being on your case rather than being on your side.

1. These people are never satisfied with their performance, and their self-confidence is affected.
2. Because everything seems to be less than they had hoped, they are miserable, tense, and unhappy.
3. Unconsciously, they treat others the same way they treat themselves—overly critical, picky, negative, and never satisfied.

Most individuals who are hard on themselves are blindsided to the problems inherent in their personal leadership style. Sometimes they require a wake-up call to alert them to the serious impact this kind of pattern has on their ultimate performance and well-being. If you recognize yourself in the above profile, answer a simple question: What percentage of the time are you on your case instead of on your side? Use a scale of 1 to 100. You can tell if you or others have a faulty evaluation system if after *every* performance you establish that you should have had:

- better effort
- higher quality
- faster delivery.

The manifestation of this kind of attitude is typically feeling scolded by yourself for failing to live up to your abilities. It's almost like you take out your whip and begin snapping yourself into shape. You may even say or think, "How could I be so stupid? When am I going to finally learn? What is wrong with me?" More, better, faster, more, better, faster: this becomes an automatic, negative self-evaluation system.

Andrea's Story

Andrea was an executive in an agency and constantly felt she was behind in everything—e-mails went unanswered, voice mails were not returned, one-on-ones with staff were cancelled or rescheduled. Her self-evaluation system was harsh and unforgiving in spite of many of the positive things she was initiating at the agency. Andrea often spent her first moments with an employee apologizing for something she had failed to get around to. Her confidence was affected, and her negative self-evaluation started to influence others. Perhaps she wasn't as competent as they had thought she was. . . .

In one of our coaching sessions Andrea achieved a breakthrough when I pointed out that she had apologized three times in 30 minutes. It was obvious she was overly critical of herself. She became painfully aware of how automatic this self-evaluation system was and, more importantly, recognized that it was quite possibly inaccurate. Andrea also became aware of how pervasive this pattern was in all her interactions and that it undermined her leadership abilities as well.

Andrea started out saying she was on her own case 80 percent of the time. Through talking about this pattern's impact and building awareness, she was able to get it down to about 40 percent. It was important for her to understand that she was not trying to eliminate being on her case, but rather reframing it into being on her side. With some real commitment and practice she developed the ability to catch the pattern faster and redirect it from the former to the latter. Andrea became more on her side and, as a result, was less demanding of her staff and more on their side as well.

Changing our self-evaluation greatly improves how confident we feel and allows us greater awareness of how we evaluate others.

Redirecting Questions

The best way to change from being on your case to being on your side is first to notice how you behave and then turn the evaluation into a *learning and action plan*. Below are some examples of whipping statements and statements that will help you redirect yourself to being on your side.

"On Your Case" Whipping

- How could I be so lame?
- Don't I know better than this?
- I'm an idiot for doing this!
- Why didn't I start this sooner?
- I could have done a much better job!
- What is wrong with me?
- I should have known better!

"On Your Side" (Phrases That Redirect Your Habit)

- Which parts of this performance went well?
- What didn't turn out the way I wanted it to?
- What exactly didn't work out here?
- Which part is under my influence?
- Is there anything I could have done differently?
- What will I have to do to accept this performance and not beat myself up?
- What can I learn from this performance?

- What will I have to improve next time?
- Is there any learning, training, or help I need to improve my performance?
- What will be my next step?
- How will I make sure I stay on track?

What was your reaction in hearing these questions? It is important to first acknowledge what went well in order to establish the proper perspective in your evaluation and to curtail the "more, better, faster" pattern. This chart shows the difference between the two self-evaluations.

	On Your Case	On Your Side
Quality	demanding	respectful
	damaging	constructive
	irrational	rational
	overgeneralized	realistic
Results	dissatisfied	encouraged
	less confident	energized
	overwhelmed	confident for the future

Questions and Actions to Be More on Your Side

- Circle the terms above you have experienced the most.
- How accurate is your evaluation system?
- On a scale of 1 to 100, what percentage of the time are you on your case?
- How do you feel after you've been on your case?
- What are the consequences for you and others for being on your case?
- Do you treat others as harshly as you do yourself?
- If you don't change this, what do you stand to lose or miss out on?
- Keep track of the times you have stopped being on your case and then redirected to being on your side. How did you do it?
- What is most difficult about being on your side?
- What helps you to be on your side?
- Record in your planner the percentage of time you are on your side each day, from 1 to 100, and reward yourself.

Your calculator *can* be fixed, and you will subsequently feel more confident and ready for new risks.

ABOUT THE AUTHOR

Dr. Relly Nadler is a licensed psychologist, executive coach, corporate trainer, and author. His books, *Leaders' Playbook: How to Apply Emotional Intelligence-Keys to Great Leadership* and the *Leadership Keys Field Guide*, are full of emotional intelligence (EI) secrets, strategies, tools, and profiles of leaders. Relly has coached CEOs, presidents, and their staffs and has developed and delivered innovative leadership programs and facilitated team trainings for Fortune 100 companies. He is recognized around the world for his expertise in linking emotional intelligence and experiential learning to business objectives. Go to http://www.truenorthleadership.com for more information and *free* EI secrets.

88

Stop the Negative Self-Talk!

Anne K. Crothers

Melody Beattie has a book called *Stop Being Mean to Yourself* that I often lend to clients because it's a good book and because I love the title. It is *hard* to feel happy when we are so critical and judgmental of ourselves. No wonder we don't feel good enough. We live with a mean voice in our heads that puts us down all the time.

It's like a soap opera in there! For some people, negative self-talk occurs only in high-pressure situations, like a public event; for others, it's all day, every day. We monitor our words, our behavior, and our appearance, and we always find ourselves wanting. We say the wrong thing, wear the wrong thing, and do the wrong thing. We never measure up to ourselves. We look at other people with envy or awe and believe that they know secrets that we don't. We compare and come up wanting.

If you marked down throughout one day how many of your thoughts about yourself were negative and how many positive, it would probably depress you. We *are* mean to ourselves. It's an epidemic in my practice! We seem to feel that if we believe positive things about ourselves, we are conceited or vain. It's not okay to praise ourselves, ever. It is okay, however, to doubt our abilities, punish ourselves for mistakes, and accept other people's opinions of us as more important than our own. We are not on our own side.

A client said to me recently that she was participating in a church group, and as a part of it, group members were encouraged to do affirmations at home. Affirmations are positive self-statements like "I am a valuable person." She found that she couldn't do them and said she was surprised as she is usually open-minded about trying new techniques. When I asked her what the problem was, she said, "They're stupid . . . aren't they?" To her surprise, I replied, "No!"

I asked her which message would be a better way to raise her daughter, to praise her or to call her fat and stupid. She understood then immediately. We always understand when it's about someone else, especially someone we love. We don't treat our children or our friends or even our pets the way we treat ourselves. Why not? Because we know it's not okay. We know it hurts them. Yet we hurt ourselves constantly.

Anyone who saw the movie *What the Bleep Do We Know* was probably drawn to the scene with the water exhibit, where simply writing a negative statement changed the water molecules to be grotesque. In the movie the heroine writes positive statements all over herself to counteract all the negative self-talk that she does. Maybe instead of getting tattoos of skulls and hearts with daggers, we should be marking ourselves with affirmations. It might inoculate us from the self-criticism.

Are affirmations brainwashing? Well, maybe our brains need a little washing! They seem to be filled with ugly words and images. Could we possibly be as bad as we think we are? Nope. We are all, all of us, just right. We are doing the best we can—and that is always good enough. We are not to blame for our early wounds; we have nothing to be ashamed of. Shame, in fact, is the problem.

Shame keeps us from being authentic. Terrified that others will see the real us and declare us hideous, we hide away our real beauty, convinced of our own unworthiness. We are all ugly ducklings who feel different, lonely, left behind. Other people seem more together, smoother, smarter, cooler than us. If only we could learn to believe in ourselves, to be on our own side.

The first thing we can do is to view ourselves with compassion. We are not perfect. We will always make mistakes. That's okay. In fact, that's the way it's supposed to be. Unconditional love is hard, and unconditional self-love is even harder. We want to attach strings, to love ourselves *if* we just lose a few pounds or quit smoking. We will approve of ourselves as soon as we earn a little more or meet the perfect mate. But it doesn't work like that. The mark keeps moving, and we never get there. It's a trick.

What if we are already everything we need to be? What if we are part of God? I believe that, I just don't believe it all the time. I slip in and out of knowing who I am. I get sucked back in by shame and self-doubt. Do you?

I have found that believing in myself means that I need to slow down, to trust my instincts, to wait and see. When I wait instead of evaluate, I can see the rightness of what happens. When I judge myself harshly, I feel ashamed, and I stop looking and listening. I don't want to know. It is in this way that I become disconnected from myself and from everyone. I am so busy being ashamed and hiding myself and my shame that I don't have time for anyone else.

Loving ourselves helps us to be open to life and available to others. If we stumble, maybe we were meant to. If we forget, maybe it wasn't right for us. If we drop it, maybe it was time to let go. Having faith that things are the way they are meant to be helps us believe that we are just right, too. We are all God's children, or children of the universe. We have a point and a plan, and we are supposed to be here just the way we are. Do you believe that? Try!

At least one thing is clear: negative self-talk never helps us do anything better. It just wastes our time and energy. So say those affirmations, change the criticism to self-praise, and stop putting yourself down. Push the bad mood out of your head. Don't stay in a state of shame or fear. When you find yourself there, get out! Have hope, and have faith. Be loving. Stop the negative self-talk!

ABOUT THE AUTHOR

Anne K. Crothers, MEd, is a therapist in private practice in Allentown, Pennsylvania. Her mission statement for her business, Healing Works, is to eliminate fear and shame and increase love of self, of the Higher Power, of each other, and of the earth. An expert in trauma and sexual abuse, Anne has a gift with children and adolescents. She uses expressive therapies and a spiritual focus. She also provides invitational-style interventions for addiction and training on play therapy, childhood obesity, and more. For more information on Anne, see her Web site at http://www.healingworksallentown.com.

89

SIGNALS

The Power of Qs

Theresa Cordova & Annette M. Bau

Have you ever wondered why some people's lives seem to unfold effortlessly while others face one disaster after another? Is it simply fate, or are there ways of controlling and improving the outcome of one's life? By understanding the laws of the universe and the capacity of personal power, you can tap into this power and create a life filled with blessings, joy, abundance, love, and wealth—truly, anything your heart desires.

The Power of Qs

The first step is to understand the Power of Qs (cues). Qs are life's signals that lead us to transform and transcend the daily struggles and thoughts that often misguide our direction and leave us feeling frustrated and unhappy. Qs are readily available to guide us toward greater health, wonderful relationships, and abundance in all we do. But how do we recognize these Qs? You may find them in the form of hunches, thoughts, ideas, insights, and intuition. They arise within us and outside us; they appear in multiple forms. They may come from people delivering messages, words said on TV, in movies, or in newspapers, or through the vibrations of nature. There is no limit to the Qs we are given or the ways in which they come. Our job is learning to recognize and receive them. While they are always present (whether we recognize them or not), the key is to improve one's ability to catch the numerous Qs that come our way. To receive Qs, we need to develop the capacity of tuning in.

Tuning In

The first step to tuning in is to take time each day to quiet your mind and listen to your heart. The easiest way to quiet your mind is through focused breathing. By focusing on slow, abdominal breathing for at least 15 minutes, the space in your mind expands, allowing greater access to the Qs that are there to guide you to a better life. Don't worry if thoughts get in the way—simply refocus on your breathing to increase the space. Once you have the space to tune in, you are then ready to ask.

Asking

Whether you have a question about a relationship, money, or a new job, the key is to simply ask and wait to see the results. For instance, if you are contemplating a new career, ask the question, "What is the perfect career decision?" Then, without attachment to the outcome, wait for the Qs that will lead you to the answer.

The amazing thing about Qs is that they come. All you need to do is listen and trust. Once you practice tuning in and asking, it is imperative to learn how to recognize the answers and the various forms in which they come.

Forms

One of the biggest challenges is not becoming attached to a particular form in which Qs come. We may have expectations of how Qs should look or what messages they should convey. An illustration of this is the story of St. Peter and John. Whenever John had a problem, he would call on St. Peter. When John heard that a flood was coming, he was not afraid because St. Peter had always provided him with guidance and protection.

Before the flood arrived a man drove by and offered John a ride to safety. John smiled and said, "Thanks for the offer, but St. Peter will save me from the flood." When the waters began rising, a man on a boat rowed by and offered John a ride. John replied, "Thanks for the offer, but St. Peter will save me." A few hours passed, and the waters became so high that John had to get on the roof of his home. A helicopter came by and dropped a rope down for John to climb up. John yelled, "Thanks, but St. Peter will save me." The helicopter left, and John waited. The water kept rising, and eventually, John drowned.

When John got to heaven, he was greeted by St. Peter. John angrily said, "St. Peter, I trusted you to save me. Instead, you let me die."

St. Peter responded, "John, I sent a car, a boat, and a helicopter to rescue you, but you declined them all."

John stood in shock and replied, "I thought you were coming to get me; I never considered you would send someone else."

The moral of the story is not to be attached to how the outcome *should* look. In fact, one of the most common forms of Qs comes in coincidences.

Coincidences

Once we understand Qs, we realize that coincidences are often the greatest tools to lead us forward. A funny example occurred with Theresa's daughter, Sophia. One night, while watching television, Sophia asked her mother whether she thought it was a good idea for Sophia to go to Disneyland over spring break. Just as she finished the question, the shout of a group of football players who'd just won the Super Bowl leaped out at them from a TV commercial, saying, "I'm going to Disneyland!"

Many people would chalk this up to a funny coincidence. However, many answers come precisely in that form. As we learn to pay attention to coincidences as Qs, our lives receive answers and direction. The way becomes clear and smooth. Sophia knows this. She chose to follow her hunch, went to Disneyland, and had the time of her life.

Signals

Signals are another form of Qs in the universe. We may be on a particular course and we start getting signals—either everything seems to click, or nothing clicks. We may believe we are supposed to pursue a career in interior decorating, but nothing is coming together, and all the while, Qs are directing us toward becoming a builder. Pay attention to signals because they direct us to the perfect situation. When we don't pay attention, we often move in the wrong direction and find ourselves miserable, losing self-worth and money, and often, losing hope. Remember: the struggle is the problem. Qs in the form of signals tell you when your direction is right or wrong.

Wait, Listen, and Trust

Now that you have a basic understanding of the process, sit back, tune in, and ask your question. Then wait and listen for the answer without attachment, and experience your life unfolding simply and perfectly by following the Qs that the universe so willingly provides. The wisdom of the ages will guide you. When you receive what you perceive as an answer, ask for validation in the form of two or more Qs to convince you that this is, indeed, the right way to go. Then relax, stay alert, and trust in the answer that comes. Herein lies the key to a life filled with purpose, love, and joy.

ABOUT THE AUTHOR

Theresa Cordova and Annette M. Bau, CFP, are partners of The Power of Qs.com, a company dedicated to teaching people and organizations the power of identifying and following the ever-present signals that create a pathway toward building a wonderful life. To receive your free report, "Tapping into Your 7 Greatest Powers," go to http://www.ThePowerofQs.com. Annette is also the founder of http://www.MillionaireSeries.com and http://www.LifeTransitions.info. She is the author of *The 7 Principles of Becoming a Millionaire for Life* and *If Only I Had Known . . . What You Need to Do Now to Avoid Devastating Financial Mistakes.*

90

SMALL TALK

Make Small Talk?
I'd Rather Eat Worms!

Signe A. Dayhoff

Small talk is any superficial personal communication between two or more people. It is the vehicle through which you approach people to test to see if you share interests, attitudes, philosophies, values, histories, and experiences on which you and the other person can build. It is the method by which you discover if you are interested in getting to know the other person better.

You can make small talk during in-person meetings, in chat rooms, on bulletin boards, on voice mail, and in text messaging. However, it is important to note that the more impersonal forms of communication are not as effective as face-to-face communication because they lack the texture, depth, and richness of in-person interaction which is essential to developing relationships.

But "small" talk is a misnomer. There is nothing small or trivial about it. It is the basis and beginning of *every* relationship, from personal to professional to business; that is, it is virtually impossible to meet and get to know people without the aid of simple, casual conversation in some format.

Yet, surprisingly, at least 95 percent of Americans report being uncomfortable conversing with strangers. Why?

Small talk is a form of speaking in public, which, according to polls, is still our number one fear. Children are repeatedly warned not to talk to strangers. Today, much of our communication is automated and anonymous so that our everyday, in-person communication skills with new people become rusty. We become shy and unsure about how to act. Consequently, we discount the necessity of small talk and try to avoid it.

Small talk is like a casual game of tennis. The goal is to keep the conversational ball in the air while giving both participants an equal opportunity to hit the ball. You strive for a comfortable rhythm. Playing to your partner's strengths is more important than concentrating on your own. Making fancy shots or acing out the other player will likely bring the conversation to a speedy conclusion. The object of the game: everyone's satisfaction, a good workout, and the mutual desire for another game.

When you work on small talk, it is essential that you focus on the *process*, not on the outcome. This means you need to develop skills in both approaching and speaking with others and make a plan to use these skills. This is what Pauline did.

Pauline was tired of staying home or standing on the periphery of conversations at social gatherings, so she decided to become more socially effective. She began to think of being with a group of strangers as being in a rowboat in a sea of interaction *possibilities*. To move herself forward, she needed to use an *oar*—the first principle of small talk—*observing* others, *asking* questions, and *revealing* something about yourself.

She began by developing eye contact, a smile, and open body positions to make her more approachable. Next, she wrote a brief but interesting introduction for herself (e.g., "Hi, I'm Pauline, and I coach people to laugh."). Sometimes the introduction included an interest, hobby, activity, work, etc. Once she had heard the other person's name, she repeated it to get it right and remember it.

In order to make knowledgeable small talk in each new circumstance, she learned about the event and the people likely to be present beforehand. She examined her reasons for going and what benefit she wanted to receive (e.g., contacts, fun, making friends, business) so she could determine afterward if she had achieved her goal. Furthermore, she took time to be up on current events, scanning a paper daily, to give her more possibilities for finding topics and similarities.

She discovered that she needed to have icebreakers ready. Using a short list of boilerplate small talk examples, she could tailor a conversation opener to any situation or person. They reflected a variety of open-ended questions and comments for each of three basic topic areas:

- **event, circumstance, or environment** (weather, what's going on in the news, or the actual physical environs of the event, like the lighting, colors, artwork, music, furniture, architecture, accessories)
- **the other person** (name, accent, appearance, attire, belongings)
- **yourself** (name, job, hobbies, interests, attire, background, belongings).

The event and environment were guaranteed to give her something in common with the other person because they were experiencing these things together.

Pauline found that she shouldn't discount the weather as a topic. She would make it into amusing anecdotes or into something with which the other person could identify. One she liked: "I was in such a hurry to get here before the rain started that I left my bag on the roof of the car but didn't realize it until it began to pour, and the soggy bag slithered down the windshield onto my wipers."

In her initial conversations she kept her topics neutral so as not to engender strong emotions and polarize the conversation. Since this is all very tentative at the beginning, when she was not sure there was a match, she remained somewhat impersonal; that is, while she was upbeat and enthusiastic, and disclosing to a degree, she did not immediately pour out her innermost dreams and desires to this new person because too much personal sharing too soon can be overwhelming.

When she first arrived, she stationed herself by the door and greeted people as they entered. Her acting as a host, not as a guest, created an immediately friendly and positive first impression. If they had been wearing name tags, it would have given her the opportunity to see and say their names and to determine if there were certain people with whom she wished to speak later. She then would have been able to locate them with relative ease, and they would have recognized her. She found that the buffet table and bar offered similar opportunities.

Pauline discovered that she could give herself more control in an interaction by introducing herself first. She would choose the person and prepare what to say and how to say it. This allowed her to direct the topic by making the first statement or asking the first question. Being first also removed the anxiety-producing anticipation of waiting for someone to speak to her and not knowing what would be asked or how to respond. The rest was listening, dovetailing what the other said, and disclosing a little about herself.

Her maiden voyage into the world of small talk was at a photographic gallery opening. While she felt a little awkward at first, she found that remaining relaxed, focusing on the other person, and looking for and commenting on commonalities made it a very pleasant experience. She even made some acquaintances with whom she could follow up.

As Pauline learned, the whole object of small talk is to find bonds on which you and the other person can build. Once you find them, you can explore them and expand on them. When you reframe small talk as *the* relationship generator and acknowledge what it can do for you, you can begin to make it your own most powerful social effectiveness strategy.

ABOUT THE AUTHOR

Known as the Social Effectiveness Guru, Signe A. Dayhoff, PhD, has helped thousands transform their self-presentation anxiety into social effectiveness. She is a psychologist, coach, trainer, and President of Effectiveness-Plus, LLC. As a former social phobic, she can show you how to replace your fear of small talk, networking, public speaking, personal marketing, and selling with presentation confidence. She is the author of five books and over 100 published articles. Her latest book is *Diagonally Parked in a Parallel Universe: Working Through Social Anxiety*. Discover what she can do for you and claim your free newsletter at http://www.effectiveness-plus.com.

91

Ten Steps to Oratory Eloquence

Craig L. Howe

As you hang up the telephone, the icy fingertips of panic grip your stomach; your heart races. Your most recent project was delivered on time, within budget, and is approaching payback one year ahead of schedule. Your industry association wants you to address their annual convention.

Relax: they believe you have something to offer. Here are 10 rules to ease your palpitations.

As you think about your speech, remember the second rule: all great speeches, and even some good ones, require *shape*. As a practitioner of the forensic form, I find the old saw is hard to beat: "Tell them what you will tell them; tell them; then tell them what you told them."

Wait a minute, you say. What is the first step? "*Shake hands* with the audience" is the answer. I already did it by noting that you have something worthy of being said. Former Ambassador Robert Strauss used to begin his addresses like this: "Before I begin this speech, I have something to say." This passage was always composed in a style that enabled him to reclaim a powerful tone for the instructive portion of his remarks. Make the first step a quick one. Put on your smile; calm your nerves, then get to work.

Your skeleton now needs flesh and blood to spring to life; structure needs a *pulse*. A good speech needs a beat, a sense of movement to get the audience tapping its mental foot. One technique orators through the ages have used is *anaphora*, the repeated beginning. For example, from Reverend Jesse Jackson: "Get ready. It's morning time. From the slave ship; to the championship; it's morning time. From the outhouse; to the state house; to the courthouse; to The

White House; it's morning time. . . ." Don't overlook parallelism. It sings. It excites. It works.

What else is required? *Occasion*. There comes a dramatic time in the life of a person, party, organization, or nation that cries for the uplift and release of a speech. Someone is called on to articulate the pride, hope, or grief of it all. The speaker becomes the center of attention, and the world stops to listen.

A closely related item is *forum*. Be it the floor of the United States Senate or the dais in the convention hall, each viewer in the audience must feel like the extension of a vast audience. One-on-one may sell; one-on-a-million thrills.

The fifth required element is *focus*. A "great" speech does not need to start out great and stay great to the finish. It needs to engage your listeners, then make allowances for a dip in interest in the middle. It then builds to its climax. John Stuart Mill, the political economist, defined the orator's art: "Everything important to his purpose was said at the exact moment when he had brought the minds of his audience into the state most fitted to receive it."

To handshake, shape, pulse, occasion, forum, and focus, add *purpose*. A speech should be made for a good reason. To inspire, to instruct, to rally, or to lead are noble purposes. To sound off, to feed a speaker's ego, or to flatter or intimidate are not.

Add *theme* to the list. If you cannot answer the question "what do you want to say" in a single, declarative sentence, do yourself and your audience a favor: decline the invitation.

Delivery is the essence of eloquence. It requires practice, discipline, drilling, and timing. You can be your own trainer. As you develop self-confidence, you put the audience at ease or make them sit up. Your eye is in contact with the people, not the page. Your professional passion is contagious.

Every audience needs a sense of *completion*. It begins with a quiet, declarative sentence; it builds in a series of semicolons; it employs the puissance of parallelism; it reaches to the farthest rafter and reverberates with the action and passion of our time, and—forgetting those silly rules of short sentences and banishments against self-adulation—it grabs each conventioneer by his or her lapels and shouts to their hearts and souls to say, "This—this is the end of the best speech you will ever have the good fortune to experience."

Follow these rules, and you will experience instant, sustained applause punctuated by the occasional "bravo!" at the conclusion of your speech. Be forewarned: there is an ever present pugnacious pundit punk in every audience who wrinkles his brow and wonders aloud, "But what was really said?"

As for everyone else, they will offer their highest compliment—their undivided attention.

About the Author

Since 1987, as the Principal Consultant for Faulkner & me (http://www.faulknerandme.com), Craig L. Howe has offered financial and speech writing services to corporate and eleemosynary clients. In his spare time he operates http://www.craighowe.com, home of the Pointed Pundit. Craig was born in Buffalo, New York. He was awarded a MA degree from the Newhouse School at Syracuse University in Syracuse, New York, and a BA degree *cum laude* from Hillsdale College, Hillsdale, Michigan. He lives in Darien, Connecticut, with his wife, Cynthia. They are the parents of three grown children.

.

92

SPIRITUAL AFFINITY

Dance with Your Heart:
How to Befriend Your Heart
and the World around You

Shirley Cheng

What do you see when people dance? Is it how their hands and feet move so gracefully in such unison with one another, yet each of them sparkles individuality? Are the dancers smiling? What does that mean? They may be joyous when they move their bodies to the rhythms of the music, but that is not all. They smile because they are dancing with their hearts.

What do I mean when I say they dance with their hearts? When you are dancing with your heart, you are dancing together with your heart and dancing using your heart, and as a result, you are becoming a dancing heart.

What do you feel when you see them dance? Do you feel like dancing as well? When you dance, you will project how you feel and what you feel onto any onlookers, causing them to have a desire, a need, to mirror your feelings, then finally your actions. You set good examples of life when you dance; you are teaching true things of life, so you must lead others by dancing yourself.

To dance with your heart, you must be pure. Release all the negative feelings hammering inside you and block out the ugly voices the outside world whispers stealthily in your ears. Become friends with yourself. What qualities do you look for in a friend?

Are you ready to become your own friend and dance with your heart? Take the following dance steps on your own before you can hold hands with your heart.

- **Acceptance.** Accept who you are as a whole. Accept how you feel. Accept how you think. Accept how you look from your head to your toes. You may not like to accept yourself as you are now because you feel you are not perfect. But what is perfection anyway? Is nature perfect? If so, then you must be perfect, too. Take a look—I bet that tall tree in your backyard has at least one torn branch, but is it still majestic? Does it still deserve to be called beautiful? Perfect?
- **Openness.** Be open, truthful, and honest with yourself. Do not lie to yourself. Do not live with pretense. When something is making you unhappy, face it, do not run away from it. Change the situation with a clear and honest look. By closely examining the situation you are in, you will be able to find the root of the problem and plug it out. By remaining in the dark, you will never find that root, so turn on the lights!
- **Understanding.** Understand your feelings, thoughts, and why you behave the way you do. Find the purpose to your actions. Learn from your past and those situations that did not go as smoothly as hoped, and utilize what you learn to make your future bright.
- **Love and appreciation.** Love yourself. Honestly tell yourself, "I know I am not a bad person. I know I do my best in everything I do, and I know I am being my best, so I love myself because I am a good person with good intentions." Appreciate what you have and whom you have. Appreciate what you are able to do.
- **Positivity.** Count your blessings. Focus on the good things you do have at the present and the positive side of things. Do not dwell on bad situations, but instead, move forward and have a bright attitude and outlook for the future. You have the ability to make a positive difference to your future just by being positive. Choosing the road to positivity and happiness will give you the strength, the desire, and the motivation to take giant steps forward. Don't pick the road to misery—it will just glue you to one spot, and you wouldn't want to get the glue onto others, now would you?
- **Passion.** Be passionate about who you are and what you do. Value life; cherish every minute that is given to you. Hold on tightly to the happy moments and their memories because when they're gone, they're gone forever. Live with conviction; live with vitality.
- **Happiness.** Smile often. Smile to yourself, even if there's no good reason. Smiling will warm you up, even when the days seem dreary. Frequently treat yourself to a big smile while working or frolicking; it is the sweetest treat you can give yourself, and the best part is that there are no calories!

Once you achieve calm in your soul, you will be able to spiritually connect with your own self from deep within you, and that is where your heart lies.

What is your heart? No, it is not the muscular organ that pumps blood through your body; it is your essence, your higher self or energy. No one has the power to harm your heart, especially if you don't allow outside negativity to pollute your spirit like a thick fog.

When you twirl and swirl with your heart, you will be sharply aware of all beauties of the world, things that you had not noticed or given heed to when you were not dancing with your heart. With the dance within you, you will have a broader sense of acceptance of who you are, and therefore your acceptance of others and the world around you will grow and grow to the point that you are spiritually connected with the entire universe—every creation breathes into you and you into it, fusing everything into one.

You will feel awake and alert when you waltz with your heart. Once you start dancing, you will not want to stop because the feeling will be too good and too powerful to let go, and you will crave it when you stop dancing. You will feel at peace with yourself and with the world. You will feel friendly toward those who follow in your dance steps or even toward those who abandon your dance to be lured into darkness.

When you dance, you will feel alive and free and painless, even if your body shouts of old age. Your body will grow older, but your essence will stay as young as a newly blossomed flower, but only with much more wisdom and understanding. Your dance will never grow old with age; instead, it will grow younger and wiser as each day passes for you will connect with all surrounding power to recharge your own energy.

Do I dance with my heart? You bet I do! Many joints in my body have been disfigured by severe juvenile rheumatoid arthritis since infancy, yet my heart dances freely and openly with no restraint. As I dance, my heart tells me all things it sees, so my blindness miserably fails to make me trip on my own feet.

Thus crank up the music, take my hand in yours, and let us dance with our hearts!

ABOUT THE AUTHOR

Shirley Cheng (b. 1983), a blind and physically disabled poet and the author of three books (including *Dance with Your Heart* and *The Revelation of a Star's Endless Shine*) by age 20, has had severe juvenile rheumatoid arthritis since infancy. Owing to years of hospitalization, she received no schooling until age 11. Having achieved grade level in all areas after about 180 days in a special education class in elementary school, she was transferred to a regular sixth grade class in middle school. After a successful eye surgery she hopes to earn multiple science doctorates from Harvard University. Visit her Web site at http://www.shirleycheng.com, or contact her at shirley@shirleycheng.com.

93

Choose to Live a Stress-Less Life: The Life You Save May Be Your Own

Karen Sherman

Life is stressful—that's a basic fact. Stress comes in all shapes and sizes. Of course, major life events, such as a sickness in the family or financial woes, are universally stressful. There are other, less obvious day-to-day stresses, though, many of which impact individuals differently. (One of the key concepts regarding stress is that "stress is in the eye of the beholder.") Sometimes stress can stem from happy things. Think about how exciting moving to a new home can be or how joyous welcoming a new baby is—and how very stressful, too!

Here's another basic fact: you can't control anything that happens in life, and you can't control anybody. For many of us, that feels scary and unsettling. But there's good news: we do have some control—the control that lies within us and gives us the ability to manage our reactions.

There is clear scientific evidence that there is a relationship between stress and health. Being able to control your level of stress will improve your physical health and your quality of life.

There are several useful techniques that can help you learn to keep stress under your control.

- **Deep breathing.** Take in a breath through your nose that goes past your throat and past your chest into your solar plexus (the area right below your rib cage). Imagine taking in the kind of breath that you would if you were walking past a bakery and smelling the wonderful aromas. Hold it for a few moments. Now release it slowly through your lips, which are opened slightly.

Imagine that you are blowing on candles that are lit on a birthday cake. (It's not your birthday, though, so you can't blow them out; you can only make the flames flicker.) By breathing this way, you are taking the necessary steps to begin relaxing your body.

- **Relax your body.** When you notice that your body is tense, imagine breathing into that area, and relax it. In order to help you learn to notice when your body is tight, practice tensing up and then relaxing your body parts, starting from your toes and moving up your body. This exercise will help you become aware of the difference between how you feel when you are tense and when you are relaxed. If your body is tight, you will be less likely to flow with a stressful situation that may come your way.
- **Learn to meditate.** Mediation is a practice that helps you learn to focus your attention. Sit upright, and focus on your breath. Some people also like to count to 10 and then start again or use a mantra (a six-syllable phrase from Buddha's teachings) to assist in keeping their attention. When a thought comes, notice it, acknowledge it, and let it go. This tool takes patience and practice but is a wonderful way to help you learn to "let go" and therefore more effectively deal with stress.

There are many times when I realize I am starting to become stressed—perhaps I am in a traffic jam and I'm late for a doctor's appointment, or I've agreed to take on one project too many and am rushing to meet a deadline. Once I realize I'm becoming stressed because I can feel my body getting tense, I assess the situation and accept the fact that being stressed will be counterproductive. More specifically, I can't change the fact that there's a traffic jam, so maybe I'll enjoy the scenery. Or by being anxious about the deadline, I'm not giving the work my full attention, so I take a moment to inhale a long, slow breath (as I've outlined above) and choose to let go of what's bothering me. In just a moment's time I'm back on track and more focused.

Though stress is a part of life, it need not adversely affect it. By learning to improve the way you deal with your reactions, you will improve the quality of your life!

ABOUT THE AUTHOR

A psychologist in private practice, Dr. Karen Sherman specializes in relationships and lifestyle issues. Her first book, *Marriage Magic! Find It, Keep It, Make It Last*, was published in 2004, and *The Choice is Yours: Rewire Your Past to Create a New Future* will soon be published. She's in the media frequently for her expert opinion and also does speaking engagements, workshops, and tele-seminars. She's dedicated to helping people learn how to make choices that will offer them richer lives, both individually and in relationships. You can subscribe to her free newsletter at http://www.drkarensherman.com.

94

Are You Stressed Out?

Susan Ratynski

Do you have difficulty expressing your anger? Are you unable to say no? Are you suffering from a constant need to prove yourself or to do it all? Do you often feel tired and burned out? If so, you are probably experiencing the symptoms of stress.

Stress left unattended will lead to burnout. Aren't you tired of living an unhealthy lifestyle?

We all have different sources of stress and different ways of handling those stressors. First, what is a stressor? This is different for everyone, but more common stressors are traffic, rude people, bills, family, friends, too many activities, too few activities, job, health issues, relationships . . . the list can go on and on. What one person considers stressful, another might not. It is not so much a person, place, or situation that stresses you out as it is *how* you react to it.

Stressor + Thought + Response = STRESS!

A stressor added to your thoughts about it, added to your response, can equal stress.

Connie, a college student studying for her MBA, explains it this way: "A stressor for me is traffic. I know I hate getting caught in it, and that leads to my getting aggressive behind the wheel." Connie's thought of hate adds to her response of aggression, which only equals stress.

Signs of Stress

Some signs of stress include, but are not limited to, the following three areas.

- **Psychological.** Depression; boredom; urge to cry; worry; helpless feelings; urge to run.
- **Situational.** Fault finding/blaming; perfectionism; aggressiveness; smoking; over/under eating; reclusive behavior; argumentative attitude.
- **Physical.** Headache; muscle tension; high blood pressure; heart pounding; stomach problems; sweating; dizziness.

Stress Management

Stress management involves observing your stressor and shifting how you define your thoughts about it to respond in a nonstressful way.

Let's look at the three main areas that stress affects and learn techniques in managing your thought responses. Remember, we are not talking about stress elimination, but stress management. It is impossible to totally eliminate stress as it is part of daily life. However, it is possible to change how we react to it.

Psychological Stress

1. Manage how you talk to yourself. Listen to the words you are saying to yourself throughout the day. Are you saying, "I should know everything" or "I should never lose my temper"? These thoughts set unrealistic expectations. No one is perfect—why do you believe you should be? Counter these thoughts with their opposites, such as "I may not know everything, but I am pretty smart at some things" or "I lost my temper this time, but now I am aware of it and next time will keep calm." Simply talking to yourself and defeating the negative self-talk with positive statements helps to lift your spirits.

2. Don't take yourself so damn seriously! Life is not meant to be hard and miserable. Our lives were meant to be filled with joy and abundance as per scripture, John 10:10: "I have come that you may have life, and have it more abundantly." So choose life! Bring out your creativity. What hobbies or activities did you once enjoy that you are no longer involved in? If you once played a musical instrument, play it again. Read, sew, play tennis, watch a comedy,

socialize with positive, fun people, or read a bedtime story to a child. The point is to do something you find fun and exciting.

Situational Stress

Stress is a sign of reduced productivity through procrastination, inflexibility, poor memory recall, perfectionism, unrealistic deadlines, or disorganization. Following are some solutions on increasing your efficiency, while lowering your stress level.

1. Do only one thing at a time. Start with the biggest, hardest tasks on your to-do list, followed by the smaller, easier tasks. Too many people begin with the smaller tasks only to run out of time before starting the larger tasks, and they become overwhelmed and stressed out. Start with the biggest task because when you complete it, the sense of accomplishment will make you feel good and help you to move on quickly to the smaller tasks.

2. Group errands or tasks together. Plan your driving route for the day. Instead of driving all over town with no real plan, group your errands together to help save time. If you need to go to the post office, cleaner's, gas station, and grocery store, then plan your route for the shortest drive possible. If the post office and cleaner's are closer, then go there first on your way to the gas station, and end at the grocery store. The main purpose is not to backtrack and waste time.

3. Delegate, delegate, delegate! Probably the hardest thing for most people to do, especially perfectionists, is to delegate activities. Remember, you do *not* have to do it all. Delegate easier tasks to family members, coworkers, neighbors, or friends. You may be surprised at how willing others are to help you. Do yourself a favor and ask.

Physiological Stress

Stress affects our bodies in various ways, however, we can protect our health with the following: (1) eat balanced meals; (2) exercise regularly; and (3) learn to relax daily.

You probably have read enough informational articles on diet and exercise, but do you really know how to relax? Learning how to relax daily will help you manage your stress. I personally like meditation and prayer to put me in a relaxed state. Deep breathing is another helpful technique. Try this exercise right now: take a deep breath in through your nose for a five-second count, hold for three more seconds, and then exhale though your mouth for a count of five seconds. Repeat this entire exercise five times.

Notice how you now feel? Can you feel the relaxation seeping through your entire body? Deep breathing is easy to do anywhere, whether you are in the office, stuck in traffic, standing in line, or waiting in the doctor's office. You can use this technique today, right now.

Managing Your Stress

The main thing to remember in stress management is that you are responsible for your overall health. Know what your stressors are, and understand that your responses to them have not worked in the past and need to be redefined.

Remember Connie, our MBA college student stuck in commuting traffic? I coached her on ways to redefine her thoughts regarding traffic, and she now manages her stress in a completely different way. "When I realized that I was creating my own stress regarding the traffic, I decided I needed to stop getting angry about something that was totally out of my control. I took the time spent in my car to listen to audio books of some of my college courses, and now I'm actually ahead in my studies. I no longer get stressed out in traffic but look forward to the time in the car for listening to my classes."

ABOUT THE AUTHOR

Susan Ratynski is a sought after life coach and speaker. Founder and President of Enjoy Life! Coaching, she specializes in personal and career coaching that connects your mind, body, *and* spirit to help you achieve maximum results for a balanced lifestyle. Susan's educational background is in psychology, organizational development, and life coaching. She is a workshop and seminar leader in topics such as the Law of Attraction and stress management skills. Susan is also a contributing author for "Stimuli Art," a paperback magazine. If you are ready to attract more abundance, prosperity, and success into your life, contact Susan at http://www.EnjoyLifeCoaching.com.

95

TAKING ACTION

Action Today!

Daniel Saintjean

So far, I think you'll agree this has been a pretty upbeat book, right? Well, here's a downer. The bad news is that you won't get the opportunity to read this incredible book entitled *The Stevedore in the White Fedora*. This novel, filled to the brim with stirring passages and replete with intrigue, passion, action, suspense, and hot romance, was going to captivate your imagination and take you on a breathtaking adventure to some of the most infamous ports of the world.

The only problem is that the book has not yet been written. And it never will be. That's because Isaac Will, who had the whole splendid script in his head and who was going to take time off to write it *someday*, died of a heart attack four days ago. Mr. I. Will's funeral will take place at 3:30 today, in Somerset Cemetery. Those who knew him well selected for his tombstone a fitting poem by James Albery:

> He slept beneath the moon,
> He basked beneath the sun,
> Lived a life of going-to-do soon,
> And died with nothing done.

Most people think of cemeteries as sad places. I do, too, but for a different reason. When I drive by one, I don't just see grass, flowers, monuments, and mourners. I see unwritten books that were going to enthrall their readers and unfinished plays that would have enchanted their viewers. Never written good-bye letters. Never started paintings and sculptures. Never completed love songs. It was Oliver Wendell Holmes who said, "Most people go to their graves with their songs still unsung."

Many people are saddened by the daily news of disappearing species. But equally sad is the fact that each and every day, around the world and around the clock, thousands of ideas, projects, products, inventions, and solutions disappear forever when they are buried with the people who died without ever realizing their dreams. Remember these words from Stephen Sondheim: "A dream is just a dream, if it's only in your head. If no one gets to see it, it's just as good as dead."

So I beg of you, if you have something inside you that you want to bring out into the world, start working on it now. Today. Action today, my friends. Please, don't wait, or your story might sound like this one. . . .

On Wednesday, December 3, 2003, I walked into Margarita Pizza to buy one of their famous Italian pizzas. I've been stopping there for the same reason every other week for the last 30-some years. But there was something different that day. For the first time ever, Attilio, the owner, was not behind the counter.

A friendly woman informed me that she and her husband had just acquired the business a few days earlier. After owning the business for 40 years, 76-year-old Attilio Janiello finally decided to sell it and enjoy the fruits of his labor.

The deal had been signed and money had changed hands on the previous Friday. His friend told me that on the way home from the bank that afternoon Attilio stopped at a travel agency to enquire about plane tickets for a trip to Italy he was planning to make in the coming months.

On Tuesday, at about 8:00 A.M., while having breakfast with his wife and reading his *Corriere Italiano*, Attilio died of a heart attack. He enjoyed the fruits of 40 years of labor for less than 100 hours, and yet I've heard since that visit that he had been willing and ready to sell about 15 years earlier. Perhaps he was waiting for the time to be *just right*, but he waited too long.

Don't wait, or one day, you might regret it . . . like Alexa Whitehorse, a Native girl from northern British Columbia, Canada, who I first met when she was 12, a young girl figure skating late at night on the village hockey rink, alone—it was too cold for the boys to play hockey.

She was very good at it. And she loved it. Everybody was urging her to become a professional skater. She skated until she was 16, winning local competitions, regional ones, and even a northern BC championship. But then she slowed down and eventually stopped. She let go of her dream. She told a friend she was waiting for "everything in her life to be right" before pursuing her dream again.

On January 4, 1993, a car accident left this vibrant 20-year-old paralyzed from the waist down. It brought tears to my eyes when I saw her again.

I talked to her a few months ago. Now 33, she's adapted to her new life. But she told me she often dreams of a genie coming to her in the middle of the night to offer her one wish. "I'd give anything for one more chance to lace up my skates—yes, those that pinched my toes when I put on extra socks to keep warm. I'd give anything for one more night out on the rink, all by myself, with the numbing wind, the bumpy ice, the scratchy PA system playing my music— "Someday My Prince Will Come." I'd give everything for that privilege, even the rest of my life. . . ." Alexa Whitehorse's biggest dream is to be able to skate again one day.

What is *your* biggest wish, *your* lifelong dream . . . and what's keeping you from going after it? Are you waiting for "everything in your life to be right"? It'll never happen. You're never going to have it all together.

Here's the best recipe I know for getting rid of procrastination. It's two simple words: DOn't waIT!

Whatever your big five-year, three-year, or one-year goal is that will change the rest of your life . . . do something about it *every single day*, even if it's just a little thing like making a phone call, reading an article, or subscribing to a newsletter. At least *one* thing. Every day.

What helps me—and Laurel, my wife and business partner—is we have a special section on our to-do list that says "MUST." The task in there is written in a different color so it stands out from the other 10 or 20 items on the list. The dictionary defines "must" as "be obliged to, be certain to, ought to." For us, MUST is an acronym that defines that to-do task in relation to reaching our *big goal*: Mandatory, Urgent, Smart, Transformational. We take our "must-do" task very seriously, as if our "new" life depended on it—and it does!

On January 1, 2006, we set a very *big goal* for us to achieve by December 31, 2006. It will change our life. So every day, we make sure there's at least one task under MUST. Sometimes there are more. But at least one. Every day. And we don't go to bed or sit down for dinner until it's *done*.

Does it work 100 percent of the time? No. But close. Hey, we're only human. But we're on schedule and on target to reach our goal *before* the end of the year. And we owe it mostly to our daily obsession with crossing off our must-do item. Try it. It works.

So, my friends, to use the words of Nike®'s marketing people, whatever it is that will make your life what you want it to be, go ahead, *just do it*! It's a MUST!

ABOUT THE AUTHOR

Daniel Saintjean is half of The BizzBoosters, Inc. (the other, "better half" is Laurel R. Simmons, accomplished businesswoman, outstanding coach, and femme extraordinaire). As The BizzBoosters, the two teach professionals and businesspeople QISS—quick, inexpensive, simple, and sensible—tips to help them boost their businesses and to improve the person as well in the process. You can reach Daniel and Laurel at results@thebizzboosters.com, or visit http://www.TheBizzBoosters.com. There you can subscribe to their "awesomsational" eBizzLetter™ they publish twice a month or purchase one of their many e-books in a series entitled *Your Road to BUSINE$$ SUCCE$$*.

96

TAKING CONTROL

Make a Splash, One Ripple at a Time!

Pauline Fleming

People often find themselves caught in the minute details of their day-to-day routines and experience a sense of disconnection from what is really important. Where your focus goes, your results flow! (Negative focus equals negative results; positive focus equals positive results.) Are you happy with your results on a daily basis? Stop the sink-or-swim approach to life and start making a big enough splash to achieve the life you really want. To avoid being sucked into a downward spiral, you need to make your own waves—the Ripple Effect.

The Importance of Your Ripples

Sometimes the thought of catching a wave can be overwhelming. Know that it all starts with a simple ripple. Each ripple creates the one following it, until finally, the ripples expand farther than expected, reaching a distant shore outside your comfort zone. This creates more time and energy in your day and ultimately more money and fun since you get to consciously choose the ripples.

You can "catch the wave" by implementing the following success formula—it works because it is an inside-out coach approach:

what you have (*W*)(*A*) + what is missing (*E*)
= your desired outcomes (*V*).

In other words, first you need to identify who (*W*) you really are and make attitude adjustments (*A*) to boost your belief. Then design a vision (*V*) of your desired outcomes with actions that align each of the previous ripples. Finally, it is vital to execute (*E*) these chosen actions.

Find the Right Pebble
W is for Who: Identify and Clarify

Before you can create ripples, you need a pebble. The pebble is *you*. Having the right pebble requires clarity around your core: *who*. What are your strengths and core values? What inspires you? Ready to make a splash? Be forewarned: You might get wet!

Focus on Your Strengths to Get Stronger

As a society, we spend far too much time focusing on our weaknesses. The energy drain from the negative self-talk we create drowns our self-esteem in disbelief. When we focus on our weaknesses, we set ourselves up for failure and struggle. When we focus on our strengths, we get stronger. The first step you need to make to create a Ripple Effect is to identify your core strengths. The following strength booster will help you become more aware of the strengths you have.

- Write out 50 of your strengths. Yes, I said 50! The first five are generally easy. When you go further, you uncover strengths you have forgotten—the ones that boost your confidence, define you, and make a positive impression, that splash you're looking for. No one gets to the ocean of opportunities by sitting on the shoreline. What better place to get your feet wet than by focusing on your best qualities?
- Highlight your top five, put them on a Post-It, and place that on the mirror where you brush your teeth morning and night. What a great way to start and end your day.

Need an Attitude Adjustment?
A is for Attitude: Believe in Your Authentic You

Attitude isn't just about having a positive attitude. It needs to go deeper than that. What gets in the way of making things happen is a lack of confidence in ourselves. We need to switch from an "*I can't*" attitude to one of "*I can.*" Absolutely no one has ever achieved anything significant by staying stuck in an "I can't" space. Complete the following belief booster.

- Put a line down the middle of a blank piece of paper.
- Think of a challenge you are facing and write it at the top.

366

- On the left, write out the details of the challenge—the "I can'ts"—the negative blocks that are holding you back.
- On the right, write out the opposite of each detail on the left, the positive version, the 180 degree perspective shift—the "I can" list. Having difficulty figuring out what those are? Physically turn yourself around 180 degrees and look at the challenge as if you have already solved it. Now, what do you see? How does this action alter your attitude toward creating results?
- To take it a step further, add an "I am" column, and use your strengths to continue the attitude adjustment.

Attitude complements the *who*. It can play an important role in determining in which pond your pebble makes ripples. You want to make sure you are in the right pond, or you can make all the ripples you want and you will never reach the ocean of opportunities!

Where Is Your Wave Taking You?
V is for Vision: Align with Where You Want to Be

Instead of rowing upriver without a paddle, envision a waterfall flowing smoothly into the pool where you float effortlessly. You see barrels passing by you. Some of them are marked with the words "shoulda," "coulda," and "if only." You choose to let these pass and say no to them. Some other barrels have "possibilities" written on their sides. Your curiosity is piqued, so you look inside. You are welcome to hang on to these possibilities or trust that they will return when you are ready for them. Meanwhile, higher up the waterfall, you see a large, wonderfully painted barrel with a big bright bow on top. You know in your heart of hearts that it contains what you really, truly desire, and it is floating right toward you. This is your vision of success, something that puts a big smile on your face anytime you think about it. Take a moment, close your eyes, and see what is inside the barrel. What is your vision of success? Complete the following success booster.

- Write down your vision in present tense as if you already have it. Make sure the description isn't just about numbers—it needs to capture the experience and be written in full detail.
- How does your vision make you feel?
- How will you know when you have it?
- What is stopping you from having it today?

- Place your vision where you can see it so it adds to your motivation and momentum ripples on a daily basis.

Bridge the Gap
E is for Execute: Real Results Come through Accountability to Actions

Execution is the step often missed to bridge the gap between where you are and where you want to be. People get very creative, have big ideas, and then wonder why they aren't seeing the results they really want. The truth? They didn't execute the next ripple—the action ripple.

What stops us? Lack of focus, or more importantly, not focusing on what is truly important. We shift our focus to more mundane, nonmeaningful actions, or we *get busy*! We need to create simple actions that honor our *who*, or the pebble will become a huge boulder that can't be moved. Complete the following results booster.

- Wake up each day and ask yourself, "What one action can I take today that will make the biggest difference?"
- Then execute it to get the right results.
- Imagine trying to create 100 ripples at once—how successful do you think that would be in reaching farther out? Commit to *one* main focus per day. Know that you *will* be productive, and your focus will reward you with many more ripples extended outward from this one focused execution.

Catch the Wave One Ripple at a Time

Imagine a group of concentric circles—the four progressive ripples of *who*, *attitude*, *vision*, and *execute* flowing outward to reach farther than one ripple on its own. See how the simple focus on one ripple at a time can help you reach the shores of abundance?

Now that you understand more about *how* to create a Ripple Effect in your life, you have a choice. You can continue to focus on what isn't working and what you don't have, or you can carry out the booster actions and reach more of the right results. Keep this question at the forefront of your mind each day: What one action can I take today that will make the biggest difference? Align these actions with your core *who*, apply a proactive *attitude*, and see your *vision* coming closer as you *execute*. You only live once—make a splash.

ABOUT THE AUTHOR

Pauline Fleming is a proactive change catalyst for individuals and organizations ready to Reach their Next Level of excellence. Hire coach Pauline when you want an experienced, independent sounding board; stronger leadership skills; high-performance results; executive retreats; more powerful presentations; a motivational speaker; and more of what you are capable of. Contact coach Pauline to find out more at coach@paulinefleming.com or toll-free at (866) 564–5534. As a gift for reading this far, receive your Bonus Boosters: visit http://www.paulinefleming.com and sign up for Pauline's free, five-day mini e-course on how to boost your focus.

97

TELEVISION

How to Use the TV to Help You Save Time

Teresa Bolen

Have you ever been told to turn off the TV, or has anyone ever told you that watching TV is detrimental to your studies, your health, your spirit, or your financial statement? Have you ever found yourself plopped down in front of the TV when you know you need to be reading, or studying, or being attentive to your family, or doing something else important—and yet you prefer to zone out in front of the TV anyway? Not only that, but you're bored doing it? Even though you may have some 500 channels or so, if you were to be completely honest with yourself at that moment, there is nothing on that truly interests you and excites you, right? You know the best thing to do would be to just turn it off, and yet you continue to sit there—seconds turn into minutes, minutes turn into hours, perhaps even an embarrassing number of hours if you allowed yourself to keep track.

This used to happen to me, too, my friend. In fact, worse yet, I was so lonely that I used the TV to keep me company! Finally, one day, I realized that if I wanted more friends and better relationships, it would need to happen outside the digital box. I would have to create them, one conversation at a time. That was a first step to reclaiming all those lost hours. The major breakthrough came when I figured out how to use the TV to help me *save* time, and that's the secret I'd like to share with you today.

I like the TV; I think it can be a powerful tool for learning and gathering important information as well as a tool for relaxation, so I'm not going to tell you to turn it off. I'm going to tell you to go ahead and watch whatever you truly want to watch. The key is to treat the TV like a rare spice, say, saffron. Saffron is quite valuable and rare, isn't it? You can buy saffron for between $40 and $65 an ounce. Silver is currently priced between $10 and $11 per ounce. Are you

370

shocked to learn that saffron—the stigmas of a flower—is valued at four to six times more than silver? I was.

Saffron is lovely, it's tasty, it's fragrant, it creates a wonderful golden yellow coloration in food, but you wouldn't want to use it in everything you cook, right? A little saffron in your rice with an Indian meal is sumptuous, but saffron appetizers, saffron curry, saffron naan, saffron butter, saffron rice, a saffron drink, followed by saffron ice cream for dessert? Bleh! No thank you. That is a *mind-numbing* amount of saffron. Way too much of a good thing!

If you were cooking and wanted to include this rare, exotic spice in your meal, you would plan exactly when and how much saffron to use, wouldn't you? You wouldn't use it as the foundation of the meal. You wouldn't attempt to use saffron as your protein dish. You wouldn't use it as a starch, or even as a vegetable. It's a high note. It's the piccolo of the orchestra. It's something special added in small amounts that gives your meal a unique and wonderful flavor.

You can do exactly the same thing with your TV viewing. Orchestrate your time for the incredibly valuable gift that it is. Just as with the saffron, decide how much and when you want to use your TV. The key again is to be sure to use it as a "*spice*" for your life and not as a *replacement* for your life. The characters on the screen are strangers and forever will be. How much of your time do you really want to give them? Which programs are enlightening and are helping you to reach your higher goals?

When you plan and schedule in your TV viewing, you are going to find that you enjoy the shows you choose to watch much more than ever before. You are taking more control over what kinds of images and messages you are feeding your other-than-conscious mind, thus creating a better future for yourself and for everyone you touch. You also have created much more time for your family, friends, studies, special projects, and whatever else you enjoy doing. Not only that, but you are also going to find that you have more energy than ever before because you are making better choices that support your growth.

Now you are a "master chef" of your time. Before you turn the page or begin anything else, while it is still fresh in your mind, get a copy of your TV schedule and your weekly or monthly planner. Decide how much time you are willing to give to TV viewing, then look through the guide and choose the programs that are uplifting, empowering, or will in some way contribute to your reaching your higher goals. Write them in your calendar.

Go ahead and watch whatever you truly want to watch. As a master of your time, you will want to be certain that you use the TV "spice" according to the "recipe" you created. The TV is on only for the shows that you have planned to watch, and the rest of the time, "the cap is on the TV spice jar" and the TV is a silent witness to your commitment to your higher goals.

Here's to your success!

ABOUT THE AUTHOR

Teresa Bolen, a.k.a. "Success Genie," is a teacher at the prestigious Todaiji Academy, one of the top five schools in Japan, and she is the author of *Master Plan to Master Exams: How to Discover Your Hidden Abilities to Create the Success You Desire*. She has a passion for helping you to unlock the keys to your success. To maximize your learning potential and to discover a foolproof way in which you can substantially improve your ability to learn and reconnect with your own genius abilities, please visit http://www.MasterPlanToMasterExams.com. Claim your free gift by subscribing to her "Academic Excellence Report."

98

How to Stay True to Yourself Above the Opinionated *Roar* of Others

Cari Vollmer

How do you stay true to yourself when you're surrounded by friends and family that have an opinion on *everything* you do? Who constantly offer their opinions, whether you asked for them or not? Who seem to imply that they "know better"?

It's not easy! However, if you're going to lead the life *you* really want, you're bound to run into a few folks who won't, or can't, understand where you're coming from. Don't let their strong opinions back you into a corner or guide your choices. Stay true to yourself by tuning out the naysayers and tuning in to the only opinion that really matters—your own. *These tips will help.*

1. **Value yourself and your choices.** When you do, others will, too. People can see how you value yourself by your presence: how you walk, talk, and relate to the world around you. If you speak confidently and walk with your head held high, people will look at you as someone who has something to offer. If, on the other hand, you avoid eye contact and slink into a corner when someone approaches you, you're sending a very different message. Your presence is determined in large part by the belief you have in yourself and the life you're leading.

   Own the choices you make in your life. Be proud of yourself and your unique view of the world. When you doubt yourself, others will doubt you. When you believe in yourself, others will believe in you, too.

2. **Realize opinions are more about the person giving them than they are about you.** Each person sees the world only as he can see it. Your best friend

may think quitting your job to start your own business is too risky and a foolish move. She may tell you, in no uncertain terms, that you're foolish to leave a well-paying job with great benefits to start a business when so many small businesses fail.

Your friend's passionate opinion doesn't mean she's right, better, or smarter than you. She simply has a different set of values, beliefs, and life experiences. She views life through a different lens. And to be sure, that lens is also distorted with her personal fears and insecurities. It's up to you to decide whether her personal opinion holds water, whether it is valid or invalid. It's up to you to decide how outside opinions fit your life.

3. **Take time off.** Too many people telling you what they think? Take time for yourself. To hear the whispers of your heart, you have to be quiet and listen closely. You can't hear what your heart wants *you* to hear if you drown it out by giving others too much airtime in your life.

   Think of it this way: Is it up to the stadium to tell the Olympic figure skater how to do her routine? She has a team of coaches who help her fine-tune her routine and rehearse her moves to perfection. But when it comes time for her to compete for the gold medal, she stands alone. She must find it within herself to do what she must do to win the gold. She must be able to hear her own voice and tap into her own strength and wisdom. She must tune out the world around her so she can do what she must do.

4. **Know yourself.** Be willing to deepen your sense of self. Create a personal philosophy for living. Know your values and what you care about most. Doing so will increase your confidence and thus affect how people look at you. It will also keep you out of all sorts of sticky situations.

   You'll say yes to opportunities and requests that fit your life and goals and say no to those that don't. More importantly, you'll do so with confidence. You'll make decisions more quickly and easily. Others will respect your position because you respected yourself by staying true to yourself and the vision you have for your life.

5. **Set boundaries.** Some people just go too far. It's okay to respectfully listen, but it's also okay to set boundaries for areas of your life that are off limits.

Does your mother-in-law have too many opinions about how you manage your family? Does your brother try to tell you how you should invest your money? Set boundaries by respectfully acknowledging their points of view, but let them know you're making choices how you see fit. It may take a few tries, but in time they'll get the message and back off.

6. **Stand by *your* side.** Our friends and family will often say they want the best for us and want us to be happy. But *they* also want to be happy. If your mother knows you're looking for a new home to buy and are considering one within a few miles of her *and* one across town, isn't there a good chance her advice to you will be influenced by her desire to have you closer to her?

Others may not be there for you when you most need them. It's very hard for those closest to us to remain objective, especially when their lives may also be impacted by the decisions we make. The solution: when faced with a big decision, keep it close to home for a while before you share it with others. By doing so, you'll gain confidence in your choices and will be less likely to be swayed by the emotional responses and opinions of others.

7. **Value the *pause* between someone's *opinion* and your *response*.** If somebody really steps on your toes, it's easy to react quickly out of anger and frustration. Don't! Of all the things you can do to stay true to yourself while filtering through the opinions of the world around you, one of the most important is to *stop* before you react.

Listen to what others have to say, but value the moment after they've said it as time to recenter yourself and regain your composure. Instead of jumping in with words of disagreement or frustration, let silence reign. Pause, consider what you've just heard, pay attention to your bodily sensations and emotions, and then offer your response. By doing so, you'll react from a place of power and value for yourself. You'll give yourself the opportunity to think before you speak.

The point is, nobody can guide you better than you can guide yourself. Listening to and learning from others has immeasurable value, but ultimately, your decisions are yours alone. Realize the naysayers, or those with strong opinions, are fearful of life in their own ways and for their own reasons. Learn to decipher the difference between opinions you should consider and those you should let go of.

ABOUT THE AUTHOR

Cari Vollmer is the founder of LifeOnTrack.com and publisher of InspireYourSuccess.com. Sign up for LifeOnTrack.com's *free special report* and e-course "5 Great Starting Places for Creating and Leading a Life That Feels Great NOW" at http://www.LifeOnTrack.com.

99

VALUES

Give People What They Are Longing For!

Suzanne Schell

Making the world (your world) a finer place does not need to be overwhelming. Investing in people all around you, in your family, in your workplace, in your neighborhood, and in your world, returns to you a world that is finer. I am not referring to a financial investment, however; I am referring to value.

> No man becomes rich unless he enriches others.
> – Andrew Carnegie

People must feel valued. If they do not feel valued, they wilt and become stifled.

A child needs to know that his parents love him, believe in him, and are there to support him. As a child makes mistakes, he will grow and become positive about trying new things if given recognition for his strengths and improvements. The result for the parent is a happy and motivated child. If the child only hears about his weaknesses and mistakes, the result for the parent is an unmotivated child that will begin to believe he is a failure. There must be a balance of positive recognition with the necessary correction and negative interactions that parenting brings. This holds true in all relationships.

All people are born with the longing to be loved. When you positively deliver recognition or inform a person that he is important to you, that you value him and respect him, you are giving that person what he is longing for.

Imagine that all individuals have a light bulb inside of them and that you have the power to brighten them or dim them. You do have that power. As you recognize strengths and goodness in people, make sure you tell them, and as soon as you do, their light bulbs will brighten. There is a bonus to this—your light bulb will brighten, too! The world has become a better place.

A very special friend of mine was an amazing person that truly brightened everyone's light bulb. If you were in a room she entered, you were soon happy to be there. She would approach each person in her path with an energy and aura that was full of what we all long for. With sincerity and passion she naturally would find an attribute or action of yours and speak to you about it in a positive conversation. It could be something small or very significant about you or your life, and my special friend would find it and make you feel bright, proud, and confident. No matter how negative or down a person could be, she would seek out the positive and engage in brightening his being and his world. Unfortunately, this extraordinary person passed away too early in her life. She fought and suffered with cancer for a difficult year. During her fight she continued to enhance everyone around her, making him feel special, valued, and bright. She selected a verse to be read at her own funeral service that spoke to each of us on how we individually could impact others' lives with positive recognition and gratitude. She will always continue to inspire people to give others what they are longing for.

Unfortunately, it is easier for us to recognize the negative, the errors, and the weaknesses in people. Think about the last time you observed something in another person that wasn't right or was a weakness that needed correcting—it was likely quite recently. Did you correct that person or point out the mistake? Finding fault and weakness seems effortless, and you can be quick to criticize. This is your power to be able to dim an individual's light bulb and consequently, dim yours as well. As a result, the world is not a finer place. Without that balance of positive and negative recognition you are left with a very dim person.

Life travels at a fast speed and doesn't seem to give much time for reflecting on people in your life to find their strengths, their good work, the positive, and then taking the time to let them know.

Think of someone significant in your life. Write his or her name here: _____.

Write down three pleasing attributes he or she has, or three commendable actions he or she took recently, or a combination of both.

Have you ever told this person that he or she possesses these attributes and that you value them? Did you praise this person's actions?

It is highly possible that you answered no. You now have the opportunity to brighten this person's light bulb and to make your world a finer place. Go ahead—give this person what he or she is longing for, then watch and feel what happens.

Positive recognition of another person raises you to a higher level. Why is it so difficult to give positive recognition? While it is what everyone needs, it is medicine for self-esteem and fuel for motivation. It is what we are all longing for.

ABOUT THE AUTHOR

Suzanne Schell is the founder of *Business Excellence*, which implements processes and change for businesses and people that are critical to positively impacting results. Suzanne is a writer and professional speaker and delivers fun, effective, and energetic presentations. Visit her Web site at http://www.suzanneschell.com, or e-mail her at Suzanne@suzanneschell.com.

100

WEALTH PLAN

The Key to Creating Your Own Wealth Creation Plan

Bill White

The number of people who don't dream of becoming wealthy are few and far between. While money isn't everything, it sure does make life easier. Both having too little and too much money can create problems, but wouldn't you rather have problems with too much money? I've looked all over the world at different methods or claims of creating wealth. It's a shame that there are so many people out there who are using the method of telling someone how to become rich to become rich themselves. As an honest person, I cannot tell you any guaranteed way to become wealthy. Quite honestly, there is no magic formula for doing so because everyone will have unique experiences as part of his individual circumstances. That said, I'll share with you the techniques I've used to construct my own wealth plan. It's something I've created an acronym for: **LACED™**. The LACED principle is fairly straightforward. LACED stands for:

- **Leverage**d
- **Automated**
- **Compounding**
- **Ethical**
- **Duplicable**.

If you create a plan using all these principles, you'll likely have a strong plan.

I've heard many wealthy people speak about leverage. Basically, you'll want to use as much leverage as possible to build wealth. You can do so by utilizing vehicles that allow you to control large assets with smaller assets. One example of this is buying an investment piece of real estate with 10 percent down. This is incredible leverage if you think in terms of the fact that you can control $180,000 worth of property for $18,000. In some cases you may be able to control real estate with absolutely no money down! Another example would be buying stock options. In this case you purchase the right to buy or sell stock, but not the obligation. This is a highly risky proposition and should not be tried without extreme due diligence and some understanding of how options work. Suffice it to say that with options you can control 100 shares of stock (one contract) for a small fraction of the price of the underlying security. By the same token, a small movement in the right direction on the underlying security can magnify the value of the option considerably.

Next, you should try to automate as much of your plan as possible. Anything that doesn't require you to actively work on it will free your time to build greater momentum toward your wealth goals. The Internet has greatly enabled strides in this way. Consider how quickly you can buy and sell stocks online, research real estate information, or even sell products completely online through an automated payment process. You can automate your purchase of shares in a 401(k) or start purchasing stocks using DRPs (know as drips), which allow you to buy portions of shares if you have less money at a time to invest. More conservative but somewhat effective still is to simply have a portion of your paycheck put into a savings account. Putting your wealth creation on autopilot will help you stay on track without having to think about it.

Compounding is one of the most powerful tools we can use to build wealth. There are a lot of different strategies for compounding. You may want to reinvest profits in your business to grow the business larger. You may reinvest your returns in the stock market to grow your portfolio more quickly. The more you are able to make your existing assets work for you, the faster you will propel yourself toward wealth. Some common ways to use compounding are compound interest earned on savings accounts, CDs, stocks, or that 401(k) you contribute to weekly. The pivotal interest rate you should try to achieve is at least eight percent because at that rate and higher the accumulation is significant enough to fight off inflation.

Some might say that doing things ethically is more of a moral choice than an actual tool for wealth creation, but I will counter with the fact that every major religion on earth I've studied has in some way said what goes around comes around. In other words, if you cheat, eventually you're going to lose. Deal with everyone honestly, and you'll get wealthy more quickly. An interesting take on this is something many people won't think about. When you don't have a lot of cash, you don't want to spend money on CPAs, attorneys, or other professionals to help you grow your wealth. You'd like to have their services, but you don't want to pay the price. This isn't ethical. You wouldn't want to give your labor away, and yet you feel they should. This is where those ethics are really going to make a difference! You get what you pay for, and if you try to be cheap, you'll very likely get cheap advice. Additionally, you may think you are getting over on your employer by slacking off at work when the boss isn't around or by "borrowing" company supplies for home use. The reality is that by doing that, you may very well get passed over for that promotion that could put an extra $5000 a year in your pocket. Do what's right!

Finally, you want to make sure the core components are as duplicable as possible. If something works one time, it may get you a large gain, but if it doesn't work twice, it may give you a huge loss the second time around. Many of my mentors have told me that a lot of small gains are much better than having one big home run. Don't fall prey to the guy at work who gives you that "can't lose" stock tip. Don't put all your eggs in one basket. Diversify your funds to protect them. Most of all, don't throw more money at an investment that isn't giving you returns. If you bought a stock at $5 a share and it's selling at $2.50, don't think it can't sink lower. If your 401(k) lost five percent last year, switch plans.

Find things that leverage, compound, and are as automated as possible, and then pick those that are duplicatable, and you will have an astonishing wealth-building machine in place. Don't wait until later because time is your most valuable commodity. Always pay yourself first. Whether you are employed or an employer, a janitor or an oil tycoon, these principles will still apply.

I hope you can take this lesson and build your own wealth plan with it. It may sound vague, and it is, but I believe it holds all of the secret ingredients you'll need to work your way toward having your wealthy future all LACED up!

About the Author

Bill White is one of the nation's top e-business coaches and is the world's #1 synchronicity expert. His techniques will unlock the hero or heroine in *you*! Bill has a newly released and free course called "Discover Your Destiny" that will help you transform your life, *and* he will give you a free, 10-minute Success Assessment by quickly going to: http://www.synchronicity-expert.com/bookoffer.htm.

101

WRITING

How Can Writing Improve Your Life?

Kelly Robbins

From ancient storytelling and hieroglyphics to modern-day therapy and prescribed journaling, writing is one of the oldest and most effective ways we communicate—both with ourselves and with others.

For centuries, people have written to bring clarity and focus to problems they've been struggling with. For those who are shy or can't find the words to express themselves, writing is a great way to get their points across, especially on personal or emotional matters.

Writing adds permanency and a sense of tangibility to your thoughts. An example is goal setting: experts tell us to write our goals down. It's one thing to think about something you want to accomplish in your life or in business—to set a goal. Taking the extra time to write down that goal makes it more permanent. You are more likely to achieve it if it is written down.

You don't have to write with the intention of being published. Write for
- self-expression
- introspection
- pleasure
- growth
- clarity
- emotional relief
- storytelling
- communicating

Writing adds another dimension to your thoughts. It expands on the experience and adds depth to the thought, making it much more likely to become a reality.

When doing anything in your life, I encourage you to use as many of your senses as you can. It enriches the experience and makes the reality of it more vivid. Writing adds the sense of touch and sight to your thoughts. Read your writing out loud—you add hearing. In business I teach my clients to incorporate as many of the senses into their marketing as they can: touch, hearing, sight, smell, and taste. Writing your goals down adds another dimension to the goal. You use another one of those senses and are thus much more likely to accomplish that goal . . . because you made it more tangible, more real.

Whether writing for pleasure or to fill your deep-seated desire to write the great American novel, many people find that the hardest part of writing is getting started. Determining what to write about is simply a daunting task for some. Staring at the blank page makes it worse. Part of what makes writing fun is seeing your thoughts flowing easily and effortlessly onto the page. But getting to that point—the effortless place where creativity and your individual thoughts come together on the page—can be tough in the beginning.

As I am writing this piece, my nine-year-old daughter is writing the final draft of a story she wrote in class. When she first brought this story home a few days ago, she was bubbling with excitement and enthusiasm. She had written an in-depth, five-page story, and many of her classmates only wrote a paragraph or two in the same amount of time. Her story was awesome, and she knew it. She started writing, and the words just flew onto the page; before she knew it, class was over. She's upset now because she has to edit and rewrite 10 times as much as her classmates before her next class. (She quickly realized it could be a bad thing if she were to continue to write that much.)

My point is that once you are in the flow—when you're in a good place and thoughts and ideas are flowing without effort—writing can be pure joy. The key is to train yourself to get to that place without effort. Following are some things to help you find that free-flowing place.

- Develop a routine, but don't make your routine difficult.
- Use a crisp pad of paper. (I always need to have a legal size pad of yellow paper. No crinkled edges. No torn pages.)
- Is your laptop better?

- Write in a quiet house or room.
- Get out of the house. Maybe sit at the local coffee shop or under a tree.
- Notice what *isn't* working so you can get away from it. The kids running madly around the house stresses me out.
- Write at the same time every day—maybe right after your first cup of coffee.
- Do you wake up early at exactly the same time every morning? Like 3:00 A.M.? If you actually take the time to get out of bed, that is a very calm time of day and can be a great time for you to be alone with yourself and do some writing.
- At the end of a stressful day a glass of wine and a pad of paper can be a great way to relax and work through some of your issues. Brainstorm ideas; gather thoughts . . . something as simple as dumping out a list of everything you need to do for the next few days can be a relief and help you to relax if you're stressed (I lovingly call this my brain-dump).
- Set a goal for yourself: 1 hour, 15 minutes, 20 pages, 1 chapter. Find what works for you.
- Write in something special—a beautifully bound journal with an expensive pen you splurged on. Make your writing time special and joyous.
- When you are writing, don't worry about spelling and punctuation. Just get your thoughts down. Let your thoughts flow freely.
- Try different things until you find what works for you.

These are just suggestions to get you started. You are not going to know what works for you if you don't just start writing. I am a writer by trade, and I coach people that want to make a living as a writer. I see them procrastinate over and over again, and the one thing I tell them over and over again is to *just start writing*. Once you get into the flow, you'll see your life improve in more ways than you can count.

ABOUT THE AUTHOR

Kelly Robbins is a healthcare copywriter and marketing coach and consultant. Kelly was the recipient of the 2004 "40 under 40" award, given annually by the *Denver Business Journal*, which recognized her as a leader in the business community. Kelly is the author of *The Essential Healthcare Copywriters Toolkit* and publishes *The Healthcare Marketing Connection* (http://www.healthcaremarketingconnection.com), an e-zine which provides marketing tips to healthcare and nonprofit organizations across the world. Kelly is a nationally known speaker, author, and columnist on copywriting and marketing topics. Kelly can be reached at http://www.KellyRobbinsLLC.com or at (303) 460–0285.

ABOUT SELFGROWTH.COM

SelfGrowth.com is an Internet super-site for self-improvement and personal growth. It is part of a network of Web sites owned and operated by Self Improvement Online, Inc., a privately held New Jersey–based Internet company.

Our company's mission is to provide our Web site guests with high-quality self improvement and natural health information, with the one simple goal in mind: making their lives better. We provide information on topics ranging from goal setting and stress management to natural health and alternative medicine.

If you want to get a sense for our Web site's visibility on the Internet, you can start by going to Google, Yahoo, America Online, Lycos, or just about any search engine on the World Wide Web and typing the words "self-improvement." SelfGrowth.com consistently comes up as the top or one of the top Web sites for self-improvement.

OTHER FACTS ABOUT THE SITE

SelfGrowth.com offers a wealth of information on self-improvement. Our site:

- Publishes nine informative newsletters on self-improvement, personal growth, and natural health.
- Offers over 4,000 unique articles from more than 1,100 experts.
- Links to over 5,000 Web sites in an organized directory.
- Features an updated self-improvement store and event calendar.
- Gets visitors from over 100 countries.

CONTACT INFORMATION

ADDRESS: Self Improvement Online, Inc.
             20 Arie Drive
             Marlboro, New Jersey 07746
PHONE: (732) 761–9930
E-MAIL: webmaster@selfgrowth.com
WEB SITE: www.selfgrowth.com

Author Index

V

W

Y

ABOUT DAVID RIKLAN

David Riklan is the president and founder of Self Improvement Online, Inc., the leading provider of self-improvement and personal growth information on the Internet.

His company was founded in 1998 and now maintains four websites on self-improvement and natural health, including:

1. www.SelfGrowth.com
2. www.SelfImprovementNewsletters.com
3. www.NaturalHealthNewsletters.com
4. www.NaturalHealthWeb.com

His company also publishes nine e-mail newsletters going out to over 850,000 weekly subscribers on the topics of self improvement, natural health, personal growth, relationships, home business, sales skills, and brain improvement.

David's first book—*Self Improvement: The Top 101 Experts Who Help Us Improve Our Lives*—has been praised by leading industry experts as the "Encyclopedia of Self Improvement." That book's success motivated him to continue publishing books which, like the one you're reading now, seek to improve the lives of others.

He has a degree in chemical engineering from the State University of New York at Buffalo and has 20 years of experience in sales, marketing, management, and training for companies such as Hewlett-Packard and The Memory Training Institute.

His interest in self-improvement and personal growth began over 20 years ago and was best defined through his work as an instructor for Dale Carnegie Training, a performance-based training company.

David is a self-professed self-improvement junkie – and proud of it. His house is full of self-improvement books and tapes. He took his first self-improvement class, an Evelyn Wood speed-reading course, when he was 16 years old, and his interest hasn't ceased yet.

He lives and works in New Jersey with his wife and business partner, Michelle Riklan. Together, they run Self Improvement Online, Inc. and are raising three wonderful children: Joshua, Jonathan, and Rachel.